A Guide to the Reading Workshop, Primary Grades

Lucy Calkins

Photography by Peter Cunningham

HEINEMANN ◆ PORTSMOUTH, NH

Dedicated to Heinemann's stunning, amazing, perfect team of editors.

Heinemann
361 Hanover Street
Portsmouth, NH 03801–3912
www.heinemann.com

Offices and agents throughout the world

The author and publisher wish to thank those who have generously given permission to reprint borrowed material:

Excerpt from *Frog's Lunch* by Dee Lillegard. Copyright © Houghton Mifflin Harcourt Publishing Company. All rights reserved. Used by permission of the publisher, Houghton Mifflin Harcourt Publishing Company.

Sam the Garbage Hound, by Charnan Simon. Copyright © 1996 by Charnan Simon. All rights reserved. Reprinted by permission of Children's Press an imprint of Scholastic Library Publishing, Inc.

Bella Likes Purple, by Michele Dufresne. Pioneer Valley Books, 2011. Used by permission of the publisher.

Food for Bella, by Michele Dufresne. Pioneer Valley Books, 2011. Used by permission of the publisher.

Cataloging-in-Publication data is on file with the Library of Congress.

ISBN-13: 978-0-325-07740-6

Series editorial team: Anna Gratz Cockerille, Karen Kawaguchi, Tracy Wells, Felicia O'Brien, Debra Doorack, Jean Lawler, Marielle Palombo, and Sue Paro
Production: Elizabeth Valway, David Stirling, and Abigail Heim
Cover and interior designs: Jenny Jensen Greenleaf
Photography: Peter Cunningham
Composition: Publishers' Design and Production Services, Inc.
Manufacturing: Steve Bernier

Printed in the United States of America on acid-free paper
19 18 17 16   PAH   3 4 5

Contents

*READ

Acknowledgments

THIS GUIDE, and indeed this series, grows out of the Teachers College Reading and Writing Project's collective community and out of decades of research, teaching, and continuous inquiry. The intellectual DNA of literally thousands of brilliant teachers from all corners of the world is here, in the pages of this book and in the series that accompanies it. People tell me that quilting becomes a symbolic, deeply significant enterprise when each square of fabric that is stitched together bears the imprint of a well-loved person and a special moment: here's a bit from Miles' iconic baby outfit; here's one from Evan's outrageous Halloween costume we all laugh to remember; here is a bit from the pillow we used to have on the couch. I hear that and say, "I know what you mean," because as I read over this book and so many of the books in this series, I recall the sources for each bit with love and gratitude.

By the time ideas get onto these pages, many of them have passed through so many hands that none of us can recall the originator. The Project brings perhaps two score of leading researchers and theorists and teachers to us each year, and we learn from each—their ideas are here, in the mix. Thanks especially to Tim Rasinski, Donald Bear, Pat Cunningham, Ellin Keene, Steph Harvey, Nancy Anderson, Yvonne Rodriguez, Mary Howard, David Booth, Mary Cappelini, and many, many others. We regard the late Marie Clay as a hero and thank her for her many visits to us and for her books. We are grateful to other distant mentors, too, including Gay Su Pinnell and Irene Fountas.

Mostly, I am grateful to colleagues who helped allowed me to tap their minds, experiences, and insights onto these pages. There are, in a sense, a dozen coauthors to this book, each one helping with a different chapter. Beth Moore's brilliance is evident in the assessment chapter; Rachel Rothman and Christine Cook, the phonics chapter; Natalie Louis, Christine Cook, and Joe Yukish, the development chapter; Liz Dunford Franco and Brianna Parlitsis, small groups and management; Katie Wears and Natalie Louis, the shared reading chapter; Amanda Hartman, reading aloud; Jen DeSutter, differentiation; Lindsay Barton and Havilah Jesperson, research. Katie Wears, Liz Dunford Franco, Joe Yukish, and Amanda Hartman have also combed their expertise and judgment through every chapter, adding insights, clarification, and examples.

All of this knowledge stands on the shoulders of current and former Project staff members. We are grateful to Kathy Collins, who was a full-time member of our team for years and is now still family but lives apart from us. Similarly, Joe Yukish has been an invaluable member of our team for a decade and brought his wisdom to those pages. Our thinking about primary literacy benefits from the entire organization's knowledge base. In the teaching of reading, no one is more original, more generative, than Kathleen Tolan, Senior Deputy Director.

All of our work is made possible by the people who connect us to schools, who organize our comings and goings, and who help us to reach our people, and no one does that more and better than our Senior Deputy Director, Laurie Pessah. We are forever thankful for her organizational leadership and emotional support. Her work allows us to learn from leading institutes and think tanks and conference days and working in classrooms, and all of this allows us to rub shoulders with superintendents, principals, teachers, and kids. We are grateful also to them, and to none more than Carmen Farina, Chancellor of the New York City schools. Carmen was first a teacher, then a principal, then a superintendent within our community, and always was a break-the-mold thinker who influenced our organization because of her bold innovative and authentic leadership. Now, as Chancellor, she is bringing joy back to teachers' and children's lives and turning New York City schools toward relationships of collaboration, shared generosity, and mission-driven resolve.

All that I know about writing has been influenced by a few mentors who will always mean the world to me. I am forever grateful especially to Don Murray, Pulitzer Prize–winning writer, and to Kate Montgomery, who was my editor for years, and led the effort to create the Units of Study line of work.

Finally, we are grateful to all the people at Heinemann who have the same high ideals and capacity for work that characterize the Project. This book came very late in the effort, when I've been pulled in many directions, and it fell to Marielle Palombo, the book's primary editor, to do more than the usual amount of smoothing, problem solving, and filling in. She has been exacting, thoughtful, and resourceful in her work with the manuscript, and I thank her. Because this book overlaps a bit with the grades 3–5 guide and Tracy Wells took the helm of that project, Marielle has received terrific support from Tracy, who also worked on some of the more challenging chapters and gave the entire book another read-through. Anna Gratz Cockerille has been particularly helpful; she came into a few rough chapters and helped to bring the lion from the marble. Meanwhile, on the production side, David Stirling has again worked his magic with photographs. Elizabeth Valway is a wizard who turns Google Docs documents into our beautiful pages. She is a genius at this effort and works with steady grace under enormous pressure. Lisa Bingen owns the marketing side of this effort and brings heroic amounts of energy, vision, and zeal to that work. Amanda Bondi has kept all the wheels turning for the entire Heinemann team throughout the process. All in all, this book and this project are blessed indeed.

A Note to My Readers

IN A MOMENT, I'm going to ask that you step with me into this series, into this effort to give young people the richest possible education as readers. I couldn't be more delighted to be sharing this work with you, as well as the sister effort to support units of study in writing. It is the understatement of a lifetime to say that Units of Study for Teaching Reading grows out of *years* of work in thousands of classrooms. The series actually grows out of *decades* of work and out of the greatest minds and most beautiful teaching that I've seen anywhere. To write this, we have done what teachers throughout the world do all the time. We've taken all that we know—the processes, sequences, wheels, continua, books, levels, lessons, methods, principles, and strategies . . . the works—and we've made a path for children, a path that draws all we know into a cohesive, organic progression; a path that brings children along to the place where they can make sense out of text and can live together as joyous, thoughtful readers.

The series bears the characteristic brand of all the Teachers College Reading and Writing Project (TCRWP) curriculum work. Like Units of Study in Opinion, Information, and Narrative Writing, this series supports your year-long teaching with four units of study for each grade. These, the heart of the series, are written to capture the quirky, real-life, handmade quality of masterful teaching. Each of the units of study is carried along by eighteen to twenty ten-minute minilessons. I know these resources will help you teach with greater efficiency and power.

If you have not been teaching reading through a workshop structure, you will find that there is great power in rallying a community of readers to work with earnest intensity on goals that are big enough for your whole community to embrace. To imagine the power of whole-group minilessons in your reading workshop, think of times when you have gathered the class to story-tell. Remember your children's big-eyed attentiveness as you told them about that giant who roared, "Fee-fi-fo-fum! I smell the blood of an Englishman."

Remember their gales of laughter when Trixie pulled her mother's bra from the washing machine and swung it overhead. Remember the times you heard your students repeating those lines and recalling those moments, long afterward. The promise of Units of Study for Teaching Reading is this. The series will allow you to teach high-frequency words and one-to-one matching, looking across the whole word and relying on patterns, predicting and inferring, with the intensity and power that you know from times the class has pulled close around you to participate in shared reading and read-alouds. Just as those occasions have filled the classroom with refrains that thread through the year—with children reenacting and referencing "Fee-fi-fo-fum!" all year long during their work and play—so, too, your minilessons can leave lasting refrains and chorus lines.

Of course, the workshop contains many parts, and all those are supported within this series. You'll get state-of the art help with reading aloud and shared reading, and you'll learn ways to expand your repertoire of small-group work. The minilessons in this series are written to be brief—less than ten minutes—and absolutely engaging. You'll teach kids that they can read nonfiction texts in such a way that they can grow big ideas even from a penny. Imagine distributing pennies into cupped hands and showing your kids that they can read those pennies closely—noticing, wondering, and connecting. Minutes later, you'll channel your children to read their books with the same close attentiveness. Imagine bringing a fortune cookie to your minilessons and showing kids that inside, there is a teeny tiny life lesson and then pointing out that stories are like fortune cookies: sometimes when you open up a story, you find a little life lesson hidden inside. Imagine teaching children that they can learn about the kind of person a character is from watching how that character responds to a problem and then rallying the class to reread a bit of the Frog and Toad series with you, finding that Toad responds to his messy house by covering his head with his bedspread and saying, "Come back tomorrow!"

Just as powerfully constructed units of study in writing have brought along even the wiggliest young writers, so, too, this reading series will sweep your young readers into pathways toward proficiency. The minilessons in this series are a bit different than those in the writing Units of Study. By popular request, we've made these considerably shorter and increased avenues for kids to dramatize, sing, act, gesture, and join into refrains. But in both the reading and the writing units of study, the real power of the unit comes not from the words that you say, but from the work that children do. It is no small feat to imagine ways that a classroom full of diverse children can all throw themselves with heart and soul into work that is not only doable for the most emergent, but also challenging to the most proficient—but of course, planning teaching that has breadth and scope is exactly what master teachers do.

The Teachers College Reading and Writing Project staff members are well equipped to think about ways to invite diverse learners into the big and important work of a reading community. After all, staff developers at the Project are fortunate enough to work in an enormous range of contexts and classrooms. We work in some of the world's most high-achieving schools as well as in some of the neediest districts, both urban and rural, in the United States. We work in International Baccalaureate schools, Montessori Schools, KIPP schools, in many Blue Ribbon Schools, in tiny rural schools and giant urban schools, and in scores of different nations, include Finland, Singapore, Dubai, Brazil, France and a score of others. In addition, Project staff work in some of the world's best pre–K programs, supporting innovative work to help teachers construct a vision of what quality, developmentally appropriate reading instruction looks like for our youngest readers.

You will find that when you teach kindergartners, for example, that they can rely on superpowers such as pointing power and snap words power and pattern power to actually *read*. Children who are just learning one-to-one

matching will be with you—perhaps reading a text with colored dots under the words to support their pointing—as will your conventional readers be with you. And "with you" is an understatement. Teachers who have piloted this unit describe it, saying, "I have never seen youngsters more engaged. Kids rush to the meeting area, looking forward to learning the day's new power. And the miracle is they don't forget what we teach earlier. As the unit progresses, my kindergartners used each power with more mastery."

These units offer an alternative for those who currently rely on small-group instruction for teaching everything that matters about reading. Writing, like reading, could be taught exclusively through small groups. But think how much would be lost from your writing workshops if, instead of convening all of your writers together to teach them that authors find the beauty in the small moments of their lives, hold those moments in their hands, and tell those moments across their fingers, you instead rush among small groups of writers, trying to get each group to understand narrative writing. When small-group instruction carries the entire instructional load of a curriculum, those groups strain under that pressure. Sometimes as a result, small-group time doesn't provide a laboratory within which you can work in out-of-the-box ways to explore a hunch or to try a new way to support those needing that support. If the groups are carrying too much instructional load, it's hard to be as responsive as you need to be.

Your small-group instruction will be transformed when this one structure is no longer carrying the stress of an entire instructional load. Now, small groups will become an extension of your minilessons as well as a potent force for reaching your outliers, those who need extra scaffolding or extra challenge. They'll also become a seedbed for new and innovative teaching for you. You'll have the luxury to adapt and be responsive within your small groups, because you won't rely on them as the only means to keep the plates spinning and the children working.

Then, too, when your teaching can lean on the work that a team of educators has spent years assembling and designing (and decades more developing), then your time outside of teaching can be spent studying your data about your children—their grubby, lopsided Post-its® that can show so much, the running records that can be so eye opening—and actually thinking through ways your teaching can support the progress of each child and each group of children. The units help you to do that. The write ups about small-group work highlight the periodic litmus tests you can give to note where your kids are in the work you have asked them to do

Everyone participates in shared reading.

and point out essential support that will make a world of difference at this or that particular point. For example, if the plan calls for you to end today's reading workshop with a song, the unit of study book may well remind you that if you listen to your children singing along with you, you can note signs that indicate which of your children need more support with phonemic awareness.

I hope these resources help you feel better prepared, too, for other components of your reading instruction: for shared reading and read-aloud. I hope you find that the teaching tools—the anchor charts and the read-aloud prompts and the examples and the scaffolds of all sorts—function like a big toolkit, the kind a plumber brings to any job, the sort of toolkit that allows

you to know that everything is there inside, ready to be pulled out at a moment's notice.

Above all, I hope that Units of Study for Teaching Reading gives you a shared framework that functions as a shared text that you and your colleagues can use and question and add to and enrich with your own inventions, ideas, and choices.

When Roland Barth, the founder of Harvard's famous Principal Center, was asked, "What really matters in a school?" his answer was that in the end, nothing matters more than the learning community among teachers. If you and your colleagues are in and out of each other's classrooms, wishing each other well as teachers, sharing insights and inventions and tools and questions, then the entire community of a school rises on the tide of that professional study.

Teaching is hard work, and this series makes no bones about that. People often say to me, "Your Units of Study series is not for the weak of heart—but yes, the units yield dramatic results." The beautiful thing is that those results are so gratifying, they can tap an energy source in you and your colleagues. Chances are that good that you'll feel a new lift to your step, a new sense of collegiality across your grade level, and a new ambitiousness to your teaching. It is beautiful work.

Chapter 1

First Things First

BEFORE YOU TURN to the ins and outs of curriculum, to the anchor charts and the comprehension strategies and the stories of children learning to read, pause for a moment to picture the face of a young person you teach—someone you know well. When you see her, skipping from the music room to lunch, do you see how she stops in the doorway of your classroom to catch your eye? She may have just left you twenty minutes earlier, yet she is so curious to see what you could be doing when you are not being her teacher. Does her face light up when you wave to her? Do you almost (not quite, but almost) want to call her in, even though this is your one free moment? And when you think of all of them, their quirky, tousled, grubby, intent faces looking up at you, do you feel a tug in your chest, that tug of feeling so responsible for them all, for how they'll succeed in school and beyond? I know you do. We feel it deeply. And this is what I want to say: *that* is the core of all that matters in teaching. Without that care, the greatest curriculum in the world is only paper and a little dry ink.

To think about designing a reading workshop that is worthy of that child, and all the others, too, think about what you want for your children as readers. As Lucille Clifton has said, "You cannot create what you cannot imagine." My hunch is that what you want is what I want as well. You want your children to become flexible, resilient readers, who read for pleasure as well as for academic purposes. You want them to carry with them, for their entire lives, the invisible knapsack of reading and writing strategies that allow them to deal with difficulty. You want them to be knowledgeable on a range of subjects from their nonfiction reading, and empathetic and thoughtful in their interactions with others from their reading of literature. You want them to read broadly and deeply, alert to the details of texts and to ways that language makes a difference in the world. You want the choices they make for the rest of their lives—for which courses to take in college, for which careers to pursue—not to be mitigated by their reading levels, but to be made with confidence that they can tackle any reading task with vigor and expertise.

That's a tall order, but that's what you need to have in mind when you plan a primary reading workshop. It's a tall order especially when you pause to think that current methods of teaching reading aren't doing the job. Yes, most children are learning to process text; they are learning the self-extending system of being able to turn marks on the page into words that add up to meaning. But too many of our children are not learning to love reading, to self-initiate reading throughout their lives, to read with acute, deep comprehension. Too often, I go into classrooms and see books strewn under the coat rack, grimy with footprints, and snarled into the darkest recesses of children's desks. A child tells me, "I read the whole book last night." Impressed, I ask, "What happened in the story?" and he scrunches up his face and looks up at the ceiling, saying "Uhhhh . . ." as he wracks his mind for some recollection of what he has read. Nothing surfaces, but he hastens to reassure me, "I read the whole thing—honest. I just can't remember it, that's all." He's not the only Teflon® reader, either. I watch a child reach the final page of *Those Shoes*, by Maribeth Boelts, and I'm ready for her to look up, to smile, to share her joy that Jeremy may not have ended up with the shoes of his dreams, but he does have his new boots, and, above all, a friend. My eyes well, thinking about what this book might mean to this student, indeed, what it means to me. She reads. For a second, she pauses. Then she snaps the book shut, slings it toward me, and says, "I'm done. What should I do now?"

I want to say to her, "You should live differently for the rest of your life because you've read that book."

How do we teach reading—the reading that makes you feel as if you are breathing some new kind of air? How do we teach the kind of reading that makes you walk through the world differently because a honeybee is no longer just a honeybee—it's wings and pollination and hives and pollution and all the rest that tumbles around that? How do we teach the power of reading—the way it allows us to see under the words, between the words, beyond words? How do we teach the intimacy of reading—of belonging to a community that has a shared vocabulary, shared stories, shared petitions and projects?

Forty years ago, Jerome Bruner suggested in his now-classic, *The Process of Education*, that "the foundations of any subject may be taught to anybody at any age in some form" (1977, 12). He went on to say that the basic ideas that lie at the heart of, and give form to, life and literature are as simple as they are powerful: "To be in command of these basic ideas, to use them effectively, requires a continued deepening of one's understanding of them that comes from learning to use them in progressively more complex forms" (13).

When there is so much at stake, it is hard to imagine a more important question than the one that powers this book. What are the norms, habits, systems, relationships, and expectations that undergird a state-of-the-art primary reading workshop?

The irony is that when it comes to teaching reading, we sometimes convince ourselves that the subject is so important that we outsource it to large for-profit companies that don't know us and don't know our kids—and don't necessarily even know how to teach well. Because we're sure that teaching children to read is the single most important thing we do, we want someone else to make the decisions about how our teaching will go. "Tell me what to do, and I'll do it," we say. And then, when the core reading program channels 19,000 little things toward us, we don't stop long enough to think, "Does this match what I know from my own experiences learning to read?" "Does this reflect what the research shows kids need?" "Does this draw upon what I've learned from all my years of teaching?" We're too intent on racing through those 19,000 steps, on doling out, checking off, drilling, monitoring, and on and on.

We need to catch our breath and to pause long enough to think, to remember, to research, and to make informed choices. Racing faster and covering more is not the answer. Years ago, when I wrote the first chapter of *The Art of Teaching Writing*, I wrote some words that have become foundational to everything I do.

> If our teaching is going to be an art, we need to remember that artistry does not come from the sheer quantity of red and yellow paint or from the amount of clay or marble, but from the organizing vision that shapes the use of those materials. It's not the number of good ideas that will turn our teaching into something significant and beautiful, but the selection, balance, coherence, and design of those ideas. (Calkins 1994, 2001)

Perhaps the place to start is by thinking about our own lives as readers for a minute. (Don't worry—it will take just a minute.) Think for just a minute about the times in your life when reading was the pits, and then think about times when reading was the best thing in the world. What were the conditions that made reading so bad? What made it so good?

I imagine you might be saying that reading works for you when you choose books that matter to you, when you have lots of time to actually eyes-on-print read, and when you can finish one chapter and, instead of answering twenty questions, read the next chapter. If you've had the exquisite pleasure of sharing reading—in a book club, a Bible study group, a women's group, a writing group, or in a friendship that includes books—then the social fabric of reading will be part of what makes reading work for you. And I'm pretty sure that when reading has been the pits for you, someone else told you what to read, what to think about, and what to do when you finished reading. You probably felt as if your every move was monitored and judged, making reading a performance for someone else.

How can it be that thousands and thousands of teachers, principals, and reading researchers are clear about the conditions that have made reading be the pits, the worst thing in the world, for us—and yet we allow a big publishing company to establish a gigantic system around the teaching of reading that results in us teaching in ways that exactly replicate the worst of what has been done to us? How can it be that half the teachers in America have been convinced to teach in ways that directly counter what we know kids need? Above all, how can this system perpetuate itself when it clearly hasn't worked? The longer kids stay in school, the less they like to read. The average college graduate in this country reads one book a year.

These are important times in the teaching of reading, though. There's been a gigantic crack in the system. Judgment is no longer pending. The verdict is in. Not one of those core reading programs, mandated under No Child Left Behind, has been shown to work reliably. After reviewing the evidence that supports even programs that regularly proclaim themselves to be "research based," Richard Allington wrote, "There is a long-standing federal enthusiasm for packaged reading reform. Unfortunately, we have fifty years of research showing that packaged reading reforms simply do not seem reliable to improve student achievement" (2011, 16). He continues, saying, "None of the proven programs that generated so much excitement a decade ago has withstood the independent research review. None of the commercial reading series has either" (Allington 2011).

Meanwhile, there is an increasing sense of urgency in the air. Today's information age requires that young people develop literacy skills that are significantly higher than those that have ever been required of young people before—and this education needs to be for all students, not just for the elite. Consider this statistic (it is but one of many that can take a person's breath away): between 1997 and 2002, the amount of new information produced in the world was equal to the amount produced over the entire previous history of the world (Darling-Hammond et al. 2008). New technical information is being produced at such a rapidly increasing rate that it is predicted soon to double every seventy-two hours (Jukes and McCain 2002). Clearly, this is a time for ambitious reform.

As this nation wakes up to the fact that the education that millions of Americans received in the past simply isn't adequate for today, more and more school systems are taking a good look at the expensive core reading programs of the past, and they're thinking, "Could it be that the emperor has no clothes on?"

Study after study shows that globalization and new information technologies have made it especially urgent for schools to chart a new mission. In their important book, *Breakthrough*, Michael Fullan, Peter Hill, and Carmel Crévola (2006) point out that the old mission for schools used to be to provide universal access to basic education and then to provide a small elite with access to university education. The world has changed, however; whereas twenty years ago 95% of jobs were low-skilled, today those jobs constitute only 10% of our entire economy (Darling-Hammond et al. 2008). It's likely that children who leave the school system without strong literacy skills will no longer find a job with a living wage waiting for them. "The new mission is to get all students to meet high standards of education and to provide them with a lifelong education that does not have built-in obsolescence of so much old-style curriculum but that equips them to be lifelong learners." Those words form the prelude of the book *Breakthrough*, and they could be the prelude to this series as well. There's been a crack in the system, and light is shining through.

The problem and the opportunity coalesce. Now is the time for a new vision for reading instruction.

THE RELATIONSHIP BETWEEN THIS SERIES, THE COMMON CORE STATE STANDARDS, AND OTHER GLOBAL STANDARDS AND ASSESSMENTS

A number of years ago, a third-grader named Jake wrote a memoir about his childhood—it always gets to me when an *eight-year-old* reminisces about "the good old days"—and in this memoir, Jake wrote:

> I'm still thinking back to first grade. Oh, those were the good old days! We did not have so much work back then, but now I am growing big and I am jammed full of work. Sometimes I wish time flies back to first grade. I was so smart back then.

Jake is not the only one who finds himself thinking back to the good old days when young children weren't so jammed full of work, when youngsters came to school and felt smart.

This year, New York City, like countless other places across the world, adopted universal pre–K. The irony is that as more and more schools around the world come to realize the value of early childhood education, early childhood educators are increasingly being left out of the conversation about K–12 education. Certainly this has been true of conversations around the development and adoption of the Common Core. Valerie Strauss, an education columnist at *The Washington Post*, has written that although the authors of the Common Core interacted with more than 300 language arts experts, almost none of those people were early childhood teachers or leaders. "Why were we not at the table?" early education experts ask.

That is a reasonable question, and certainly there are aspects of the Common Core that need to be adapted so the standards are as child centered and developmental as possible. This book, and indeed this series, does not attempt to take up the question of the extent to which the standards on the Common Core are appropriate for early childhood classrooms. Certainly, we worry over interpretations of the Common Core that are all too common. We worry when we see kindergarten being viewed primarily as a step toward college readiness. We worry when we see kindergartners spending ever-larger portions of their day doing worksheets. And we worry about reading workshops in which the only focus is to move children up levels of text difficulty, whether or not they enjoy reading or engaging in grand conversations about books or coming to think of reading as one of the best parts of the day. To the question, "Is this series aligned to the Common Core?" and "Is the Common Core appropriate for young children?" we answer that it depends on how you translate the standards into practice. We are resolved that there can't be a conflict between the best developmentally appropriate early childhood instruction and the Common Core or other iterations of global standards. We think, in fact, that the only way

to bring children to exciting heights as readers and writers is to teach in ways that are as developmentally sensitive as possible.

Attacks on the Common Core usually question overly zealous interpretations of them and the punitive nature of their rollout. The standards have too often been caged in judgment, fear, shame, and panic, in talk of compliance and of ratings, and in pressure to make reading myopic and teacher-controlled, with test-like questions masquerading as text-based questions. In far too many places, kids now spend their entire reading time inching through teacher-selected, test-like passages, answering swarms of little questions with sentences copied from the text as "evidence." Like many other educators, we look in dismay at those developments, asking, "Is this the way to create state-of-the-art schools—places where teachers, principals, and kids innovate, invent, problem solve, take risks, create, dream, and achieve?"

Some places have rejected the Common Core State Standards altogether, replacing them with other standards, most of which are similar to the CCSS. Other places, like New York City, have called for a reset of the Common Core to achieve new pathways of implementation. Either way, this much is certain: our children are growing up in a world that expects dramatically more of youngsters as readers and writers. And when they are given the richest possible invitation into the world of joyfully rich literacy, the work they do is astonishing.

Units of Study for Teaching Reading aims to achieve a balance. On the one hand, the Common Core's call for students to read a greater balance between information and fiction makes sense, as does the call for students to read more closely, rather than simply glossing over texts. And certainly, students will need to read in ways that allow them to handle progressively more complex texts. Most of all, what makes sense is the reminder that achieving high literacy standards needs to be a mission shared by all the K–12 educators in a district. So, yes, this series provides teachers with the tools to move students expeditiously toward the new expectations while supporting their self-concepts as readers, and their enthusiasm, tenacity, and sense of personal agency and power.

On the other hand, however, the series does take a stand *against* a position some advocates of the CCSS espouse. Some interpret the Common Core to mean that young readers should spend reading time persevering with grade level complex texts even in instances when those texts are well beyond that child's reach. Everything we know about reading development tells us that when working with children who need to make rapid progress as readers, we must work efficiently to make every moment count so students can read the most complex texts possible. Students thrive when they are given opportunities to develop a self-correcting reading system that allows them to cross-check information gleaned from meaning, syntax, and visual sources (letters). And for that to happen, they need to read texts that are within reach for them. So this series advocates an assessment-based approach to teaching reading.

THE MISSION

The work we need to do is clear. Children deserve the richest, happiest, most powerful literacy education that we can give them, and for that to happen, teachers also need the richest, happiest, most powerful professional education that we can give them. Years ago, Seymour Sarason (1996), that great champion of school reform, wrote, "The notion that teachers can create conditions which are vital and alive for students when those same conditions do not exist for teachers has no warrant in the history of mankind." The most important thing we can do to help our children become the readers and writers that we want them to be is to turn schools into vibrant communities of professional learning.

Research is clear on the reason why commercial reading series and packaged reform programs haven't yielded results. Any reform effort that seeks to improve education by bypassing teachers, by trusting programs rather than professionals, will always fail. The U.S. Department of Education recently released a study showing that the single most important thing that can be done to lift the level of student achievement in our classrooms is to support the development and retention of good teachers. In fact, access to good teachers is more important to the likelihood that students will do well than anything else. It is more important than a student's background, small class size, or the overall quality of a school. A mountain of research confirms what all of us already know: the single most important resource a school can provide to its students is an effective teacher. And yet most of the money that has been spent over the past decade to improve the teaching of reading has been spent on large commercial reading programs that aim to teacher-proof reading instruction. What's needed is exactly the opposite.

In his book, *Time for Meaning*, Randy Bomer, a professor at the University of Texas, describes what it was like for him to enter teaching as a second career. On his first day of orientation, the district lined the new teachers up like children. Randy and the others marched single file onto a yellow school bus and were toured through the district. Randy and the other teachers didn't know each other. Each of them sat, as children are apt to do, one per seat, each in a separate box, in a fashion that Randy would later see as emblematic of his experience in that district. The new teachers were brought to the high school and led into the music room—an amphitheater of chairs on risers—where they sat as if in a chorus, although no one opened his mouth. The superintendent took his place on a swivel chair at the front of the room, sitting as if he was a conductor, and offered the new teachers some advice. "When anyone talks back to you, when a kid steps out of line, just write the person's name like so." To illustrate, he called on Randy, elicited his name, and then wrote R-A-N-D-Y in large letters across the board. "Each time the kid talks back, just erase one letter," he said, and he proceeded to turn R-A-N-D-Y into R-A-N-D, R-A-N, R-A, R, and eventually, into nothing. "Kids identify with their names. They don't like to see themselves disappearing" (Bomer 1995).

Within a few years, it became clear to Randy that this was the district's way of working with teachers as well as with students. When he protested anything at all, he was dropped from committees and no longer referred to in decisions. "The longer I stayed in the classroom, the more my voice, my judgment, my creativity were erased" (Bomer 1995). What happened to Randy is what has happened to too many teachers. Too many teachers have felt their creativity, their talent, their beliefs, and their dedication have all been erased—often by decisions that others have made to outsource reading, the heart of teaching, to corporations or to programs designed quickly by state offices of education to match the letter of the standards, dispersed through websites. It hasn't worked.

The reading workshop offers an alternative, which emphasizes providing students with the conditions that are supported by reading research (not by market research). The irony is that there are mountains of scientific studies that confirm what most of us knew just by thinking about the times in our own life when reading has been joyful and the times when reading has been the pits. The research confirms that kids get better as readers when they have time—lots of time—to read (to actually read, not to answer questions, fill in crossword puzzles, and circle the right answers). It is critical that kids read with engagement, and nothing supports engagement more than the opportunity to choose high-interest books that are within a reader's grasp. Learning to read isn't magic. It requires that teachers reflect on their own strategies as readers and reveal those strategies to kids. Good instruction involves demonstration and supported practice, and it is tailored to the learner based on the teacher's ongoing assessment.

Chapter 2

What Does the Series Contain?

T HE SERIES HAS BEEN DESIGNED so that it provides you with a curriculum to lean on and to adapt, as well as with the professional development that you need to develop a deep knowledge of reading process, of beginning reading, and of methods for teaching reading.

Each unit of study includes approximately eighteen to twenty sessions, each representing a day in the reading workshop. Each session contains a minilesson, suggestions for the conferences and small-group work you are apt to do that day, and a possible mid-workshop teaching and share session for that day. Each day's teaching builds onto the teaching from the day before, and each day's teaching is encapsulated in an illustrated over-sized Post-it or two that you can combine to create the anchor charts.

The units also contain extra teaching tools, including one-day charts, songs and games, and student tools, such as planning mats, bookmarks, cue cards, and scaffolds of various sorts. Each unit supports a stretch of read-aloud work that can be adapted to support reading aloud other texts as well, providing you with scaffolds to support state-of-the-art read-alouds. Similar supports are provided for shared reading. Each unit also includes a short list of recommended titles for independent, partner, and club reading.

Four major units have been developed this way for each grade level, and these include a foundational unit, as well as units in both fiction and nonfiction reading. In addition, there are six additional units of study in the *If . . . Then . . . Curriculum: Assessment-Based Instruction, Grades K–2* book, as well as detailed advice for how you can alter the progression of units and draw on those units if the bulk of your students are reading considerably below or above benchmark.

In each unit of study, you will learn a rich repertoire of ways to provide focused and explicit instruction on a handful of skills and strategies. Within one unit, for example, you'll rally all your students to read nonfiction texts, reading not only the words, but also the charts, pictures, and diagrams, and adding together knowledge from all those sources. Minilessons will help you rally your students to tackle this important work, regardless of their zones of proximal development. For children who are reading the most accessible texts, information can be acquired not only from the sentence or two on the page, but from the illustrations and photographs. Children reading more complex texts will learn to hold onto details from each chapter and then to leaf back over those pages after reading them to think about how they all fit together. Like any other essential reading skills, synthesis of information is not something readers learn to do once and for all. Instead, this skill develops along a pathway. This means that an entire community of readers can be invited to work toward a particular reading skill. No reader will ever stop working to determine the main idea, synthesize, or predict, for example. It's just that the texts in which readers do this work and the nature of the work itself will become increasingly complex, and the scaffolds you provide will vary.

To help you support diverse learners as each one works in her way toward shared goals, the series will show you how to collect data you value and to work together with colleagues to provide data-informed instruction in which you scaffold your students' learning so each works in his zone of proximal development. You will also learn ways to assess children, to help you understand a specific child's characteristic ways of working with texts, and to use the structures of the reading workshop to create individualized supports.

One of the distinguishing features of this series is the way it welds theory and practice. Too often, practical, nuts-and-bolts instruction is divorced from theory. Too often, teachers need to choose between books that embrace research and theory and books that are grounded in real-life classrooms. The Units of Study for Teaching Reading and its sister series for teaching writing instead weave theory and practice together, showing state-of-the-art teaching and then pulling the curtain back from this teaching to reveal the principles that informed the teaching decisions, the alternatives that could have been considered instead, and the transferable methods that underlie this powerful instruction. The books also aim to give you opportunities to receive both strong scaffolding and on-the-job professional development and graduate education in reading development.

A SERIES BUILT ON DECADES OF TEACHING AND RESEARCH

This series builds on decades of teaching and research—in literally tens of thousands of schools. In states across the country and countries across the world, this curriculum has already given young people extraordinary power, not only as readers but also as thinkers. When young people are explicitly taught the skills and strategies of proficient reading and are invited to live as richly literate people do, carrying books everywhere, bringing reading into every nook and corner of their lives, the results are dramatic.

The work has spread from one district to another. When teachers receive support in teaching reading and are consequently able to provide students with clear, sequenced, vibrant instruction in the skills and strategies of proficient reading (as well as opportunities to read with others), it makes a dramatic difference in students' abilities and attitudes as readers. Good teaching pays off. When you provide students with constant opportunities to read and to write, and when you actively and assertively cultivate their best efforts through focused instruction, their literacy development will astonish you, their parents, the school administrators, and best of all, the students themselves.

It is not only *student's* work that is transformed when teachers are supported in the teaching of reading; *teachers'* work is also transformed. One of the beautiful things about teaching literacy is that no one needs to make a choice between responsive, student-centered teaching and results-oriented, data-based teaching. When young people share their reading with you and with each other, it's easy to track their progress in higher-level comprehension skills. Schools can be characterized by that cycle of continuous improvement that is the real source of good teaching.

The good news is that when a community of teachers embraces reform in the teaching of reading and writing, teachers become reinvigorated and renewed in the process. My expectation is that you will describe this teaching to others, saying, "It is not the easiest way of teaching—it asks a lot of me—but you know what? Somehow, the approach also gives me energy. I'm finding this way of teaching taps a new energy source in me." Over the years, teachers have repeatedly told me just that. They say that this kind of teaching has given them new energy, clarity, and compassion, reminding them why they went into teaching in the first place. I understand what these teachers mean, for it has done all this—and more—for me as well.

As school systems come to realize that you and your colleagues are in fact the secret to higher standards—that the only way for a school to teach reading really well is for the professionals in that school to be immersed in a cycle of continuous improvement—this will create an escalating demand for professional development. This series aims to meet that demand by providing, you could say, professional development in a box.

A SERIES PROVIDING BOTH CURRICULUM *AND* PROFESSIONAL DEVELOPMENT

Both the Units of Study for Teaching Reading and the sister publication, Units of Study in Argument/Opinion, Information, and Narrative Writing, series have been written in ways that double as both curricular support and professional development. Each day's instruction in both reading and writing is designed according to research-based principles. For example, you will see that all of the teaching follows the "gradual release of responsibility" model of teaching. Students first learn from a demonstration (accompanied by an explicit explanation), then from guided practice, and then finally from support transferring what they have learned to another text, another day. When students attempt something new, they are given scaffolding, and this is lightened and then removed over time. They continue, however, to receive feedback on their independent work. Over time, strategies that are learned in concrete step-by-step ways become more layered and implicit, fluid and responsive.

The progressions that undergird this curriculum are always carefully chosen and explicitly explained. Our goal is not just to provide you with a coherent, principled curriculum; it is also to teach you knowledge of reading development and methods of teaching reading. Because my colleagues and I have spent thirty

years helping hundreds of thousands of teachers learn to teach reading and writing, and because we have studied that work, reflecting on it as we engage in a continual process of revision, we know a lot about how to provide professional development in literacy teaching—and that is the aim of this series. While the units scaffold your teaching, they also help you develop finesse and flexibility to invent other English Language Acquisition (ELA) units, and to transfer this kind of teaching to other disciplines.

The wonderful thing about learning to teach reading well is that there are just a few teaching methods that one needs to know and be able to use effectively. Better yet, the methods are similar to those used for teaching writing. This means that as you become adept at teaching within a writing workshop, these teaching methods you learn transfer to a reading workshop. In this series, we provide crystal clear advice on how to lead efficient and effective minilessons, conferences, and small-group strategy sessions. We do so, knowing that as you travel through the series, encountering scores of minilessons, conferences, small-group sessions, book clubs, read-aloud conversations, and the like, you will learn not only from explicit instruction but also from immersion. *A Guide to the Reading Workshop, Primary Grades* details the architecture of minilessons, conferences, guided reading, and small-group strategy sessions and articulates the management techniques that make reading and writing workshops possible. You'll also find chapters about assessment systems that make teaching and learning more robust, goal-directed, data-based, and responsive. The unit books put the methods, the principles, and the curriculum into your hands, so that you can bring all this to life with your own students. The book *If . . . Then . . . Curriculum: Assessment-Based Instruction, Grades K–2* helps you adjust your teaching plans to meet the particular needs of your students.

Ideally, you and every other teacher in the world should have the opportunity not only to implement exemplary teaching, but also to do so with a coach nearby, highlighting the way the teaching puts into action a collection of guiding principles. Therefore, as you witness our teaching, I will from time to time act as a coach (or a colleague will), underscoring aspects of the teaching that seem especially essential. The italicized comments on minilessons are one of many ways we help to extrapolate guidelines and methods as you observe this teaching, so that you'll be positioned to invent more in your own teaching. The end goal is not the teaching that we've described here, but the teaching that you, your colleagues, and your students invent together.

AN OVERVIEW OF THE SERIES' CONTENTS

The intent of this series is to provide systemic schoolwide support to enable the students across your school become engaged, purposeful, strategic readers. To support this work, each grade level box for the K–2 series contains:

- *A Guide to the Reading Workshop, Primary Grades*

- Four units of study. There is an equal division between fiction and information reading across the units and a great deal of support for foundational skills.

- A book containing additional units: *If . . . Then . . . Curriculum: Assessment-Based Instruction, Grades K–2.* This book is written to help you adjust your curriculum to your standards, your interests, and your students' needs and interests. It also helps you differentiate curriculum by supporting small-group work and one-to-one conferring.

- *Online Resources for Teaching Reading.* This treasure chest of additional resources includes a range of tools: bibliographies, student tools, reading logs, short texts, artistic renderings of charts, reproducible checklists, homework, mentor texts, and Web links.

- A five-day plan for both read-alouds and shared reading lessons accompanying each unit of study. These plans both use a transferable structure that you can adapt so that it also supports subsequent lessons.

- Anchor charts that evolve across each bend and unit. Each unit supplies large Post-its that provide clear visuals and accessible language to support students' independent practice and build a repertoire of strategies.

An assumption behind this series is the idea that if you are truly going to bring all of your students to the ambitious levels of any of today's global standards, there needs to be vertical alignment in the instruction children receive, so that teachers at any one grade level can count on students entering their classrooms with some foundational skills that can then be built upon. Teachers and kids, too, need to speak a common language so they can reference and build on the work done previously.

The days of each teacher functioning as a lone ranger need to be at an end. Imagine how impractical it would be if each first-grade math teacher used a different word for borrowing and carrying, and each first-grade teacher decided on her own whether or not to teach place value: second-grade teachers who received students from several different first-grade classrooms would find that half the class would have little knowledge or vocabulary around subtraction, and the other half would be ready, with some review, to move toward subtraction with regrouping. Of course, almost every school *does* have a math curriculum that supports vertical alignment, allowing teachers to extend and build on previous instruction. This series provides a similar curriculum in support of skills such as retelling, summarizing, inference, and interpretation.

In this series, instruction builds on itself. You might teach a skill first within fiction reading, then transfer that skill to a unit on high-interest nonfiction reading, and then help students also use that skill with poetry. You might say, "In your earlier unit of study, you learned that when you get stuck on a hard word, it helps to look at the picture to think about what word might fit. Today I want to teach you that as your books are become more challenging, the pictures become less helpful. Instead of looking at the picture for clues, you can think about what's happening in the story to figure out a word that would make sense." In this way, students are brought to higher levels of achievement because teaching stands on the shoulders of prior instruction. One month's or one year's instruction recalls and builds upon the previous instruction. A teacher might say, "I know that last year, you learned to become a more fluent reader by rereading the text to make it sound smoother. This year I want to teach you that there are other ways to do this. You can reread to notice punctuation and where to scoop words, and you can reread to notice the tone and then match your voice to make your reading sound smooth." Because the units of study books fit tongue-and-groove alongside each other, they help students learn and then consolidate and apply what they have learned in new contexts, doing so in ways that allow those students to meet and exceed any iteration of global standards.

Later in this book, I will discuss a recent study by Bembry and others, which shows that if a child has access to a strong teacher for three consecutive years, that child's scores on standardized reading tests will be as much as 40% higher than the scores of students who have not had such access to strong teachers. That data shows not just the effect of a good teacher, but the effect of a good school.

This series aims to support good schools. We do so, believing that the children in Bembry's study who were taught for three years in a row by good teachers are not just the recipients of good luck. Rather, they find themselves in schools that function as communities of practice, in schools that support and strengthen teachers. In these schools, a spiral curriculum allows the work of one grade level to build upon that of another. The teachers in such a school meet across the grades to talk and think about how a unit of study in character will be different in first, second, third, and fourth grades. When will the emphasis on secondary characters move front and center for all students, instead of being reserved for more proficient readers? At what grade levels will teachers tend to emphasize that characters sometimes play a symbolic role in a story? These are schools that think carefully about special support services that children receive, making sure that a child's work with a reading specialist is aligned with, and not disruptive of, the classroom work. These are schools with a systemic approach to assessment, where, for example, teachers at the end of one year make book baggies full of just-right books for each child, so that for the first two weeks of the new year, each child is reading books selected at the end of the preceding year.

I recall a visit to Portland, Oregon, when a principal spoke to me about the effects of our writing units of study, and what he said pertains to reading units of study as well. He said, "What your series has done is that it has brought my whole staff into a shared conversation. Our school has become a community of practice. We started out working 'by the book,' and now we're dancing on the edges, looping in some other work we also love, addressing some issues unique to our setting; but, because of the units, we're doing this together, in a cohesive community of practice." I can't imagine a more significant accolade.

It is critical that teachers across a school take up shared methods of teaching, because this means that when one teacher has special finesse with that method, others can use prep time to watch that teacher at work, learning from her. It means, too, that one teacher can head across the country to study from an expert, with everyone in the school awaiting the goods when that teacher returns, arms full of new information.

It is especially important for schools to become communities of practice, because methods of teaching are also methods of learning. If every year, every teacher needs to induct kids into whole new ways of acting in a classroom, into whole new cultures and expectations, then kids spend half their time trying to adapt to the whims of each new classroom. How much better it is for a school to decide upon some shared methods and to think about how children's roles over time will become more proactive, more complex, and more responsible!

The Unit Books: The Heart of the Series

Each unit of study book represents about four to six weeks of teaching. Within that time, the unit supports students reading lots of books, with the assumption that those who are reading the shorter and more accessible texts will read them at a faster clip than those reading longer and more complex texts. So some students may read and reread fifty books in a unit, while others will read twenty, or perhaps seven. During every unit, students are matched to books that represent the high end of what they can handle, and they move through those books at different rates. Many books take children no more than seven or eight minutes to read.

It is an understatement to say the Units of Study have been piloted many times. The teaching in these books has been planned, taught, revised, and retaught through a cycle of improvement involving literally thousands of classrooms in schools dotting the globe. Early iterations of these units were summarized in the "Curricular Plans" that the Teachers College Reading and Writing Project drafts each year. More to the point, each of these units has had the advantage of input from scores of great educators who have lent their wisdom to the work.

The unit books are written to give you the opportunity to listen in on and observe the unit being taught with students just the age of your students. As you read them, it will seem as if you were invited into a classroom to watch and listen as my coauthors and I teach and work with young people. You will draw close as we convene the class for a ten-minute minilesson, channeling the students to sit beside partners, calling for their attention. You'll hear how we talk about and demonstrate the strategies and skills of powerful reading. Of course, you'll also overhear the stories we use to draw kids in and the directions we give to send them off to their work time. Then, too, you'll hear the ways we confer and lead small groups—guided reading groups, strategy lessons, book clubs, and partnerships. You'll watch us teach readers to self-assess their abilities to solve words, synthesize, compare and contrast, interpret, and reflect on author's craft. You'll see, too, how early in a unit of study we help students become familiar with goals for that unit, and you'll see the way that learning progressions and assessment data weave through every unit of study.

Each unit is introduced with front matter that helps you understand why, out of all that could possibly be taught at that juncture, we decided on this unit and this pathway through the unit. The art of teaching is rooted in choice. The front matter provides the rationale behind the choices that inform the storyline of the unit. How does this unit support students' reading development? What are the real goals? What is the work students will be doing in each bend? The front matter highlights what matters most in the unit.

Then you can receive help giving your students state-of-the-art *minilessons*. When you read the transcripts of my colleagues' and my teaching, you'll hear the language that we use, and then you will want to use that support to help you teach. It is okay to literally open the book up, hold it on your lap, and to read it aloud, if you need to do that. Over the years, that will change. You'll become so comfortable that you'll know the gist of the minilessons in your bones, and you'll feel free to ad lib.

Each minilesson follows the same structure, which is described in more detail in Chapter 7. This is also the same structure that the writing units of study follow.

The *conferring and small-group work* takes place after you send students off to their work. Each day, you'll see that my colleagues and I help you with the work we think you're likely do that day. More often than not, this section will be like a miniature professional development workshop, showing you ways to anticipate the challenges your students are likely to encounter. That teaching will be punctuated with *mid-workshop teaching* that you will offer to the whole class part way through reading time. Often this teaching builds on the minilesson, extending it by providing a next step or a follow-up point. Other times, the mid-workshop teaching counterbalances the minilesson or broadcasts lessons being taught in conferences or small groups. Next, in kindergarten and first grade, comes *partner time*, when students get together midway through the workshop to read books together and talk about them. We also describe the whole-class share session that culminates the workshop. For readers in grades 2–5, the share is the time for partners or sometimes clubs to work together. We know, of course, that you will very likely invent your own share sessions that respond to your own students and their work.

The Design and Rationale for the Curriculum

When you teach the units of study in this series, you will provide your students with instruction, opportunities for practice, and concrete, achievable goals so they can progress expeditiously to meet and exceed any set of high standards. The units will help you aim not only for grade level standards, but also beyond them. Runners don't aim to stop at the finish line; they aim to run right through it, keeping up the pace until the finish line is well behind them. We, too, want to aim beyond the finish line—bringing every reader with us as we do so.

How were the four units per year decided upon?

The units of study books have been written with the assumption that a year-long curriculum will contain these and other units, taken either from the *If . . . Then . . . Curriculum* book or from other sources. The Teachers College Reading and Writing Project works with a number of schools. Those schools have been teaching seven or eight units per grade level, and those units have changed somewhat over the years. As a result, when we decided to write units into books, we had many choices to draw upon. The units we selected seem to us most essential to students' progress as readers and to their mastery of the challenging goals required by the Common Core and by other iterations of global standards.

How are the units structured?

Each unit is structured into several "bends in the road." Think of a road winding up a mountainside and a biker looking up the slope. Rather than thinking of the thousand-foot climb, it's easier to think of the first bend in the road, where you may stretch and regroup, readying yourself for the next bend. That's how these bends in the reading workshop road go. For example, in the first-grade unit, *Meeting Characters and Learning Lessons: A Study of Story Elements*, the first stretch of the unit supports students in tracking the setting and plot to retell the big events of longer stories in sequence. Then the unit turns a corner, and students work for a time to dig deeper, studying the characters in the story, inferring feelings and rereading to reflect those feelings with appropriate intonation and expression. In the third bend, readers think about the whole of the story, particularly endings, to consider the lessons characters learned, as well as universal lessons the author aims to teach.

In the final bend of the unit, readers consider their own opinions about the books they've read, recommending favorites to others and passing along those important life lessons to friends.

How do the units fit the needs of my students/school/district/assessments?

As you think about your students' interests and needs, and your district and school curriculum, you'll need to make some decisions. You may decide, based on your particular situation, to teach a unit at a different grade level than it was originally intended. For example, you may choose to teach a unit that we have written for first grade to both first-graders and then, with adaptations, again to second-graders. You may decide that one of the second-grade units could be taught, for the time being, in third grade as well as in second grade, because your current third-grade students didn't get the second-grade teaching yet. Those sorts of decisions are all discussed in the *If . . . Then . . . Curriculum* book. In that book, we also point out that these units can be taught alongside other units, and we overview six alternatives. You can also draw on units contained in publications by literacy leaders such as Anne Goudvis, Debbie Miller, Kathy Collins, Stephanie Parsons, Tony Stead, and others. Certainly, the expectation is that your reading curriculum will always be a living, changing, growing compilation of best practices.

The Relationship to Units of Study in Opinion, Information, and Narrative Writing

This Units of Study for Teaching Reading series aligns with Units of Study in Opinion, Information, and Narrative Writing, although each can also be taught by itself. The most obvious alignment lies in the area of methods. Those of you who have learned to teach the writing units will find it a small step to now also teach the reading series. Although people may not think about kids, as well as teachers, having jobs to do within a particular set of methods, they do. And kids, as well as teachers, will find it a small step to now work within reading units of study.

Each session in the reading series is perhaps 30% briefer than those in the writing series, and texts play a more dominant role in the reading series. Other than those differences, however, the two series are very similar. The reading units all intersect with and reinforce the writing units and vice-versa, aligning in how they develop content, skills, and/or habits.

There are instances in which the reading and the writing units fit together, tongue and groove. For example, in the kindergarten writing series, students are taught early on to include spaces between their words to make their writing easier for readers to read. In one of the kindergarten reading units, students are taught to use the spaces between words in their books to track print as they develop one-to-one correspondence. Similarly, a second-grade book on information writing teaches students to organize information by including headings that name the main topic and then developing their piece by including information that connects to that topic. The second-grade nonfiction reading unit supports children in developing the sort of organized thinking that will make that writing unit easier to teach. Students are taught to use the headings in their nonfiction books to preview chapters, to consider what a section is mostly about, and to retell key details to provide examples of what each part of a text teaches. As in so many cases, related reading and writing activities reinforce each other.

In smaller ways, the reading units reference and rely on students' experiences as writers. For example, when teaching students to read analytically and understand that an author has written the text they are reading and made choices deliberately and purposefully, the units call upon students' own experiences as writers. When teaching students to pay close attention to an author's craft, the term "show, not tell" is brought over from the writing workshop to help readers infer a character's feelings. In these and other ways, there is reciprocity between the reading workshop and its sister, the writing workshop.

If . . . Then . . . Curriculum: Assessment-Based Instruction, Grades K–2

In addition to the four units of study for each grade level, you will find *If . . . Then . . . Curriculum: Assessment-Based Instruction, Grades K–2*, a book that helps you to move from assessing your students to planning your year-long sequence of units. For example, *If . . . Then . . . Curriculum* helps you look at your student data and think about ways you might alter the suggested sequence in the units because of that data. If you are teaching second grade, for example, and your students have no experience with any of these units, what do we recommend? If your class is reading well below benchmark level, should you vary the sequence of units that you teach? Our thoughts in response to questions such as these are in this text.

If . . . Then . . . Curriculum also offers shortened versions of half a dozen additional units of study—units that you might decide to teach before, after, or in between the units we've provided in full. For example, you might worry that your second-grade students are not yet ready for the *Series Book Clubs* unit, because most of your class is not yet reading early chapter books and needs more support with lower-level texts. In that case, you may decide to turn to an alternative unit titled "Readers Get to Know Characters by Performing Their Books." This unit could supplement *Series Book Clubs*, taught either prior to the series unit as a ramp into the work, or as a guide for small-group work with students who need extra support. If you think your students need more experience in reading nonfiction, you might decide to teach a "Reading Nonfiction Cover to Cover: Nonfiction Book Clubs" unit of study in the spring. The curriculum we've described in the full-length books only supports a portion of your reading curriculum, so you'll probably want to adapt and use some of these additional units of study.

Where can I find books for reading workshop that have engaging, relevant content and fit the needs of my readers?

Some units offer specialized book lists, included in the online resources. There are also book lists available through Booksource, in their Units of Study Libraries, that include books at a variety of levels. The nonfiction lists specialize in books on high-interest topics, many of which are structured to help readers learn to ascertain the main topic and supporting information as they read.

Online Resources for Teaching Reading: A Grade-by-Grade Collection of Digital Resources

In the Online Resources for Teaching Reading, you'll find a rich array of additional resources to support each unit of study and each grade level. These include learning progressions, rubrics, student exemplars, a small number of short video clips, websites, book lists, and additional resources to go with particular sessions. You'll also find reproducible teaching charts and other teaching tools. These resources are provided to support your teaching throughout the year.

AUTHORSHIP OF THE SERIES

Although the text reads as if one teacher created and taught the minilessons, mid-workshop teachings, small groups, and shares, the work that goes behind a unit is actually much more collaborative. I am a coauthor of some of the books and the editor of others, but either way, the process has involved more people than I could ever name. Usually the genesis of a unit begins years before we actually start writing it down. Either the entire unit or portions of it will have been taught in some form for years, often in hundreds of classrooms. As the unit is being taught, my colleagues and I continue to learn new things, to adopt new standards, to take on new goals, and to make new tools—and all of that leads to revisions of the unit.

When the decision is made that a particular unit—one from all the many units my colleagues and I have created—will be written down, then the unit is totally rethought from top to bottom. The work begins with plans for the bends and the mentor texts. Implicit in the plans for a unit are literally hundreds of decisions, and our initial plans are always revised endlessly before becoming the backbone of the unit. Part of that revision process involves passing the plans among many of us because the units that we write become essential to all the Teachers College Reading and Writing Project's work in schools, and we all need to agree on the major decisions. For this K–2 reading series, Amanda Hartman and Liz Dunford Franco played especially key roles in this process.

During the early planning portion of the process, the coauthors and I decide on mentor texts and on the bends of the unit. Then one person drafts a minilesson or two, and that minilesson is placed on Google Docs so that we can all work with it. The lesson is revised, piloted, revised again, and principles from that revision are sent out from the work with that one minilesson to all coauthors of all the K–5 books. "Just a note to point out that we're finding it helps to . . ." Each book receives help from "elves," as we call colleagues, writers, and graduate students who function like the shoemakers' elves, coming into the manuscript in the dead of night when coauthors have left it and keeping the forward progress going by lending their particular talents: one helps with "getting ready" sections and checks for consistency with other books at the grade level; another contributes to the small-group work and conferring sections; yet others triple-check the teaching against our best knowledge of reading development or standards.

On the books for which I am a coauthor, I play a very major writing role, writing at least half of the final text. On the other books, for which I am an editor, I always work intensely on the plans and also coach, revise, spot problems, and problem solve. I do whatever writing is necessary to make a first-class book. In some instances, I write a lot and in other instances, I write a little. Either way, I am part of the revision process. The manuscript goes through four or five wholesale revisions and is passed among a number of hands before it is close to being finished. Many books were revised from head to toe even after we thought they were nearly finished. All of this work reflects the care and respect we have for teachers. We want your work to be easier, more efficient, and ever more effective, leaving you energy to give your students the attention they deserve.

Although the books read as if they draw on one classroom, depicting the true story of how that unit of study unfolded in that one classroom, in truth, the classroom depicted in these books is usually a composite classroom, and the kids' voices are captured or created from all of the kids we've taught.

Chapter 3

What Does Research Say that All Readers Need?

WHAT ARE THE ESSENTIALS OF READING INSTRUCTION?

Twice, I've been part of a group of literacy leaders from across the nation who have met repeatedly for the purpose of constructing national literacy standards. Both times, the members of those think tanks were literacy leaders representing some of the nation's most influential thought collaboratives and perspectives. Yet each time I've participated in this work, I have been reminded that an important consensus has emerged around the bottom-line essentials that all children need to thrive as readers. Increasingly, people are coming together around the recognition that youngsters of all ages need a handful of key opportunities.

Above all, good teachers matter. It is important to develop teachers' abilities to teach by providing professional development and a culture of collaborative practice.

In the end, it's teachers that make the difference in kids' lives. Again and again, research shows what most of us already know to be true: good teaching makes a world of difference (Allington and Johnston 2002; Duffy 1997; Rebell and Wolff 2008, 90; Rivkin et al. 2005; Darling-Hammond and Sykes 2003; Pressley et al. 2001; Guthrie and Humenick 2004; Snow et al. 1998). Bembry, for example, found that students who were, for three years, in classrooms that provide high-quality instruction achieved scores on standardized reading tests that were 40% higher than the scores earned by students receiving lower-quality instruction (Bembry et al. 1998). That is a staggering statistic, and it is an important one, because many people believe that reading comprehension boils down to intelligence and that some kids are predisposed to understand complex texts and others aren't. Clearly, the research suggests otherwise. As Allington writes, "It has become clear that investing in effective teaching—whether in hiring decisions or professional development planning—is the most 'research–based' strategy available" (2002).

Shirley Brice Heath, Margery Bailey Professor of English and Dramatic Literature at Stanford University, has gone so far as to suggest that the single most important condition for literacy learning is having mentors who are joyfully literate people, who demonstrate what it means to live joyfully literate lives. Some lucky children grow up in households where families demonstrate the richness of a life of books, but many of our students rely on school to provide them with that image of possibility. And so it is not just nice—it is essential—that teachers bring their own love of reading into classrooms, talking about the books they love, sharing excitement over hearing an author speak, or telling students that they can't wait to curl up with a book on a rainy Saturday while the rain pelts against the windows.

As new global standards call for levels of intellectual work that many adults have never experienced, it is even more important that teachers engage with their own literacy so they are able to say to students, "Let me show you a strategy that has worked for me." When teachers are public and transparent about their own efforts to develop themselves as readers, they can model that learning to read well is a lifelong process.

Teachers grow stronger not only from studying individual readers, poring over children's books to analyze the challenges and supports those books provide, and talking with others about running records and oral language transcripts, but also from teaching alongside each other. In his article "Improving Relationships within the Schoolhouse," Roland Barth (2006) states, "One incontrovertible finding emerges from my career spent working in and around schools: The nature of relationships among the adults within a school has a greater influence on the character and quality of that school and on student accomplishment than anything else" (8). It is critically important for schools to establish "communities of practice" (Wenger 1998), where teachers work together and learn from each other's best practices with the shared goal of helping students develop into skilled, proficient, expert readers and writers.

Learners need enormous amounts of time for actual reading.

When you teach reading, you are teaching a skill—like playing the oboe or swimming. And when anyone teaches a skill, the learner needs to practice that skill. Students don't learn to play the oboe or to swim by listening to someone talk about playing the oboe or swimming. As Grant Wiggins said when he spoke at Teachers College, you don't learn to drive by taking a car apart and studying every tiny screw and cog that goes into making the car. You need to practice driving. Learners need to be playing that oboe or criss-crossing the pool. And in the same way, your students need to be reading.

A mountain of research supports the notion that teachers who teach reading and writing successfully provide their students with substantial time for actual reading and writing. Allington reports that exemplary teachers of reading have their students actually reading and writing for as much as half the school day, whereas in typical classrooms, it is not unusual to find kids reading and writing for as little as 10% of the day. In all too many schools, a ninety-minute "reading block" includes no more than ten or fifteen minutes of actual reading (Allington 2002). Students in the classrooms of more effective teachers read ten times as much as students in classrooms of less effective teachers (Allington and Johnston 2002).

Success in reading is directly related to the amount of time a person spends reading. Krashen points out that 93% of the tests on reading comprehension that collect data on volume of reading show that kids who are given more time to read do better (2004). Guthrie and Humenick (2004) found that reading volume predicted reading comprehension and that dramatic increases in reading volume are important for thoughtful literacy proficiencies. The NAEP Reading Report Card for the Nation (U.S. Department of Education 1999) showed that, at every level, reading more pages at home and at school was associated with higher reading scores. John Guthrie's study "Teaching for Literacy Engagement" (2004) illustrates that fourth-graders who read at the second-grade level spend just half an hour a day reading, while fourth-graders who read at the eighth-grade level spend four and a half hours a day reading. Anderson et al. (1988) also researched the relationship between the amount of reading done and reading achievement. They found that the amount of time reading was the best predictor of reading achievement, including a child's growth as a reader from the second to the fifth grade.

Research also suggests that both quantity and quality of reading material are important. In a study called "Does Practice Make Perfect? Independent Reading Quantity, Quality and Student Achievement" (Topping et al. 2007), data was collected on 45,670 students in grades 1–12. The results indicated that the combination of reading high-quality books in high quantity led to high academic achievement gains.

Even when the activity students are doing in lieu of reading has been shown to be useful, warning signs should go up when nonreading activities consume more than a few minutes of reading time. For example, although activating prior knowledge before reading has been shown to be useful (Pearson and Fielding 1991), spending most of a reading block doing so is not supported by research—and that's just one example. Allington suggests that three to five minutes spent activating prior knowledge is probably sufficient (Allington 2002). Similarly, a study of over 1,000 first- and second-graders (Foorman et al. 2006) documented the ways children spent their time during literacy instruction. Out of twenty ways that students spent this time, only one way of spending time was able to explain the gains children made on their post-reading test—time spent reading text.

At the very earliest stages, the time children spend reading might look different than it does at later stages. McIntyre et al. (2006) suggests that independent reading time when children are just beginning to read conventionally should be to some extent mediated by a teacher. That is to say, simply handing a book to a child and sending her off to read isn't necessarily going to help her get better as a reader. Instead, readers at this stage may spend their reading time engaged in a variety of oral reading activities such as repeated reading, partner reading, choral reading, and echo reading, in a carefully structured environment that supports the development of the child. With scaffolding and expert instruction, these readers also benefit from the opportunity to spend time reading texts.

After reviewing the overwhelming amount of research on the need for students to spend volumes of time actually reading, Allington concludes, "So how much daily in-school reading might we plan for? I would suggest one and one half hours of daily in-school reading would seem to be a minimum goal given the data provided by these studies . . . However my ninety-minute recommendation is for time actually spent reading" (2006, 47). Research by Guthrie shows what this call for more time spent reading will look like in practice. A level C book can be read in just a few minutes. This means that a student reading for thirty minutes could get through possibly ten or more books in just one sitting. If a book in The Magic Tree House series is an accessible text for a reader (if the reader can handle it with fluency and appropriate accuracy), that child can finish the book in one day and be able to read seven such books in a week. Those books contain approximately 6,000 words, and for this to be a just-right book for the reader, the child would need to be reading the book at 100–200 words per minute—hence the calculation that these books should take no more than thirty to sixty minutes to read. And the research is clear that if children have the time they need to read and to write as well as expert instruction, this bodes well.

The single most important thing we can do, then, to make schools into places where youngsters thrive as readers is to clear out the time and space so that children can learn to read by reading. This means shoveling out the

busy work; in some classrooms, when children are not actually meeting with a teacher in a small guided reading group, they are spinning dials and shaking dice to play letter-sound games, drawing pictures of word cards, or circling right answers on worksheets. Speaking at Teachers College, Allington said, with a twinkle in his eye, "*Crap* is the technical term reserved for all the nonreading and nonwriting activities that fill kids' days—the dittos, dioramas, papier-mâché maps—all that chases real reading and real writing out of the school day" (2008). Remember, exemplary teachers' students read and write as much as ten times as much as kids in other classes. It is impossible to stress enough the importance of kids "just reading." Throughout this book I will help you imagine what this means when the readers are very young.

Learners need access to books that allow them to do a high volume of high-success reading.

One fairly obvious implication of the research showing the need to provide students with a lot of time for actual reading is this: students need access to books that are accessible enough that they can engage in an enormous volume of high-success reading. That is, students need access to lots of books that they can read with high levels of accuracy, fluency, and comprehension. They need opportunities to consolidate skills so they can use skills and strategies with automaticity within fluid, engaged reading. Readers need to work with texts they can read with the smooth orchestration of sources of information that allows the magic to happen and meaning to be made. If a child holds a giant tome and stumbles through it, making swipes at some of the words, that's not reading. Novelist John Gardner describes reading this way:

It creates for us a kind of dream, a rich and vivid play in the mind. We read a few words at the beginning of the book or the particular story and suddenly we find ourselves seeing not words on a page but a train moving through Russia, an old Italian crying, or a farmhouse battered by rain. We read on—dream on—not passively but actively, worrying about the choices the characters have to make, listening in panic for some sound behind the fictional door, exalting in characters' successes, bemoaning their failures. In great fiction, the dream engages us heart and soul; we not only respond to imaginary things—sights, sounds, smells—as though they were real, we respond to fictional problems as though they were real: we sympathize, think, and judge. (Gardner 1991)

Students' reading book boxes

It's not surprising that children need opportunities to engage in high-success reading. Who among us brings giant pharmaceutical books on a long airplane flight or to the beach on a summer day? Adults rarely read a text that we can't read with 99.5% accuracy. We wouldn't read if we were constantly derailed by complexities that we couldn't assimilate, and kids aren't any different.

Over sixty years ago, Betts studied fourth-graders and found that low error rates led to improved learning (1946). In that research, independent reading levels were texts that readers could read with 98% accuracy or better, and instructional-level texts were those readers could read with 95–97% accuracy. Swanson et al.'s (1999) meta-analysis of 180 intervention studies showed that for learning-disabled students, one of the three conditions that allow for achievement is that the difficulty level of the task must be controlled enough that the learner can be successful.

This is nowhere more important than for children who are beginning readers or who struggle. Too often, only the students who can read well are given lots of opportunities in school for high-success reading, and as a result they flourish. Kids who can't read well come to school ready for the

promise of an education, and they're given impenetrable texts. They might as well be given sawdust. Many studies support this conclusion. For example, Ehri et al. (2007) studied a specific tutoring program to support struggling first-grade English language learners (ELLs), and after tracking the daily oral reading accuracy of the students, found that "the reading achievement of students who received . . . tutoring appeared to be explained primarily by one aspect of their tutoring experience—reading texts at a high level of accuracy, between 98% and 100%" (441).

The exemplary teachers in the studies by Allington and Johnston (2002) and Pressley et al. (2001) rejected district plans that required one-size-fits-all mandates, wherein all students read the same texts and answer the same questions every day. These teachers instead recognized that such mandates contradict everything that is known about effective teaching of reading. They spent their own money to provide multilevel texts, if needed, not only during language arts time, but in social studies and science as well. Allington writes, "A primary outcome of these exemplary teachers was the acceleration of literacy development in their lowest-achieving students" (Allington and Johnston 2002). While students at all achievement levels benefited from exemplary teaching, it was the lowest achievers who benefited most.

What does all this mean? It means that it is important to provision the students in your class with books they can read. If you teach second grade, you can't simply go to a publisher and purchase a set of books that some publisher has decided will be perfect for every second grade across the world. Your particular second grade will have its own characteristics: perhaps you need books in Spanish as well as English. Maybe you have many children who are still reading level C/D books. You need the books that match the readers in your classroom. As Fountas and Pinnell (2013) remind us, "To become proficient readers, students must experience successful processing daily. Not only should they be able to read books independently, building interest,

A consensus has formed around the resolve to accelerate students' progress so they can read increasingly complex texts by the time they reach college. Teachers are finding ways to provide students with access to complex texts, even if they cannot read those texts independently. Digital recordings and teacher read-alouds allow students to benefit from hearing, thinking, and talking about these texts (Elley 1989; Fountas and Pinnell 2012; Ray 2006).

It is especially important that students develop their vocabularies, not only by learning the domain-specific words that they are apt to encounter in the content areas (e.g., *life cycle, antenna, pollination*), but also through immersion in academic language, including terms such as *character, predict,* and *compare.* Figurative language, too, is a hallmark of more complex texts, and students need to wrestle with the meaning of metaphors, similes, and idioms. When students are given access to complex texts, they also are immersed in complex sentence structures, including longer sentences that contain subordinate clauses and embedded phrases. Complex texts for primary readers are often organized in more complex ways: time in narratives may not unfold sequentially but may be marked by flashbacks, gaps in time, and/or digressions. More complex expository texts are apt to have sections or chapters, main topics with supporting details, and other features that indicate how information is structured.

stamina, and fluency; they also need to tackle harder books that provide the opportunity to grow more skillful as a reader" (267). The books you provision your students with matter tremendously and are among your most powerful tools as a literacy teacher.

It takes just a moment of reflection on our own reading lives to be reminded that it's important not only that young people have access to books they *can* read, but that they also have access to books they *want* to read. In a study of over 800 students from pre-K to fifth grade, Edmunds and Bauserman (2006) interviewed children and asked them to share about a book they had recently read. Not surprisingly, the vast majority, 84% of the children, discussed a book they had selected for themselves. Chances are, you and I would do the same. Choice matters—not a little, but a lot. The goal, after all, is not only to teach kids to read, but to help them grow up to be people who value reading. Luring kids to be invested in reading is not a small goal. After all, a 2007 National Endowment for the Arts study, "To Read or Not to Read," found that Americans are reading less, with people aged fifteen to twenty-four spending less than seven minutes a day reading. If we hope to bring up a nation of readers, it is crucial to allow them to choose among high-interest books that they can read. In fact, Guthrie and Humenick (2004) did a meta-analysis of twenty-two experimental or quasi-experimental studies of reading motivation and achievement and found factors that were strongly related to student success. Ensuring that students had easy access to interesting texts was the single most influential factor, and providing children choice about what they read and whom they read with was the second most influential factor.

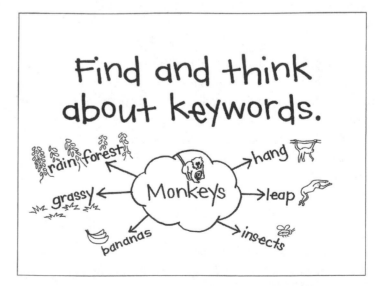

Although nothing is gained from asking a student who cannot decode a complex text to sit in front of such a text, staring at the page, there are many students who *can* decode such a text and do not have the high level strategies or the appetite for tackling this sort of difficulty. To help these students develop the muscles to handle complex texts, it is helpful to provide them with the instruction necessary to deal with complex text structures, shifting perspectives, figurative language, and the like. This instruction will involve opportunities to engage in repeated readings, to work in pairs, to pause often as one reads, to summarize and discuss meaning, and to explore word meanings (Shanahan et al. 2012).

Carol Dweck's research identifies two different mindsets for how we understand intelligence and achievement: the fixed mindset and the growth mindset. People with a fixed mindset view intelligence as a fixed trait—either you have a lot of it or you don't. Dweck noted that students with this mindset worry about whether they have enough intelligence, and this hinders them from taking risks and seeking new challenges. In contrast, people with a growth mindset view intelligence as something you can develop through active learning. Students with this mindset take more risks with their learning, welcome challenges, and don't worry about whether their performance will reveal a lack of intelligence, because they believe they can become smarter through their efforts. Dweck articulates the advantages of a growth mindset:

> This view, too, has many repercussions for students. It makes them want to learn. After all, if your intelligence can be increased why not do that? Why waste time worrying about looking smart or dumb, when you could be becoming smarter? And in fact students with this view will readily sacrifice opportunities to look smart in favor of opportunities to learn something new. (Dweck 2000, 2–4)

Dweck's research also indicates that students can be taught to adopt a growth mindset, which can help them persevere in the face of challenge. In addition, it's important that students are interested and invested enough in their reading that they are willing to work with some persistence when they encounter difficulty.

Learners need direct, explicit instruction in the strategies of proficient reading.

To grow as readers, in addition to ample time to read and access a variety of appropriate texts, children also need expert instruction. Think of an athlete practicing to improve their skills. Under the eye of a skilled coach, all of a sudden an athlete begins to improve in leaps and bounds. A simple instruction to shift some weight or hold a racquet a little differently can make all the difference. The same goes for readers. Explicit instruction in the strategies of proficient reading can make all the difference in helping readers grow in leaps and bounds.

Reading is complex. When your eyes skim across a page, you instantaneously recognize thousands of words, processing them into sentences and fluidly making meaning. What feels effortless for a proficient reader represents a world of challenge for a novice reader. To squeeze meaning from the page, a beginning reader must be able to identify and discriminate a series of little black squiggles on the page, with just the tiniest variations (think of the difference between the letter *n* and the letter *h*). They must understand that those squiggles represent dozens of different sounds and that those sounds come together to represent words, sentences, and ideas. And they must do this while still integrating the content with their own emerging understandings of the world. To do this, readers will need instruction in skills that are foundational to the development of becoming a reader: print concepts, phonological awareness, phonics and word reading strategies, and fluency.

To develop a concept of print—an understanding of how print works—children need to learn how to handle books and understand text directionality (left to right and top to bottom), one-to-one matching, the difference between letters and words, and the function of punctuation. They also need to understand that print communicates a message. These skills are foundational in learning to read because they help the reader know "where to attend, in what sequence, and how to pick up information perceptually" (Clay 1991, 153). Children learn these concepts both through explicit teaching as well as implicitly through modeling when reading texts together (Gehsmann and Templeton 2013).

Phonological awareness is the ability to hear individual words in oral language as well as smaller sounds within words, such as onsets, rimes, and syllables. Phonemic awareness is the ability to hear and manipulate phonemes—the smallest sounds within a word (e.g., /c/-/a/-/t/). Both phonemic awareness and phonological awareness are considered essential to becoming a successful reader. However, in a review of research on phonemic awareness instruction for the National Reading Panel, Ehri and colleagues (2001) caution against assuming that instruction in phonemic awareness is a "magic bullet" and emphasize that it not be taught in isolation. "Teaching phonemic awareness is not the sole key to reading success nor does it constitute a complete beginning reading program" (280). They found that phonemic instruction was more effective when it was taught alongside the instruction of letters and that it does not need to consume long periods of time to be effective. They also stress the importance of teaching kids to apply the skills they have learned within the context of reading.

Phonics is the ability to match letters with their corresponding sounds, and it requires that children have both letter recognition and a knowledge of the sounds that letters and letter combinations can make. This is called the alphabetic principle—an understanding that letter sounds connect to letters (Adams 1990; Snow et al. 1998; National Reading Panel 2000). This principle is critical in helping children learn to decode words in text. While there is no clear evidence of one best way to teach phonics, there are some examples of effective practice. In one, the most effective first-grade teachers in a research study taught letters and sounds, onsets and rime, and then the application of this knowledge in the context of reading and writing (Juel and Minden-Cupp 2000).

Fluency has been identified as a critical component of literacy instruction (Allington 2011; National Reading Panel 2000; Rasinski 2010). A definition of fluency involves two components; the ability to read text accurately and efficiently (automaticity) and to read with appropriate expression or prosody (Rasinski 2011). As early readers, many children have difficulty reading fluently. Chall (1995) describes readers at this stage as being "glued to the print." Their reading is often slow, and they read word by word as they attend carefully to the text, using their early understandings of how letters and words work to problem solve. According to Rasinski (2013), "one of our roles as educators is to help students move from purposeful decoding to word identification that is effortless and automatic" (270). This is best done through support with word recognition and by giving students ample practice reading across a variety of texts. In addition, research has found that prosody (phrasing, intonation, stress, and tempo) is particularly supportive of student's reading comprehension (Benjamin and Schwanenflugel 2010). Think about your most proficient readers—the "nose in their book" kids who truly understand the joy of reading. Chances are, these readers read in a way that is phrased and meaningful because it is absolutely essential to understanding the author's message (Clay 2005). It is our job as educators to teach this to all children.

In their report on recommendations to improve comprehension in the primary grades, Shanahan and colleagues (2010) make it clear that there is strong evidence supporting the teaching of comprehension strategies right from the earliest stages. The report highlights activating background knowledge, questioning, visualization, monitoring, inference, and retelling as key research-supported strategies to be taught in primary classrooms—all of which are found woven through the instruction in this K–2 series. In addition, the report recommends that a gradual release of responsibility model be used in this instruction.

The National Reading Panel also strongly supports explicit instruction in comprehension strategies, suggesting that the teaching of even one comprehension strategy can lead to improved comprehension, and that teaching a repertoire of strategies can make an even larger difference (National Reading Panel 2000). Allington's research yielded similar findings, noting that exemplary teachers "routinely gave direct, explicit demonstrations of the cognitive strategies that good readers use when they read" (2002, 743). It is important that strategy instruction teach students *what* the strategy is, *when* it is used, *how* it is used, and *why* it is worth using.

This is critical because many teachers think of teaching as little more than assigning and assessing work. Assigning students a task—say, one that resembles those on high-stakes assessments—and then assessing their abilities to do that task should not be confused with instruction. When imagining instruction, think instead of a progression of work that goes from "watch me, let me demonstrate" to "now you try, and I'll support you." Many researchers have detailed this form of strategy instruction. Among them are Duke and Pearson (2002), who point out that strategy instruction involves:

- Naming and describing the strategy: why, when, and how it could be used

- Modeling the strategy in action

- Using the strategy collaboratively

- Guiding practice of the strategy, gradually releasing responsibility to the student

- Providing opportunity for using the strategy independently

Rosenshine found that "The more effective teachers do not overwhelm their students by presenting too much new material at once. Rather, these teachers only present small amounts of new material at any time, and then assist the students as they practice this material" (2012, 3–14).

Duke and Pearson make an important caveat, in "Effective Practices for Developing Reading Comprehension," stating, "It is important that neither the teacher nor the students lose sight of the need to coordinate or orchestrate comprehension strategies. Strategies are not to be used singly—good readers do not read a book and only make predictions. Rather, good readers use multiple strategies constantly" (2002, 210). Allington (2002) discusses the same point when he writes, "The instructional environment must foster independent strategy transfer and use. A real concern is that when instruction becomes too explicit too much of the time, children never acquire the independent strategy transfer and use. Use of a strategy in a highly structured, teacher-directed setting is not the same as knowing how and when to profitably and successfully use the strategy when reading independently (Allington 2002)."

The voice that has perhaps made this point most clearly when it comes to the development of young readers over the last few decades is that of Marie Clay. Her work reminds us that our ultimate purpose as teachers of reading is not to simply teach strategies, but instead to teach our readers to become *strategic*, to be the kind of readers that take action, to solve problems independently by integrating all they know about reading and do so in ways that are flexible and adaptive. Reading instruction, then, needs to help children learn to act with agency. It needs to support readers in developing a system that uses multiple sources of information (meaning, structure, and visual) to monitor, search, self-correct, predict, and/or confirm as they read (Clay 2005). Reading is incredibly complex work, and it warrants thoughtful, deliberate instruction that guides children in becoming joyful, independent readers.

Learners need opportunities to talk in response to texts.

Talking and writing both provide concrete, visible ways for learners to do the thinking work that later becomes internalized and invisible. Think about it. If you want to gain insights on your teaching, your family, your life—what do you do? You meet with someone to "talk things over." If you want to become better at doing something, you bring in a coach, a tutor, or an advisor. Whoever the person is, what you will do is talk. In think tanks, study groups, inquiry projects, graduate courses, seminars—what do you do? You talk. Talk is the medium in which we all outgrow ourselves, over and over.

It was Vygotsky, more than anyone, who staked out the theory that accounts for the crucial role of social interactions in supporting learning. The key element in his theory of learning is that "all the higher functions originate as actual relationships between individuals" (1978, 957). The words that we say in conversation and the kinds of thinking we do in collaboration become internalized. If you and I had a conversation about the ending of a book, we might mull over why the author chose to end it that way and weigh how the book might have been different had it ended differently. Then another time, reading alone, I might reach the ending of a book and think to myself, "Hmm, . . . I wonder why the author decided to end this book this way." The thinking I'd be doing would be an internalized conversation.

Because teaching reading is teaching thinking, it is not surprising that social relationships are critical to a reading workshop. Conversations are especially crucial, because data suggests that not enough American students are growing up to be thoughtfully literate (Goodwin 2014). If one looks at what students spend their time doing in school, it is very easy to project the skills that they will master. If students spend their time answering low-level literal questions, filling in blanks, and recalling facts, then that will be the kind of thinking they can do well. And all too often, that is exactly what is being asked for and what is being learned in American classrooms. In study after study, researchers report that, in the typical classroom, the assigned tasks overwhelmingly emphasize copying, remembering, and reciting, with few tasks assigned that engage students in discussions about what they've read. Is it any wonder that many students do not seem adept at comparing and contrasting, analyzing, making connections, and thinking interpretively and critically? And yet this is exactly the sort of literacy that is required in the world of today—and of tomorrow. The New Commission on the Skills of the American Workforce describes the candidates that the best employers in the world will be looking for this way: "Candidates will have to be comfortable with ideas and abstractions, good at both analysis and synthesis, creative and innovative, self-disciplined and well-organized, able to learn quickly and work well as a member of a team and have the flexibility to adapt quickly to frequent changes" (2007).

One of the most powerful ways to teach children to think is to teach them to engage in thoughtful discussions, especially those that incorporate thinking under, between, and around texts. In their article "Text Talk," Beck and McKeown suggest that the key to literacy isn't "merely listening to book language but talking about ideas" (2001, 10–11), citing many researchers such as Catherine Snow who have highlighted the critical role that talk plays in children's literacy growth. In their research on exemplary teachers, both Allington

(2002) and Pressley (2001) note that the nature of talk was fundamentally different in the classrooms led by exemplary teachers. These teachers fostered more student talk, both teacher-student and student-student. The talk was not chatter, but problem-posing, problem-solving talk. In addition, recent research by Foorman and colleagues (2015) also found that oral language was a significant predictor of reading comprehension in first- and second-grade students, lending more support to the importance of children having strong oral language skills.

Talking well, like writing well, does not emerge *ex nihilo*. It is helpful to explicitly teach students to make claims that are grounded in the text, to supply evidence for those claims, and to connect the example and the claim. In a case study of young children's talk about text, Maine showed the importance of teachers modeling and then prompting students in how to have rich, text-based discussions (2013). It is helpful to teach students to develop a line of thinking through sustained talk about one subtopic and, as part of this, to elaborate using transitional phrases such as "This is important because . . ." and "I wonder why . . ." Then, too, it is important to teach readers to be able to build upon the ideas of others, following an idea to its conclusion.

Reading workshops not only support talk, but also *teach* talk. Readers are generally matched with a long-term partner—someone who is able to read, and has the interest in reading, similar books. Partners in kindergarten and first grade tend to read independently for half of the reading workshop and then spend the second half reading with a partner. Right from the beginning of kindergarten, children are taught that partners can not only read together, but they can also talk about their texts. In second grade, children spend most of the reading workshop time reading independently but in the last few minutes have the opportunity to get together with a partner to compare notes, raise and pursue questions, and learn to see the text through each other's perspectives. Readers also have the opportunity to work in small groups—inquiry groups or book clubs—so their talk can engage them not only with a partner, but with other voices and other perspectives as well. The classroom community as a whole also engages in extended conversations around texts that are read aloud.

Learners need support reading nonfiction books and building a knowledge base and academic vocabulary through information reading.

Consider how much of the reading you do in a day is nonfiction. Day in, day out, you interact with nonfiction texts. Yet research suggests that until recently, most students have had insufficient access to informational texts.

One study of first-grade classrooms found that, on average, informational texts constituted less than 10% of classroom libraries and was supported by only 3% of materials displayed on walls and other surfaces in classrooms (Duke 2000). This study also showed that first-grade classrooms studied informational texts for only an average of 3.6 minutes a day. Lower-income children logged just 1.9 minutes a day of exposure to informational texts. A study by Goodwin and Miller (2012/2013) supports these findings, suggesting that the average child in the United States spends just four minutes a day reading nonfiction.

One reason it is critical for students to increase the time they spend reading nonfiction is that the strength of a student's general knowledge has a close relationship to the student's ability to comprehend complex nonfiction texts. Students who read a great deal of nonfiction gain knowledge about the world as well as about vocabulary. Research shows that even kindergarten aged children can learn content and new language structures from exposure to informational texts (Duke et al. 2003). In addition, the same researchers show that including more informational text in the classroom also has potential benefits. In a study of first-grade children with limited letter-sound knowledge,

those in classrooms with more informational text had higher reading comprehension and writing levels by the end of the year than similar children in other classrooms. Reading nonfiction texts aloud in primary classrooms was also found to be beneficial. A study by Linda Kraemer and her colleagues (2012) demonstrated that first-grade children who were read information texts three times a week for four weeks demonstrated an increased ability to comprehend nonfiction texts in comparison to their peers. The study suggests that increased exposure to information texts at an early age will help prepare students for the challenges of the nonfiction content they'll be reading in coming years. These are just several studies in a mounting body of evidence supporting the use of nonfiction texts in our classrooms—a topic that we simply cannot afford to ignore. It is imperative that we provide our students with a wide variety of texts to read and learn from.

Learners need assessment-based instruction, including feedback that is tailored specifically to them. Children who struggle with reading especially need instruction tailored to their specific strengths and needs, as well as extra time and extra help.

Learners are not all the same, and learners do not all need the same things to progress. Teaching, then, must always be responsive, and our ideas about what works and what doesn't work must always be under construction.

Certainly, when a teacher decides to angle her teaching to support a cluster of reading skills (e.g., in nonfiction reading, focusing on keywords, asking questions, and noting and discussing important information), then teaching begins with observing, listening, and making small, informal assessments. Those assessments help us analyze what it is that our learners can do, can almost do, and can't yet do.

By taking the time to look at students' work and to theorize about their place along a pathway of development in a cluster of skills, we gain knowledge that enables us to provide explicit, concrete, manageable guidance, so that each learner is able to progress toward clear goals. This requires a stance toward teaching that means always behaving in classrooms as researchers. We must invent ways to study kids' work—to research and reflect and discuss and imagine what good work entails. We must wrestle with what pathways toward good work might look like, and we must help kids progress along those pathways. Assessment, then, like teaching, can't be outsourced. And assessment can't be something that occurs once or twice or three times a year. Instead, assessment must be sewn into the fabric of our teaching.

Research suggests that the use of performance assessments embedded in a curriculum can support building higher-order complex skills and can improve instruction (Goldschmidt et al. 2007; Pellegrino et al. 2001; Wood et al. 2007).

In addition, a growing body of research supports the use of learning progressions to guide and raise the level of instruction. Research has demonstrated that learning progressions have important potential for educators, policy makers, and curriculum and assessment designers. Multiple policy documents and research reports published recently related to learning progressions (Daro et al. 2011; Corcoran et al. 2009; Mosher 2011) argue that the development of the Common Core State Standards have created a strong need for learning progressions. For students to have hope of meeting these standards, teachers will need to monitor student progress and know when and how to intervene to support students in reaching the standards. They will need to be aware of when students are encountering difficulty in working to reach these standards and aware of how to support students in getting back on track. In short, teachers will need to know "when to teach what to whom" (Daro et al. 2011, 12). Learning progressions, like research-based maps or pathways, can help guide educators about where to go next.

Of course, assessment is nowhere more critical than when it allows us to take our cues from students who struggle with reading. If a child enters our classroom already encumbered with labels, then we need to be clear from the start—it is our job to turn that child around so that he begins immediately to see that, in fact, learning and progress are within reach. Readers who struggle cannot wait even a week before we begin to show them that reading can make sense for them, and, yes, they can get better as readers in a palpable, observable fashion, making multiple years of growth in just a single year. The first step is for the most knowledgeable person available to assess these readers to find out what reading work they can do with success. If this is a second-grade child and he needs to be reading books at the level of *Biscuit*, then absolutely nothing is gained by giving him instead a Cam Jansen book. Halfway measures are good for naught, because with texts he can't read well, the child still won't feel everything clicking together into reading and still won't have the chance to read in ways that allow him to learn from reading. If the various stakeholders invested in this child—the people who care about him—disagree, then these adults need to come together and talk longer and think harder, so that a single, coherent plan is made that will allow the child to be a successful reader (with the texts that are within reach) and then to move forward in giant steps.

There are a few obvious things to be said.

Children who struggle with reading cannot be taken from the language arts classroom—from reading, writing, word study, or reading aloud—for extra help in language arts.

It is especially worrisome if children who are below benchmark level in reading are taken out of the general classroom for reading once or twice a week and left in the room the other days. The result of this is that when the child *is* in the classroom, she won't understand the read-aloud book or know the shared reading texts or grasp references in the minilessons prior to instruction, because she will have missed a third of reading class, leaving her with big gaps. How much better it would be if the child can receive supplementary support before school, after school, or during a time other than reading class. For these particular children to achieve success, they would benefit from a cohesive intervention program, where all the adults work together and collaborate regularly to ensure positive outcomes for the child's reading progress. This is what makes programs like Reading Recovery so successful in achieving accelerated progress with struggling readers.

Children who read below grade level need to spend 90% of their time reading books they can read with ease.

This means that guided reading can't be about propping a child up to struggle valiantly through a text that is too hard. Anyone who uses guided reading in such a fashion should review the important books on the topic by Gay Su Pinnell and Irene Fountas. It is critical that children who read below grade level are reading books within their zone of proximal development, not just during reading time, but across the day. For these readers, 90% of their reading time should be spent on books that are just right for them and perhaps as much as 10% of the time, books that are a stretch, so that *after* receiving support, they read them with approximately 96% accuracy, fluency, and comprehension.

During extra-help time, children who struggle with reading need help that is assessment-based, tailored to the particular child, and in sync with what is happening in the classroom.

It cannot be that all children who struggle with reading receive the same one-size-fits-all help during an intervention, because what we know about each one is that they are more different from one another than most readers are. Kids who struggle with reading need something, but not necessarily the same thing! For starters, some children in grades K–2 who struggle need more help with phonemic awareness and concepts of print, some in phonics and word work, and others need help in comprehension and fluency. The instruction these readers need will be utterly different.

For any learner to grow stronger, he must be provided with informative, responsive, targeted feedback. Hattie's (2008) research perhaps best supports this claim. He reviewed 180,000 studies involving 20 to 30 million students and found that of 100 factors contributing to student achievement, providing learners with feedback rates in the very top 5–10% of influences. Feedback is especially valuable if the teacher helps the learner know where he is going, what progress he has made so far, and what specific activities he can do next to progress toward the goal. Ideally, learners also receive help in refining and seeking more challenging goals. This is what conferring is—working one-on-one with an individual child, listening and looking to understand her work and intentions, and then helping her make productive use of the instruction provided through personalized direction and feedback tailored to that learner's needs.

Above all, children who struggle with reading need access to good teachers, and that means that teachers need high-quality professional development.

Readers need teachers to read aloud to them.

Read-aloud is essential to teaching reading. You read aloud to open the day, using stories and poems to convene the community and to celebrate what it means to be awake and alive together. You read aloud to embark on shared adventures, to explore new worlds, and to place provocative topics at the center of the community.

There is far more to a powerful read-aloud than simply reading the text. Beck and McKeown remind us that "although reading a story to children is not a difficult task for a literate adult, taking advantage of the read-aloud experience to develop children's literacy is complex and demanding (2001, 19). For the read-aloud to help students develop deep comprehension skills, it is important that it provide teachers with an occasion for modeling think-alouds and prompting for and then extending rich conversation. Research from Teale and Martinez (1996) suggests that there is something powerful that comes from the rich analytic talk that occurs when children are given the chance to reflect on a story. This kind of read-aloud, often referred to as interactive read-aloud, supports children as readers and thinkers.

Read-alouds are also a powerful method to teach vocabulary. We know from Hart and Risley (1995) that when children enter kindergarten, those from economically privileged homes have heard an estimated 30 million more words than children from economically disadvantaged homes. The difference is staggering. Fortunately, one of the ways we can bridge this gap is through read-aloud. Research tells us that explicit instruction of sophisticated vocabulary in read-aloud texts, along with extended interaction with these words across the day, has a positive effect on children's overall vocabulary (Zipoli et al. 2011). When teachers are explicit in using read-aloud as a vehicle for teaching comprehension, they not only teach children new words, but they also create in children a voracious appetite for noticing and learning new words.

For young children, a read-aloud is also a sneak peek into what reading can be. Rasinski (2005) describes read-aloud as being critical to fluency instruction because it provides an essential model for how reading should sound. Too often young readers develop the habit of crawling through their texts word by word and assuming that this is what reading sounds like. Frequent read-alouds dispel this notion and give readers a sense of how reading should sound so they can begin to emulate it in their own texts. Likewise, research also shows that reading aloud fosters positive attitudes toward reading in young children (Kotaman 2008), creates engagement in text (Sipe 2002), supports the development of oral language (Isbell et al. 2004), and strengthens comprehension (Kraemer et al. 2012; Trelease 2006). Of course, it also benefits children to hear a variety of texts across genres (Kraemer et al. 2012; Yopp and Yopp 2006). The fact is, as we read, we transmit more than just the story. We also model a mood, a stance, an engagement and a fluency that bring out not just the meaning, but the feeling of the texts and how they go—features that, once children *internalize* them, make their independent engagement with their own texts far more effective.

Readers need a balanced approach to language arts, one that includes a responsible approach to the teaching of writing as well as of reading.

Reading is critical, but it's not everything. In a democracy and a world that requires people to speak up, writing needs to take its rightful place alongside

reading as one of the basics. In addition, young children in particular also need foundational instruction in phonological awareness and word recognition. Children need to have a well-rounded, balanced diet of literacy instruction. Research supports this. The National Reading Panel's recommendations in 2000 supported the need for children to have balanced literacy instruction. And after writing his book on the importance of a balanced approach to teaching literacy, Pressley and his colleagues (1998) began to do research in this area, seeking out examples of exemplary teaching in the primary grades and studying the approach to instruction. In every case, whenever they found a classroom with high literacy engagement, they found balanced teaching in place (Pressley et al. 2002).

These tenets, then, have led to the reading workshop structure for teaching reading:

- Readers need teachers who demonstrate what it means to live richly literate lives, wearing a love of reading on their sleeves.

- Readers need long stretches of time to read.

- Readers need opportunities to read high-interest, accessible books of their own choosing.

- Readers need to read increasingly complex texts appropriate for their grade level.

- Readers need explicit instruction in the skills of proficient reading.

- Readers need opportunities to talk and sometimes to write in response to texts.

- Readers need support reading nonfiction books and building a knowledge base and academic vocabulary through information reading.

- Readers need assessment-based instruction, including feedback that is tailored specifically to them. Struggling readers especially need instruction that is tailored to their specific strengths and needs, as well as extra time and extra help.

- Readers need teachers to read aloud to them.

- Readers need a balanced approach to language arts, one that includes a responsible approach to the teaching of writing as well as reading.

Chapter 4

A Knowledge of Reading Development Can Power Your Teaching

LET'S START AT THE VERY BEGINNING: BUILDING A CONCEPT OF STORY

In *The Sound of Music*, Julie Andrews emphasizes starting at the beginning when teaching the von Trapp children to sing. The movie, *The Sound of Music*, is a beautiful one, and Maria's journey from a novice at the abbey to the brave stepmother, leading her children over the Alps to freedom, is a perfect metaphor for the work that primary-level teachers do year after year as they take their children into the world of literacy. But actually, when you read, you don't begin with A, B, C, but with developing a solid sense of story.

Increasingly, it seems as if many of the children in our classrooms haven't had lots of experience spinning their lives into threads of story. How many are growing up with long family suppers filled with shared stories? How many are being asked, "What'd you do in school?" and nudged to tell the stories in more detail. "Wait, how did that start? What exactly happened?" More and more, it seems that instead of sitting at the kitchen table and regaling parents and caretakers with accounts of the hamster getting loose, the toilet overflowing, the dragonfly that flew into their classroom, many children today are plugging themselves into video games, the television, the computer, the cell phone. Bill Moyers has said, "Our children are being raised by appliances," and that is true all too often.

If you ask lots of children to tell you what they did over the weekend, you'll quickly notice gigantic differences in children's abilities to tell stories. Some children can regale you with detailed, well-structured, lively narratives of their comings and goings. For others, storytelling is clearly an alien activity. You'll note this straight away, in the staccato factual answer to a question meant to elicit a story. A child may answer your question about his day by saying, "We went to the park."

"Oh, you went to the park? What did you do at the park? Tell me about it," you say. The child may simply say, "I went on the slide." You press for elaboration, "Tell me about that." Then the child stares at you, unsure how to respond.

When children don't respond to your invitation to tell a story, it is probably because they haven't had much experience doing so. In this case, they'll need more than a mere nudge. It is impossible to emphasize enough how critical it is for children to develop an internalized sense of how stories go. They need to know that there's a beginning, a big middle part, and an ending. They need to know that in a story, the person—the main character—does stuff and says stuff. Something happens to that character: he gets into some sort of trouble or she goes on an adventure. Often the character comes to an idea or learns a lesson or realizes something.

Children's sense of story can be developed in lots of ways. Particularly if your children haven't had the experience of spinning their own lives into stories, it's a good idea to ask the class to join you in telling stories about the events the class has lived through together. If one day when you are reading aloud, a mouse runs across the meeting area, be glad! You have the makings of a great story. Recruit the children to help you remember what you all were doing before the mouse showed up:

> We remember the time when our teacher was reading *Koala Lou* to us. She read about the gum tree climbing contest, and then all of a sudden we heard Ben shriek, "A mouse!" We saw a little gray mouse. He was standing at the edge of our meeting area . . .

If the class helps you tell the story once, with you asking often, "Then what happened?" and spinning the remembered fragments into a story, that one story can then be told and retold. You can nudge the class to include the important parts and the parts they usually don't tell: "Who screamed? Oh yes, it was Ben. What did he say? Oh, yes, he screamed, 'It's a mouse!' Let's tell that part again, like a storyteller would!" You needn't worry about writing each of these stories down. The important part is not that the story becomes fixed and accurate, but rather that you invite children to spin their lives into stories.

It's important to find ways to weave shared storytelling and individual stories into your children's day, and it is especially important to do that if your children don't come to school already at home with story. Perhaps the day begins with story time, as partners get together to swap stories. Perhaps children have a buddy class of fifth-graders, who each listen to (and nudge for) your children's stories and then tell their own. The work of developing a concept of how stories go will serve your students' writing, their emergent storybook retelling, and later, their conventional reading.

LET'S START AT THE VERY BEGINNING: READING FOR MEANING AND JOY

For children to take off as readers, they must *want* to read. After all, learning to read takes hard work. Children are perfectly game to work hard to learn things they regard as worth doing. They'll get onto that bike and pedal away, knowing full well they might fall and skin a knee on the blacktop. For kids, learning to ride a bike is worth the work, worth the risk. Reading needs to be equally appealing. So learning to read starts not with A, B, C, but with discovering that reading is a way to connect with others, to learn cool things, to have fun.

The first books that you'll likely read to children and give children to read to themselves will be ones you select because they are irresistible. Some may be books that second-graders are apt to read: *Corduroy, Mike Mulligan and His Steam Shovel, Bunny Cakes, The Three Billy Goats Gruff*. You'll choose these and other books because they are seductive. You might choose not only grand stories, but also books with beautiful illustrations and cool features—flaps and pop-ups and inside views. Your goal will be to entice kids into being readers by showing them all that books can be.

Of course, the thing that will draw kids into those books and into reading will be the invitation to participate. Remember, these books will be closer to the K/L/M band than to level A, so the participation you encourage won't involve conventional reading. Instead, you'll point to pictures and recruit children to talk about the characters, places, and events. You might set children up to be the peddler in *Caps for Sale*, shaking his fists at the monkeys who've stolen all the caps he intended to sell. Half of your class may play that peddler, shaking a hand at the imaginary monkeys in the treetop above and calling, "Give me my caps!" The other half of the class may pretend to be the monkeys, each wearing a brightly colored cap, mimicking the peddler, shaking their hands at him and calling, "Tsz, tsz, tsz."

Soon, you and the reader can look at the title page and talk about the presence of an author and an illustrator. You might say, "What a funny title the author came up with!" Whether you are reading with the whole class or one-on-one, there will be times when you say to students, "Let's look at this first picture. What's happening in the picture?" The prompt "What's happening in the picture?" will elicit a story (whereas the question you may have asked earlier, "What do you see in the picture?" will only elicit labels or a list).

Throughout all of this, children will also "read" books independently, and you will support them to incorporate all they've learned from your demonstrations. You'll be glad when you see them starting at the front cover, reading the title, then flipping to the title page and onward, talking about the pictures and saying words that match what is happening on the page or what the book is about.

All of this is to say that although singing may well begin with *do, re, me,* reading does *not* actually begin with A, B, C.

LET'S START AT THE VERY BEGINNING: EMERGENT STORYBOOK READING HELPS STUDENTS UNDERSTAND HOW STORIES GO AND HOW BOOKS TALK

It's important not only to support your students in becoming adept at spinning their lives into stories, but also to help them use storytelling as a way to make meaning as they read. To do this, we rely on Elizabeth Sulzby's work on what she refers to as "emergent storybook reading." In a nutshell, Sulzby suggests that a teacher reread a few beloved narratives repeatedly to kids. The reading should mimic a "bedtime" reading, cover to cover, with natural reactions and gestures. You will want to choose stories that follow conventional story structure and have illustrations that clearly match the words on each page. Stories with repeating lines and/or plot are often easier for students to retell. Favorites might include *Caps for Sale, The Three Billy Goats Gruff, The Carrot Seed,* or *Harry the Dirty Dog.* Once children have heard a story several times, the teacher gives them opportunities to reread or retell those stories as best they can. Sulzby has studied the rereadings that children do and identified eleven subcategories that start with commenting and labeling and end with reading conventionally. (You can find the emergent storybook stages in the online resources that accompany this series.)

For the purpose of supporting instruction, we have consolidated Elizabeth Sulzby's eleven subcategories (or levels) into four major categories that we think you need to watch for and support. Category 1 represents Sulzby's levels 1 and 2, where a student's rereading of the story does not sound like a story at all, but more like a commentary about each page. Category 2 represents Sulzby's levels 3 and 4. Now as the child returns to that familiar storybook, his effort to reread or to story-tell does sound like a story, but he uses his own natural oral language, rather than book language. In category 3, representing Sulzby's levels 5–7, the child retells the book so that it sounds like a story and the talk sounds like written language. Category 4 represents levels 8–11

in Sulzby's classification scheme. In this final stage, the child recognizes that the print actually holds the words on the page. At this point the child may refuse to tell the story because she is worried that her talk won't match the print, or she may locate some known words on the page and attach the told story to the written one at those points. The child at this level may even start to read the text conventionally.

Once you know the ways children's emergent storybook language develops, you will see indicators that show you that some of your children are in each of these stages. Even after you have read a rich storybook to children multiple times, children whose concepts of story are in the first category will merely comment on what they see, rather than re-create—or retell—the story. If, for example, you have read *Caps for Sale* several times, these children might point to the peddler and say, "Look. Huh? Hats. He's got hats on his head!" This youngster might even notice the action and say, "The guy's walking." Instead of linking one page with another, they may talk about each page as if it is a separate item. It is helpful to say to kids at this stage, "Can you tell us what's happening in the picture?" That prompt, rather than "What do you see in the picture?," elicits a storyline with action.

Children who are in the second category—those whose sense of story is developed but whose speech sounds more like conversation instead of the written word—might turn the pages and say, "Look! The monkeys took his caps. They went up the tree." Some students' speech may be a mix of oral language and written language. "You monkeys you, you give me back my caps. He was mad, he shook his hands."

As children either become more knowledgeable about this one story or develop their concept of story, they enter the third category. Now, when they "read" *Caps for Sale,* the retelling sounds so much like the book, in word and intonation, that a listener may be fooled into thinking that the child is actually reading. The same part of *Caps for Sale* might now sound like, "This made the peddler really angry, so he shook both hands and said, 'You monkeys you, you give me back my caps!'"

Category 4 brings in an attentiveness to the print on the page—the written words—along with everything else. Now if a child chimes in on the refrain, "You monkeys you," she may point to those words as she reads them. Of course, reading the words will be easier in a sparse story like *The Carrot Seed,* by Ruth Krauss, than in a more developed story like *Caps for Sale.* The student may try to actually read the words on the page and refuse to retell the page for fear that she is now not actually reading.

By supporting this work—work Sulzby refers to as emergent storybook work—you help students develop oral language and learn to use meaning and syntax as they read. Readers learn to preview the text: the cover tells them who is in the story, where the story takes place, and what might happen. They learn that pages of a story go together to build the entire story and that the pictures and print hold meaning. Students learn how stories work: that there are characters with feelings and problems who go on adventures. Finally, they learn that the written word is different than oral language, that books talk a certain way. It is a natural way for kids to build a love and joy for reading and an understanding that we read for meaning. Through this engagement, they soon discover that the words they are saying are actually on the page, thus sparking a curiosity about print. Marie Clay reiterates the importance of emergent storybook work when she says, "Attention to the formal properties of print and correspondence with sound segments, is the final steps in a progression, not the entry point to understanding what written language is" (Clay 1991, 33). This work is so important that you may want to continue it long after your students are conventionally reading.

Kindergartners falling in love with books

LET'S START AT THE VERY BEGINNING: DEVELOPING CONCEPTS OF PRINT AND PHONOLOGICAL/PHONEMIC AWARENESS BEFORE CONVENTIONAL READING OF LEVEL A/B BOOKS BEGINS

It is crucial to help a child learn what some refer to as the mechanics of reading—high-frequency words, letter-sound relationships, and the like—but charging straight at that work can sometimes shortchange the work that Marie Clay refers to as "learning to look at print."

It's a breeze for you to look at a page and know how to approach it. There's no effort involved in starting at the front cover of the book and proceeding to page 1, page 2. It takes no brain cells for you to start reading in the upper left corner and to proceed left to right, line by line. But none of this can be assumed for the young child learning to read, and if a child can't yet navigate a line of print, it's superfluous to teach that child a collection of high-frequency words. The successful reading journey begins as you make sure that your students know how to look at print, and only after that will you expect them to use letter-sound relationships to problem solve words or a knowledge of high-frequency words to match words they see on the page to words they say.

When a teacher opens a book to the first page, sees that the page begins with the word *my*, instructs a five-year-old, "Read the first word," and then, after silence asks, "What is the sound of that first letter?" and the child just stares in response, what conclusions can be drawn? Does the child's response to the teacher's question, "What is the sound of the first letter?" suggest the child needs instruction in the letter *m*? Perhaps. Might this child be anxious or obstinate? Perhaps. But it is just as likely—or frankly, more likely—that the child doesn't know what is meant by "the first word." What is a word? Where does a word start or end, anyway? What is a letter?

When Marie Clay's Reading Recovery Program came to the United States, she stressed the importance of explicitly teaching concepts of print at the get-go of reading. On the Teachers College Reading and Writing Project website are a variety of assessments that you can access without cost. One of them is a concept about print assessment. Examine this assessment and discover that the concepts of print encompass the following behaviors:

Concepts of Print Behaviors

1. Book orientation
   a. Front of the book
   b. Back of the book

c. Opening book to the first page

2. Locating print on page and differentiating it from the picture

3. Orientation within text

   a. Finding the beginning of one line of text and realizing this is where to begin reading

   b. Movement across a line of print from left to right

4. Orientation within a word

   a. Locating a letter in a line of text

   b. Locating a word in a line of text

   c. Locating the first letter in a word

   d. Locating the last letter in a word

5. Demonstrating the return sweep to a new line on a page with two lines of text

6. Pointing to words in a line of text that the teacher reads with one-to-one matching

7. Identifying the punctuation marks (. ? !) and stating their purpose

Many teachers who see this list of behaviors for the first time think, "Gee, I never really thought about teaching *those* things. I think my kids can already do that!" It is true that many children come to school with strong concepts of print. But children who were never exposed to print at home or given opportunities to notice print can't do these things, and they must be taught. Much of the teaching about how to look at print can be accomplished by teaching concepts of print while children read level A/B books. But there are things that can be explicitly taught about concepts of print *before* children begin reading level A/B books, and these skills can be taught while you work to develop a love of reading using the emergent read-aloud techniques discussed in previous sections and while you support beginning writing.

Above all, your students' phonological awareness will develop during the writing workshop. Clay (1993) states that learning to write letters, words, and sentences helps the child make the visual discriminations of detail in print that he will use in his reading. Children who write are required to pay attention to letter detail, letter order, sound sequences, letter sequences, and the links between messages in oral language and messages in printed language. It is particularly important that children learn to hear the sounds in words

they want to write and find appropriate ways to write these sounds down. The writing knowledge serves as a resource of information that can help the reader (10).

Writing is the best possible venue for teaching children the relationship between meaning, syntax, and phonics (MSV), because when a child writes, the meaning is her own. She will work hard at the visual—at getting the letters onto the page—because it is *her* story, and she wants the world to be able to access her meaning. She'll stretch the word and listen to the sounds and write a sound and then reread and hear and record more sounds and reread again—all to write one word. She'll reread that one word and recall what she wants to say next, then stretch that next word out, recording the sounds, and then reread yet again, two words this time. She'll do this work to inch across the page, because she wants to communicate her own thoughts.

When you work with that child, make sure that you encourage lots of rereading. The writer rereads to regain her place while in the middle of writing a word, then rereads when she is finished writing a word to recall the next word. Support the writer in stretching out a word, saying it slowly, because that is crucial phonemic awareness work. Initially, if a child is having trouble hearing multiple sounds in a word, it can help if you write a dash or box for each phoneme in the word to assist him in hearing sounds from left to right in a word. Eventually, let the writer write the word alone, articulating every sound to figure out the needed letters. For more information on this type of work see the discussion of Elkonin boxes in Clay (1993, 32–35).

Sometimes we see children in a writing workshop who draw pictures to represent their stories but don't write anything to accompany those pictures. The child may point to a picture and say, "That's me." If I ask the child's teacher why the child is not writing as well as drawing, the teacher sometimes says to me, "I'm still waiting for her to be ready."

Let me caution you that writing development is actually not something you *wait* for. It is something you *teach toward*. If your kindergartner has drawn a picture and has not labeled it, you can ask, "Who is that?" and "What are you holding?" If you learn that the picture is the child and she is holding a balloon, you might say, "I thought it was a hula hoop! I had no idea! You need to write *balloon*, so I know. Let's try doing that, okay? So everyone knows this is a balloon!" Then you can tell the child, "Let's say that word slowly." Watch while the child does that. Give her some space. If she needs support, your voice should be quieter than hers, under hers, and temporary. Just once, you might say, "bb-aaa /bbb/," and then, "You say it." Make sure you do not do the work for the child. It can't be you who does the sounding out!

If you find a child writing marks that appear to be random strings of letters, then watch as the child writes in front of you. Suppose the child tells you he wants to write a sentence: "I ate ice cream." As you watch him just throw a string of letters onto the page, stop him and ask, "What was that? What did you just do?" If the child explains that he just wrote, show him how to isolate the first word, to say it slowly and listen for the first sound, to reread that sound and listen for the next sound, and so on. This writing work can be a source of great strength as children develop a repertoire of concepts about print behaviors that will support them when they are taken into conventional reading of level A/B books.

If you examine the list of concept about print behaviors above, you can create other nonreading activities that also help establish concepts of print behaviors. For example, you could tape circles of colored paper in rows on a white piece of construction paper. Then you can ask children to read the colors one at a time across the rows, pointing to each one. (The same activity can happen with pictures of simple objects pasted in rows.) That work can help a child learn how to sweep to the beginning of the next line.

Once a child is holding level A/B books and attempting to read those books, she may have difficulty with one-to-one matching. Some children will memorize the repetitive sentences in level A/B books and be able to produce those sentences. One child announced to his teacher, "I can read this book with my eyes closed!" He had looked at the pictures, remembered the pattern, and then with closed eyes, recited the words on the page. Fortunately, his teachers stressed how important it was for him to read with his eyes open, pointing to each word as he said it. That poses new challenges!

The teacher of that youngster was experienced, and she knew to bring out one of the sheets of paper with colored circles in a row and to say, "Remember how you read the color circles on this sheet, one by one, saying the name of

Children exploring words during word study

each? Reading words in books is done the same way." She demonstrated one-to-one matching in text and then asked the child to do it. It wasn't long before he was orchestrating the one-to-one matching process in all his reading, freed up to focus on other things. This is explicit teaching!

With a firm understanding of the behaviors involved in "learning to look at print," teachers will recognize how they can emphasize them in the other components of their literacy program that operate before conventional reading begins—shared reading, interactive writing, and so forth.

For example, phonemic awareness is one of the most important things to teach while your students are in the emergent reading stage of development. Phonological awareness is "the conscious awareness that words are made up of segments of our own speech that are represented with letters in an alphabetic orthograph" (Moats 2000, 234). Phonemic awareness, however, is "a subset of phonological awareness and includes both the understanding that words are made up of individual phonemes and the ability to manipulate phonemes" (Shanahan and Lonigan 2013, 236). The National Reading Panel suggests that children require eighteen hours of instruction in this across the entire kindergarten year, which translates to about five minutes a day. This is instruction you can do while kids are lining up for lunch or while you are greeting them at the start of the day. This instruction can include songs, rhyming play, and clapping games. Although this sounds light and playful—and it is—often when children fail to thrive in early reading, it is because this critical work has been overlooked. If a child can't rhyme and can't hear sounds within a word, that child doesn't have the foundation needed for further reading development. Later instruction won't stick because this foundation is missing. A resource we recommend on this critical topic is Diane Snowball and Faye Boltons' *Spelling K–8*, Chapter 5 (1999). That chapter summarizes games you can play with children to support six skills crucial to phonemic awareness (such as segmenting and blending, for example).

THE READING WORK THAT READERS OF LEVEL A/B BOOKS NEED TO DO

The books that are labeled A/B are designed to help students develop concepts about print such as left to right and one-to-one correspondence. These books encourage readers to come to know a few high-frequency words and to use those words to help anchor their reading. At levels A and B, students will rely on many familiar texts (especially texts read in shared reading and texts created in shared writing) to be able to approximate reading.

There are a few key challenges to keep in mind while helping readers progress from emergent storybook reading into level A/B books.

Challenges for Readers of Level A/B Books

- Children must be able to locate one word as a unit in a line of print. Then, they must locate two words.

- Children continue to draw on a sense of story, book language, and concepts of print. Meanwhile, their reading begins to be constrained by what the text says, and especially by language patterns.

- Children must begin to match their voice to print, so one spoken word matches one written word, using one-to-one correspondence.

- As children work on reading with one-to-one matching, as well as carrying a pattern across the book, they will also work on using the pictures and what is happening in the text to help them solve words. Books that work for these readers are written and illustrated in such a way that they provide this support.

- Children need to learn a few high-frequency words (such as *the*, *and*, and so on) so they can recognize them quickly.

- After children can identify a word as a unit and before they move to the next level, they should be able to identify the first and last letter in a word.

- Although children are not using letter-sound correspondence to read books in levels A/B, they should be able to identify a core of upper- and lowercase forms of letters and locate these letters in words.

- Children should be learning sounds for consonant letters. (*Note*: This is an ongoing process. Not knowing the sounds of all consonant letters should not be used as a reason to hold students in level A/B books.) (Adapted from Fountas and Pinnell 2006)

Building on Children's Developing Skills and Concepts

When children move from emergent reading (which might involve reading well-loved story books) to reading books that are leveled A/B, both you and the kids need to remember that all the skills your students drew on to produce renditions of books like *Caps for Sale* are still important now as they read books with one line of print per page. Their work with level A/B books is not something altogether new, but rather a continuation of the work they were doing with familiar storybooks. The hope is that they will continue to draw on their sense of story as they get started reading these sparse, heavily patterned books. Some level A/B books actually have fairly rich storylines embedded into the illustrations, and children will bring their knowledge of stories to their work with these texts, which will help them to see and to follow those storylines. Some books will not. But it should be noted that the level A/B books that provide a balance of all three sources of information will be most helpful to kids—that is, the books that have a story and that use language that sounds like natural talk. Books that say, "one cake, two balloons, three presents" prevent children from being able to draw from their own natural language as a source of information. You want young readers to orchestrate all three sources of information while pointing to words as they read and using the pictures to help them think about what the words are saying, so it is best if your book collection doesn't contain too many level A/B books that have neither a storyline nor language patterns that will be familiar to your children.

Meanwhile, as your students work on locating known words on the page and using the pictures to solve new words, the patterns in the books they read will be especially supportive. Prior to now, when children looked at stories like *Caps for Sale*, they looked at the pictures, thought about how stories go, remembered that particular story, and then essentially made up the story. Back then, the text supported that process but didn't constrain it as much as happens now.

Now the hope is that children will pay closer attention to the words on the page. That is why these texts have fewer words and sentences. The books are written so that readers can try to read with one-to-one matching (saying one word for every print word)—no more, no less. The goal is to track the print. At these very early stages of reading development, reading words accurately is not essential.

To support your students who are reading books at levels A/B, you'll need to find a few ways to help them grasp the language pattern in a book that they do not already know well. When they were rereading storybooks at the emergent literacy stage, they knew how the book sounded because you'd read it to them, over and over. Now, when reading books at levels A/B, they continue to need similar help. Because level A/B readers are not yet conventional readers, they may only be able to produce a text that is *similar* to that which is in the book. It is helpful, therefore, to introduce some of these texts through shared reading and interactive writing. Some of these texts can also be introduced by providing a meaning-based book introduction.

Let's think, for example, about the book *Can I Have a Pet?*, by Gwendolyn Hudson Hooks. If you read through the book, which won't take long, you'll see that on every page, the little girl asks her mother, "Can I have . . . ?" a different animal: a monkey, a tiger, a zebra. The story ends with the girl asking "Can I have a fish?" and the answer, "Yes."

Perhaps you might be tempted to do an introduction to this story by encouraging the child reading it to memorize the repeated language stem. You might say, "The book goes like this . . ." and then you read it, accentuating the repeating line, then say, "Can you repeat that?" and the child recites back the refrain, "Can I have a . . . ?" Although that introduction does provide syntactical support (the S in MSV) by highlighting the language pattern, it is not a meaning-based text introduction, which is what I recommend.

A more helpful introduction would highlight the *meaning* in the story. A close look at the book reveals that the girl and her mother are at the zoo together. So, as the girl asks the question, "Can I have a . . . ?," she and her mother travel from animal to animal at the zoo. A sign even points out that the girl will first travel to the monkey, the zebra, the tiger, which is the sequence that the book follows.

In a meaning-based introduction to this book, then, you'd say to the child, "This book is about a little girl who wants a pet. She asks her mom, 'Can I have a . . . ?' But then, they go to the zoo. So when she gets to the monkey cage, instead of asking her mom, 'Can I have a pet?' I bet you know what she will ask for. So when she asks her mom, 'Can I have a . . . ?' what do you think she will say?"

Note that in this instance, you are providing the child with syntactical support (one of the three needed sources of support—meaning, syntax, visual) and also with meaning support (telling the story about the girl at the zoo). The child will likely say the word *monkey*, drawing on the picture to support her in reading that word.

When you and the child read the next page, you can look at the picture of the girl and her mother walking up to the tiger, and you can say to the child, "I bet you know what she says on this page! She wants a pet, so what does she say?" That prompt is far more helpful to a child than "Do you remember the pattern for this page?" Children are best at using meaning to help them read, so engage them in doing so when you can!

This detailed discussion addresses the introduction for just one book, and hopefully, your students will have ten books in their baggies and a new collection of ten books each week. (After all, each book takes just a few minutes to read.) You may be wondering how on earth it's possible to provide this sort of support to all those books for the entire class.

Know straight away that it won't be, and you'll just do the best you can. Remember, at the start, children can become familiar with many of these texts through shared reading. The good news is that, as children return to these books and reread them, they'll discover more themselves. Across these days, you'll also have repeated opportunities to introduce the books. Introductions need not all be done prior to children working on their own in a book.

But here are a few suggestions. First, some of your kindergartners could start level A/B books earlier in the year than others. Some will be ready for these levels during the first week of the school year. Don't wait. Avoid launching all your students into this work at the same time.

If you have a shortage of books, you may have only five books in each child's baggie. In that case, make sure that partners share the books in their baggies with each other. That gives an individual reader access to ten books at a time, and it means there are half the number of books in play for you to support. Of course, it is ideal to have multiple copies of level A/B books so you can give book introductions to a small group of readers at one time, then challenge them all to continue reading on their own, but this is not apt to happen. If you populate your shelves with duplicate copies, you'll need twice as many books.

When children are shopping for books, make sure that you are engaged in that work and that you give little book introductions as they gather books up into their baggies.

Finally, you can make little books out of familiar songs and poems. For instance, you might make books out of the song, "Twinkle, Twinkle, Little Star." These types of books, songs, and chants give children some texts in their baggies that they can start on right away.

Supporting New Skill Development

The next challenge for readers of level A/B books revolves around one-to-one matching. At these levels, you'll begin to help your students match their voices to print, so that one spoken word matches one blob of print (one written word) in a one-to-one fashion. Remember that when children were generating their own made-up stories to accompany the pictures in storybooks, they were producing their own language. They weren't constrained by someone else's language. Now your book introductions can help children stay with the printed page.

You can draw on an array of methods to support that learning. Reading with these children, you may say, "Each time I say something, I will point to a word—one word said, one word touched." Tell them that one-to-one matching applies to writing as well as to reading. "If I want to write, 'I love my mom,' how many words do I need to make to write that?" You can record four blanks. "Let's touch these and read them back to see if we did this right." Then touch each of the four words as you read the sentence together. There are other ways to teach the concept of one-to-one matching; the important thing to note is that generally children learn this easily. But that doesn't mean that they'll read every level A/B book accurately. They won't. You need not keep children reading at these levels until they do so with accuracy. Once children grasp one-to-one matching, you can graduate them to levels C/D. While at those levels, they'll begin to read with more accuracy.

For example, a child may read a page that says, "Can I have a tiger?" and say, "Can I have a lion?" and you may think, "No, that is wrong." Had the child read the sentence, "Can I have a duck?" then it would be fair to call this incorrect—a duck looks nothing like a tiger, and therefore the child who says duck is not using the picture to help solve the word. In this instance, however, the child reading the word *tiger* as *lion* is not a problem. Although she may have confused the name of the two animals, she did make a syntactically correct substitution. You are not yet asking children to look at V (letter-sound relationships) in level A/B books, and both *lion* and *tiger* fit the syntax (they are names of animals) and the meaning (they're both from the cat family) of the sentence. Later, when the child begins reading level C/D books, you can go back to this one and teach to the mismatch of beginning letter sounds in *tiger* and *lion*.

Another way to support students at this level is to do interactive writing with them. For example, you might support a child or a small group in learning how to read and write with one-to-one matching by writing a book, with the child's help, that names the parts of the child's bedroom, recruiting the child to illustrate it. "I like my bed. I like my bureau. I like my chair. I like my cat." If the child is a soccer player, she can help you write a book that goes, "I like to kick. I like to pass . . ."

It's helpful to do lots of repeated work around one-to-one matching. When a child reads without matching, you might say, "Oh, no, something's wrong. You need to make it match. Watch me make it match, then you try to make it match."

match." When the child reads in a way that doesn't match, you could mimic what the child did, again not making it match, and ask the child to help you. "You read like this," you might say, and read without matching. "Does that match? Can we try it again?"

It's enormously important for children to learn to recognize a few words instantly. These are referred to as *known words*. If a child recognizes *the* and *and*, and is trying to read with one-to-one matching, those words anchor the matching. You'll probably want to teach a few high-frequency words (*snap words*) during word study time, and then those words can be posted on a word wall in your room. Many teachers teach students to become familiar with those words by teaching them to look at the words, say the letters, write the word while it's covered, and then check it: look, say, cover, write, check. In any case, support students in using these words as anchors when they read. For students to move beyond books at level B, they may need to recognize twelve to twenty words.

It is exciting to see a child discover a word that she is learning in a book she is reading, exclaiming "Here's *the*! It's that word wall word! It's right here in my book!" To allow this discovery to happen and to ensure that readers are really "learning to look at print," ensure from the very beginning that level A/B readers are pointing *under* the words as they read them, not *on* the words.

Some level A books and most level B books have two lines of print. Readers at levels A and B need to be taught the return sweep to a second line. In addition, many students need to learn that sentences can continue onto the next line and that, when this happens, they need to move their eyes (and thus fingers) to the next line of print as they continue to read.

Do not expect on a first reading of a text that students will read with much fluency. As students are rereading their texts several times, you can coach them to begin to work on better phrasing, and you can expect more automaticity in reading the words on the page.

Generally, children are in and out of these levels of text complexity within two to four weeks, rather than a few months. You may find that some children are in between levels—they read level A/B texts just fine but can't independently read level C. This is a common stage. Do not let them languish in these level A/B books, but instead support them in moving into level C books. Most likely, they will need the skills demanded by the next level to be able to move forward, so it's helpful to teach students to use those skills in level A/B books as well as level C texts.

While children read level A/B books, you'll be teaching them phonics (sound-symbol relationships), and that knowledge will be important for them to draw upon when they shift to reading level C books. These books are designed so that the reader must use the first consonant to identify the object in the picture or the action that is happening in the story. The text in one level C book reads, "A truck takes the dirt away." The truck could be carrying many different things. In this book, the reader must recall that the previous pages told about dirt being put into the truck by a "loader." Bringing that information forward, they look at the unknown word *dirt*, say the beginning sound /d/, and read *dirt*. Your phonics instruction may, for example, teach children a letter a day. Children will listen to hear the sound of the letter, and then they'll write the letter. When they learn these letter-sound relationships, the journey through level C/D books becomes easier.

The important thing to keep in mind is that while readers don't progress up a notch of text difficulty unless they are generally reading books with about 94% accuracy, moving to levels C/D is an exception. Children are not expected to read level A/B books with accuracy on their own. If the picture shows two striped snakes and a child reads "I see stripes" as "I see snakes," that is considered just fine. Onward.

THE READING WORK THAT READERS OF LEVEL C/D BOOKS NEED TO DO

The move from level B to C is a significant jump with regard to meaning, syntax, and visual information. Most texts at levels A/B are nonnarrative texts, or concept books, where the reader can think about what the book is mostly about—team sports, things that kids can do, and so on. An entry level C book may also consist of similar nonnarrative structures, but narrative texts are also now introduced, asking students to do more challenging meaning work with regard to comprehension. Students will now need to consider character feelings and motivation. With regard to structure, level A/B texts are written with a child's natural language. The child's natural language is preserved in the beginning books at this level, but as the child progresses within level C and into level D books, the language may transition to more book language (for example, in a beginning level C book the text might say, "The tiger went up the tree." An exit level C book might read, "Up went the tiger!"). Another important structural change for level C/D readers is the use of prepositional phrases. Students at level C must use visual information, not just meaning and syntax, to read the correct word. Level C books are designed to challenge the reader to cross-check visuals so that their reading now makes sense, sounds like it would in a book, and looks right. Additionally, the number of high-frequency words significantly increases in level C and D books.

Because of the myriad new challenges at level C, you need recognize all of the meaning, syntax, and visual changes and pick books for guided reading that are appropriate for the individual child.

Challenges for Readers of Level C/D Books

- Illustrations become more involved and do not support all words in a text, requiring readers to rely on known sight words or beginning word analysis. (Example: "I can see the pizza." The illustration does not support reading the word *can*.)

- The fact that text patterns begin to change at least once in level C books requires that students "comprehend" what is going on in the illustrations to be able to deal with the pattern switch.

- Dialogue statements by characters are introduced in level C books. The character's statement is followed by the word *said*. ("'Help!' said Marco. 'My cat can't get down.'")

- Language patterns repeat as they did in level A and level B books, but sentences are longer. A new syntactic characteristic in level C books is that prepositional phrases are introduced in longer sentences. ("He went to see the rabbit." "The mice go down to the ice.")

- Multiple lines of text are common in level C books, but the text is often formatted to support students reading in phrases. ("I am looking / for a home.")

- A range of punctuation is introduced, and students must be taught the function of these new punctuation marks, words in bold text, commas, quotation marks, question marks, exclamation points, ellipses, and apostrophes in possessive forms of words or contractions.

- Students to have a wider range of high-frequency words under control. They should be able to read these words instantly with automaticity.

- Students must know the meaning and/or function of all high-frequency words and know how this creates meaning or determines how the words are used in the sentence structure.

- Students need to use the first letter to read the words that are in the book.

- In level D books, consonant blends at the beginnings of words are introduced.

Supporting Readers in Building an Increasing Variety of High-Frequency Words

It's a good idea to look through the sets of books you are using with your children, noting the type of high-frequency word they contain as well as choosing words from a list you were given. You'll probably notice that these books are chock full of words with irregular phonemic patterns: *was, said, here, come*. Other high-frequency words contain vowel rules that have not been taught yet in your word study program: *like, came, look, play*. The difficulty of these new high-frequency words requires explicit teaching and practice in isolation during word study time and in context in shared reading and interactive writing.

If you have students entering level C books well before the rest of the class, you may choose to give them the new, challenging high-frequency cards during small-group instruction and ask them to be on the lookout for these words during independent reading time. These students might use these more challenging high-frequency words during word study time. When half the class or more is transitioning into level C, you may want to make sure that the high-frequency words that you are teaching the whole class represent the words they need to read at this level.

Supporting Readers in Using Multiple Sources of Information

Reading level C/D books requires readers to be proficient using early concepts about print behaviors so they can focus on the new challenges of integrating meaning into their reading of stories that become more involved and using some letter-sound relationships to support accurate reading. They must be pointing under words, specifically under the first letter of the word, to focus their attention on first letter sounds. They must realize that analyzing the illustrations is becoming important to get full meaning from the story. The following examples from Michele Dufresne's book *Bella Likes Purple* illustrates these new challenges:

Page	Text on the page	Illustration accompanying the text
page 2	I like purple.	Photograph shows little Bella the dog.
page 4	Look at the goggles. The goggles are purple.	Photograph shows purple goggles.
page 6	Look at me. I like the purple goggles.	Photograph shows Bella wearing the purple goggles.
page 8	Look at the hat. The hat is purple.	Photograph shows a purple hat.

This level C book may be described as an entry-level C book. The meaning is familiar and it is a nonnarrative book, just like those students are used to at levels A/B. It contains just two sentences on most pages. The sentences are simple and use a natural language pattern. The text sounds like the way a child would talk. The text does not contain the prepositional phrases that we see in harder level C books.

The work that this text requires, however, does lift the level from A/B in two major ways. First, instead of following a consistent pattern across all pages, the pattern changes. The different patterns use the same high-frequency words, but in a different order, requiring the reader to carefully check that the words she is saying match what is printed in the book. This text also requires the reader to do new beginning level work with visual information. A child who looks at the picture on page 7 and says "Sunglasses," will now have to think about what is happening in the text and also check the beginning letter of the word to make sure the word that she said "looks right."

After a lean "check it" prompt, you might coach the child by saying, "*Sunglasses* does make sense, but what letter would we expect to see at the beginning of the word *sunglasses*?" You might then instruct the child that the words we say need to make sense with what is happening in the book, but we also have to something new. We now need to check the beginning letter of the word to check if our guess matches the letters that are written. If it does not, we need to think of another word that fits with the book and looks like the written word on the page. The work of using and cross-checking with visual information is repeated on page 8 when the child encounters the word *hat*.

A perfect place to practice cross-checking visual information is during whole-class or small-group shared reading time. Simply cover words like *goggles* and *hat* and have students check their guess when you reveal the covered word.

Another level C text, *Food for Bella*, also by Michele Dufresne, represents a text with several more challenges.

Page	Text on the page	Illustration accompanying the text
page 2	"Look," said Bella. "I can see pizza. Yum! Yum!"	Photograph shows Bella on the table leaning over a pizza.
page 3	"No," said Rosie. "The pizza is not for you."	Photograph shows Rosie, the new dog, at the table with Bella.
page 4	"Look," said Bella. "I can see the chicken. Yum! Yum!"	Photograph shows Bella on the table smelling a whole roasted chicken.

In this text, as in many level C books, the reader is invited into the world of story. There are characters, Bella and Rosie, and Bella wants something. She wants to eat the food on the table! Bella's friend Rosie knows they are not supposed to eat the food and repeatedly yells, "No!" and "It's not for you!" The comprehension work required is more complex than previously. The reader needs to think about the characters' feelings, what the characters want, and why they might do or say things. All readers can benefit from explicit teaching about this inferential work and work involving how stories go, because it sets a model for the thinking beyond letters and words to meaning that will be critical in future reading.

Because readers at level C are now reading stories, another new challenge will be reading simple dialogue and seeing how it is punctuated with quotation marks and commas and assigned with the speaker tag *said*. In addition, there are many sentences with prepositional phrases now ("The pizza is not *for you*. The bones are *for you and me!*"). The use of these prepositional phrases marks the transition from oral to written language.

Although this book does not present particularly challenging book language, there are several other level C books that do. We all know the books that sound like "In went the socks," "Up went the cat," or "Shall we come to dinner?" When you find books with a challenging structure, point it out to your young readers and explain that books do not always talk the way we do. The more students read and are read to, the more familiar they will become with book language and be able to anticipate how their own book might talk—just one more reason to continue the emergent storybook work even after students are conventionally reading!

In addition to the ongoing work that readers will need to do visually, using and cross-checking with the first letter, students will also have to figure out words that do not appear in the picture. In this book, one such word is *can*. Your students should know the high-frequency word *an* before they enter level C. You could begin showing them on a white board how the word *an* changes when you add the letter *c*. Always take them back to the text to see how the word fits into the sentence, "I can see the pizza." Emphasize what *can* means in that sentence.

Another way to approach this work is to grab your magnetic letters and practice making and breaking words so that students are able to see that they can change the beginning of a word to make a new word. After reading this text in guided reading you might go back to the word *can* and say, "Let's look at this word. We already know *an*." Add the letter *c* and show how it becomes *can*. Then show what happens when you go back to *an* and add the letter *m* to the beginning.

The work moving from levels A/B to level C described above is monumental for some children, but level D books allow them to further master and orchestrate this work, because level D books have minimal changes in difficulty. Comprehension and thinking about story characters and events continues to develop. A bigger change is that letter-sound work at the beginning of the word requires students to use consonant blends and digraphs to read the correct word.

THE READING WORK THAT READERS OF LEVEL E/F BOOKS NEED TO DO

The slope from levels C/D to E/F is a steep one. The length and complexity of books at levels E/F/G are great enough that many children won't have enough knowledge of phonics or high-frequency words to be able to rely on decoding alone to read these books. Instead, it will only be by coupling those skills with strong comprehension skills that most readers can make headway through these books. And then, their experience reading these books will provide practice and exposure that helps those developing readers grow into the work they are doing.

There are some key challenges to keep in mind while helping readers progress from reading level C/D books to reading level E/F books.

Challenges for Readers of Level E/F Books

Meaning Changes:

- Stories become more complex, with a clear beginning, a series of events, and an ending.

- Illustrations become more complex, with many things happening in the picture. Students must select the important content that will assist them in comprehending the story and word solving.

- Longer stretches of dialogue, often split dialogue, are common.

- Dialogue statements begin to be assigned with words other than *said* (*cried*, *shouted*).

- Since level E books have a series of episodes, students must recall the important, big events, ruling out minor details.

Structure Changes:

- Sentences become longer and often contain multiple embedded phrases. Commas are introduced in dialogue statements, placing items or statements in a series, and parenthetical statements.

- A new structural change at level E is sentences in which the verb precedes the subject ("Ring, ring went the phone."). Sentences written in a question format are very common ("Can I play with you?")

Visual Changes:

- Books have easy, predictable letter-sound relationships and spelling patterns, but using the first letter(s) is not enough. Readers must begin to look at the beginning part of the word, rather than across the word.

- Compound words are introduced at level E.

- Words with inflectional endings (*-ed*, *-ing*, *-s*) are quite common.

When helping children read a page of a level E book, you can ask them to think hard about what is likely to happen next in the book. That thinking allows a child to generate almost a private, made-for-the-moment word wall of options. Then, when the child turns to the next page, she can read to see which of those options works best.

The fact that readers of level E/F books rely heavily on comprehension to support their work explains why it will be important for you to emphasize the need for children to think deeply about level C/D books. Prior to getting into level E/F books, it is important that children are already accustomed to stopping and thinking as they read, mulling over what is going on, and generating more language about the content as they do so. This process of pausing to think about a text pays off in a big way for readers of level E/F books.

Suppose a reader is reading the book *Frog's Lunch*, by Dee Lillegard. It begins like this:

> Frog was sitting on a lily pad in the middle of the pond. "It's lunchtime," said Frog.
> Along came a fly. "Mmmm, lunch," said Frog.

It is likely that a reader of this book will get stuck on some of these words. Chances are good that this reader has never encountered the word *middle* before now. This is one of those words that causes some readers to slam on the brakes. At these levels, you can count on the book containing a number of words like this. A reader might read the opening page of *Frog's Lunch* like this, omitting the word *middle*.

> Frog was sitting on a lily pad in the ____ of the pond. "It's lunchtime," said Frog.

Some suggest telling students to skip the word and read the remainder of the sentence, probably because they are a competent adult reader and do this themselves. At levels E/F/G, readers have not developed the reading savvy of adults who use this strategy. Readers of E, F, and G books are not ready to skip the word and read on and need a better means of problem solving words. Wise teachers ask their children to use the following strategy when coming to a difficult word in level E, F, and G, books:

1. Stop at the difficult word and think aloud about what is going on in the story right now. Check the illustration if necessary. ("That frog is sitting on something in the pond. It looks like a green leaf.")

2. Look at the words up to the tricky word. ("'The frog sat in the _____.' Hmm, . . . it looks like the missing word is going to tell where the frog is. The name of something. I remember that the name of something often comes after the word *the* when I write stories.")

3. Next, teach the student to say the sounds of the consonant(s) plus the next two letters (/m/ + /id/). Note that the word is *consonant(s)*,

because sometimes a word begins with a two or three letter blend. If the word has a vowel digraph (*ai, oa,* and so on) after the consonant(s), the child reads the next three letters. (Example: "c + *oun*" to read the word *counted*. Notice how important it is to teach "vowel teams" when readers begin reading level E, F, and G books.)

4. Next, tell the child to go back to the beginning of the sentence and read up to the tricky word, saying that first part. (It has been our experience that, if the word is in the student's vocabulary, she'll get it correct most of the time.)

This is the part most teachers forget:

5. Ask the child, "Did it make sense to call that word *middle*? Why?"

6. Then direct the child to the word *middle* and say, "Run your finger under the letters and see if the right letters are there for the sounds you hear all the way across the word." (This prompt is important, especially in level G books, because you will want to begin teaching readers to go across the word with their eyes, checking "word parts" or "chunks.")

The strategy instruction above is demanding of teacher time and student attention. But explicit teaching takes time and attention to pay off. The mini-lesson, shared reading, and teaching point at the end of small-group work and conferences are places where this explicit teaching can happen. It is important that children don't progress to third grade as "first letter guessers." This strategy for reading beyond the first letter is the first step toward stamping out "first letter guessers."

During word study time, readers who are working at these levels of text difficulty profit from working on inflectional endings, such as *-ing, -er,* and *-ed*. Children need to learn that a word they know by heart can add on an ending—say, *-ing*—and still be the same essential word.

THE READING WORK THAT READERS OF LEVEL G/H/I/J BOOKS NEED TO DO

The jump between books at levels E/F to those at levels G/H (kids reading at the latter levels are known as transitional readers) is not an especially large one. But moving to level I from F/G/H requires readers to handle a host of changes. To make the jump to level I books, students must be very efficient at word solving, and self-corrections should be made at the point of error. This requires that students self-monitor to ensure that the words they read sound like they would in a book, make sense, and look right. Self-monitoring comprehension to know when meaning fits with story events or noting that meaning has broken down is also critical, because stories become longer and more complex at this level. Some people call putting all these things together to monitor one's reading *self-regulation*. Characters are no longer one-dimensional. In addition, success at these levels forms a foundation for moving on to books at level J, where we groom our readers for the next big jump to level K/L books, expecting at least mastery of level M books at the end of second grade.

There are some key challenges to keep in mind while helping readers progress from reading level E/F books to reading level G/H/I/J books.

Challenges for Readers of Level G/H/I/J Books

Meaning Changes:

- The books are much longer (eleven to twenty-four pages); some may be illustrated chapter books.

- Level I books have different episodes that may not be within the experiential background of the readers, and the episodes are more elaborate.

- Dialogue statements become an integral part of the story, and the variety of words used to assign dialogue increases (*replied, shouted, yelled, laughed, whispered*). Often, adverbs are used to describe the dialogue (*quietly, loudly*). This requires students to comprehend the interaction between characters and the character's feelings if they are to read dialogue statements with fluency.

- Literary language (similes, metaphors, and so on) begins to appear.

Structure Changes:

- Many sentences with embedded clauses and phrases occur in level I books. Sentences in earlier books mainly contained one embedded prepositional phrase, and few or no clauses were used. Books at this level can have multiple phrases in the same sentence.

Visual Changes:

- A full range of phonics knowledge must be mastered and used automatically: long/short vowel sounds, consonant blends/digraphs, dipthongs (/oi/, /ew/, and so on), r-controlled vowels, vowels that are silent in some words. And the variations in different sounds for the same consonant or vowel.

- The amount of print on the pages of a book is another change at level I. Most books have ten lines of print.

- Books, especially short, illustrated chapter books and nonfiction books, have a table of contents, a glossary, and two or more graphics on a page.

One of the big challenges at the level G/H/I/J text band is holding onto the story, because stories at these levels will be longer and more complex. Let's take the book *Sam, the Garbage Hound* (level G) as an example. The book's length and shape almost give the impression that it has chapters, though it doesn't. It starts like this:

Sam was a garbage hound.
He lived at the dump.
He ate canned food.
He slept in a snug bed.
He chased flies for fun.
It was a good life
But Sam was lonely.
One day Rosie and her mother came to the dump.
When they left, Sam went with them.

The story continues, with Sam taking up residence with Rosie and her mother, where he again has all the nice things he had at the garbage dump—canned food, a snug bed—but now, he isn't lonely anymore.

The important thing to notice about this story is that it is longer than lower-level texts and is divided into parts. If you ask a child, "Tell me about the story," it no longer works for the child to proceed to retell each detail: "Sam lived in the dump. He had a snug bed. He chased flies." The story is long enough that an exact retelling isn't what is called for. Instead, a successful retelling of a book at this level involves the reader standing back from the book to tell about it part by part, rather than event by event. "First, Sam lives at a dump, where life is good except for the fact that he is lonely. Then he moves to live with Rosie and life again is good, only now he isn't lonely anymore." Notice that this kind of retelling requires children to summarize and to determine importance—to think, "What are the most important parts of this story to retell?"

This requires instruction, because unless you intervene to help, kids are likely to read and talk and think page by page. They typically won't talk about collections of pages, about parts of books. You might say to them, "I'm looking for a single statement that talks about these three pages."

You might read a section of the book with a child, helping her to say something like "This part tells about Sam living in the dump. He has a good life, but it's lonely." Then you can paperclip those pages together. Moving forward, unclip the next bunch of pages before inviting the child to read the next section of the book. Once the child has read that second section, you could ask her to say one statement about that next part and then, paper clipping the two parts together, to say one statement about the two parts.

The reason it can help for children to do this sort of work with level G/H/I/J books is that soon they will be into chapter books. At that point, there will be lots of pages, and efforts to hold onto everything can result in holding onto nothing. Also, if children try to hold onto everything in a story, they have no mental energy left over to reflect on the story. They're pooped just from the effort to recall.

Before they read chapter books, children need to begin to figure out what to hold onto in a story, which has something to do with learning story structure. They also can watch for ways books signal that readers have just come to a new part. There will be a new setting or a new chapter or a transition word, such as *later*, to signal that they've come to a new part.

At these levels, students are encountering more multisyllabic words. They will need support solving these words with efficiency. Coach them to chunk parts of a word and then blend those parts together, thinking all the while what the word might be. Building on the chunking work, or

work on word parts that students learned earlier, you can help them work with spelling patterns. Look, for example, at the word *hound*. To read this word, children will work with *-ound*. Help them to approach these, not as individual phonemes, but as spelling patterns, and then to use the pattern to read other words. They can sort words that are similar to and different from *hound*.

sound show slow found low

They can follow your guidance to make words. "Start with *mound*. Change the *m* to get a kind of dog (*hound*). Take away the *h* and add a letter to learn the shape of this dog (*round*). Change the first letter, and that's where you go if you want to adopt a dog (*pound*)."

Children can also brainstorm and write collections of words that represent a spelling pattern. They can write those words in sentences. They can find them in their books. They can use magnetic letters to represent those words. All of this word study work, of course, needs to be drawn upon as children read and write, so word study is integrated, useful, and transferable to a variety of contexts.

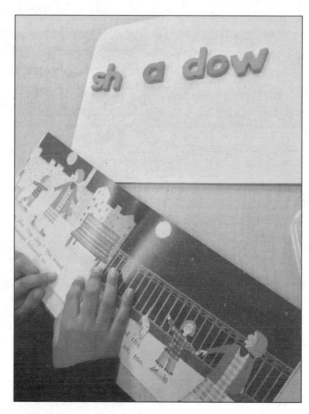

Magnetic letters used to help chunk words

Another important thing is that nonfiction becomes more dominant and important once readers can handle books at these levels. Prior to levels G/H/I/J, the challenge with nonfiction books is that to keep them accessible enough for early readers, the books can't contain a lot of unfamiliar words. As a result, however, the nonfiction books children encounter at levels E/F tend to teach about a topic like the beach, but they do so by providing information that is already obvious to the reader (e.g., the beach has sand, the beach has waves). By levels G/H/I/J, readers can begin to handle some Tier II words, which may not be part of their oral vocabulary. So now nonfiction books teach new words about topics; for example, a book about a tree frog might talk about "croaking" or "suckers."

Word Bank for Penguin Topic

habitats	brood
blubber	fledgling
rookeries	down
camouflage	molt

Tier III words chart

The nonfiction books at these levels tend not to have headings and chapters, posing other challenges. Readers often need to divide these books into parts as was suggested with *Sam, The Garbage Hound* earlier. You might say, "This first part is about what the tree frog looks like. This next part is about what he eats."

As children move toward books at level I, one of the most important differences they will find is that the books are longer. At these higher levels, on a first reading, look to see that students read with better phrasing and intonation. It may still not be perfect, but they have engaged in and developed skill in word solving and comprehension instruction, and you should note improved automaticity of word solving and using meaning

from what they read. This will support them in being able to read with fluency.

In level I, readers need to work on both phrasing and expression. To coach children in phrasing, notice the size unit in which they read, for starters. They may be reading in one-word chunks. The first pages of *Noisy Nora* may sound like this:

Jack/had/dinner/early.

Father/played/with/Kate,

If that's the way a child is reading, push for two- or three-word phrases before moving to meaning-based scoops. You might say, "You read a bit like a robot. Try reading like me." Then read with phrasing yourself, and ask children to repeat what you do.

However, for many children, following a model alone won't be enough. You may need to explicitly name what they should do as they read. "You learned to read by looking at one word, then saying that one word, then looking at the next word. Try looking at two words at a time, then saying those two words. It might not be exactly two words. You also have to watch the punctuation. So it goes like this: see two, say two, see two, say two. Try it."

Jack needed/burping.

So Nora/had to wait.

First she/banged the/window

Then she/slammed the/door.

Fluent readers don't, of course, think about the number of words they are seeing or saying, but help your students by breaking that word-by-word reading practice. You can continue to push for grouping by saying, "Let's see if you can expand what you see to half a line at a time." Or you can teach them how to identify phrases in sentences. Some teachers I work with had success with teaching students that prepositions—such as *in, on, of, into, through, with*—are "scoop up" words. When you see one of these words, you know you are going to read the part that follows them as a group. See the example on the following page. The "scoop up" words are in bold print, while the groupings are underlined.

__On__ the way __to__ Mr. Tom's barber shop, Nic and Matt saw their friend Josh __with__ a new baseball cap.

Notice how these words provide clues to readers to phrase, or *parse*, their reading into the underlined group of words. Work with prepositional phrases first. Then you can suggest that the subject of the sentence (*Nick and Matt*) plus the action word (*saw*) can be read as a group. The words *their friend* automatically become a group in this sentence.

At the same time, continue to support children in thinking about the text and being able to say one statement about a few pages in the book. After reading the pages cited above, in which Nora finds her parents busy and bangs the window and slams the door, you might say to students, "What is she doing?" The hope is not that kids repeat the words of the text: "She is banging the window, she is slamming the door." Instead, the hope is that they will make an inference from the details provided and summarize, saying, "She is trying to get attention."

This relates to another part of fluency—expression or *prosody*—because to read with expression, a reader must use her voice to register what is happening in the story and must comprehend the story events to use the right intonation. Rereading books again and again allows practice in reading with expression. Rereading is about gaining mastery by orchestrating all reading behaviors and strategies and gaining pleasure. Children reread to laugh more, to show off, or to share a reading experience. You can encourage rereading by inviting kids to turn rereading into games they play with friends. You might challenge, "Who can find the funniest page?" or "Who can find something that shows how a character feels?"

Still, at these levels, it's important to continue building students' lists of known high-frequency words, so that by level L, students will have learned somewhere around 200 words.

THE READING WORK THAT READERS OF LEVEL K/L/M BOOKS NEED TO DO

There is a big step between levels G/H/I/J and levels K/L/M. Children reading levels K/L/M are in early chapter books. At these higher levels, not only are the books longer and divided into chapters, but the role of rereading changes, which is a big deal. Readers no longer regularly read a book, then reread it, then reread it once more. Instead, readers will likely only reread if you encourage them to do so. You can suggest that readers choose favorite books to reread to find more in them to appreciate. You can say, "In this unit, you're going to be choosing some books to reread, and when you reread them, you can push yourselves to have ideas about the book, to push beyond retelling." When you push readers of level K/L/M books to have ideas about what they're reading, you can help them reflect not just on the sequence of events (which is what they're apt to be preoccupied with), but also on a character's wants or the relationships between characters or the cause-and-effect relationships between events.

There are some key challenges to keep in mind while helping readers progress from reading level G/H/I/J books to reading level K/L/M books.

Challenges for Readers of Level K/L/M Books

- Illustrations disappear across this band of levels. They provide a backdrop for the story in some level K books. An illustration appears between long stretches of text in level L books, and they are almost nonexistent in level M books.

- Children need to use what they know about story structure and elements to help them track longer, more complex stories.

- There is a greater variety of genres including, mystery, simple fantasy, fairy tales and folktales, myths, legends, and biographies.

- Nonfiction texts become more complex, with more technical language explained in text, and information is divided in sections by boldface headings and content.

- The character work at these levels becomes increasingly more difficult. Starting at level K, students may have to keep track of many characters, accumulate traits explicitly stated in the text, and also think about relationships. As readers move to level M, the traits become less explicit and the reader has to do more inferential work to figure out what the character is like.

- Sentences are longer and contain information embedded in more complex structures.

- Readers must grapple with unfamiliar vocabulary and figurative language and develop strategies for understanding what these words and phrases mean.

- Phonological and phonics skills must be well developed because words with irregular sound patterns are more common. Polysyllabic words require going across the word by word part or *chunk*.
- In essence, word work must be strong to allow for paying more attention to comprehension of more complex texts.

When readers move into books within this band of text difficulty, they find that instead of reading episodic chapter books, in which each chapter is essentially a self-contained story involving the same characters, they are now reading books in which a single storyline tends to span the entire book. At the lower end of this band, the story may be told across pages without chapters, as in *Nate the Great*, by Marjorie Weinman Sharmat. At the higher end, that might mean that the story is told across chapters, as in The Magic Tree House series, by Mary Pope Osborne. This means that readers are required to carry a lot of content across a broader swath of text, so synthesis and determining importance are critical skills. Readers profit from understanding how stories tend to go, because most fiction at these levels fits neatly into the traditional story structure of a character who has traits and motivations, runs into problems, and resolves those problems. Working with students around story structure and elements can provide helpful scaffolding as they learn to draw upon such knowledge in making meaning of longer stories.

The good news is that books at this level tend to provide youngsters with a lot of support. Both the books and the chapters (when there are chapters) tend to be short. The title of the book (and sometimes of the chapters) and the blurb on the back cover usually help readers grasp the main through line in the story, as is the case for the book *Horrible Harry and the Ant Invasion*, by Suzy Kline. Helping students make use of these features can support their reading comprehension.

The characters in books at these levels typically have a few dominant characteristics, and these are explicitly and repeatedly labeled. Horrible Harry is not horrible! He likes horrible things. The characters tend to be relatively static. They change their feelings over the course of the story, but their traits are fairly consistent. Often these traits help the character solve the problem, as in the Cam Jansen series, by David A. Adler, in which Cam uses her amazing memory to figure out the mystery. Sometimes the traits are related to the main problem. In *Harry and The Ant Invasion*, Harry likes creepy things, so

when the teacher asks, "Would you like to be the ant monitor?" things coalesce around this character trait.

In these stories, the character often wants something concrete—to take care of creepy creatures, to win the prize, to get the shoes that popular kids wear. In the books at the high end of the band, it often happens that the character ends up not getting the desired thing, but instead satisfies the deeper motivation behind wanting that concrete object in the first place. The boy does not get the shoes that all the popular kids wear, but he does get a friend and a chance to feel popular. Inviting students to think about and discuss such increasingly complex character and plot development and related themes can help them learn and practice useful comprehension strategies.

There is often a lot of dialogue in these books among several main characters. It is not always tagged and is sometimes interrupted, as in this example: "'I'm going,' Mark said, getting up to walk out. 'I won't ever come back.'" It can be helpful to support students in tracking dialogue like this.

At these levels of text, readers benefit from a nudge to do some talking or writing about chunks of the text, asking themselves, "What just happened? How does that go with the earlier part?" It's important for readers to begin doing that from the beginning of a book. Asking children to capture what's happening in part of the text on a Post-it is a useful challenge, because Post-its don't have much space, so readers will need to synthesize.

If readers can synthesize and summarize what is happening in the story, this will set them up well to be able to do inferential thinking, which becomes more and more important as children progress up the levels. Often when teachers say that a reader of early chapter books doesn't "make good inferences," the real problem is not the quality of inferential thought, but rather the fact that the reader hasn't actually grasped the storyline.

Many of these stories will have themes or life lessons, which tend not to be subtle. They are often simple and hit readers over the head a bit. Sharing is good. Try not to be mean. They may not be earth-shattering lessons, but they are actually some of the most important things a person can learn. Encouraging students to think about and discuss these themes can help them build important skills in preparation for more challenging interpretation tasks when reading more complex texts.

These book levels will pose new vocabulary work for readers, who will sometimes run into words that they have never seen in print before. Readers of books in the K/L/M band will find themselves tackling an increasing number of two- and three-syllable words. They'll find that more and more words in level K/L/M books are not words they use conversationally, and many of these will be subject-specific. A story about soccer may include words like *opponent*, *cleat*, *faceguard*, and *positions*, for example, some of which will likely be new vocabulary for these readers. Readers can use phonics to decode a word such as *opponent*, but then, once they pronounce the word, there is a new challenge. Do they know what the word means? The most important tip you can give them is that it helps to pause to ask, "Do I know what that means?" and then to work at it a bit. It can be helpful for readers to realize that coming to understand a word can be more complicated than they realize at first.

It will not just be new vocabulary words that students face at these levels. Students may also encounter unfamiliar figurative language. Books at these levels are full of metaphors, similes, hyperbole, homophones, and idioms. Students may know what each word in a phrase means, but when those words are used together, they mean something entirely new. Readers may come across phrases such as "Sophie was a volcano, ready to explode," and they will need to notice these special phrases, reread them, and use what they know about the words in the phrase, as well as what is happening in the story, to figure out what the phrases mean.

Certainly, as students reach these levels, they will have accumulated around 200 high-frequency words (and often more). They will also be continuing to develop new spelling patterns, work on long vowel patterns, and even work on prefixes and suffixes. Even on a first reading, a child will hopefully read in three- and four-word chunks that preserve the syntax of the text. When the child rereads the text, phrasing and intonation will both be strengthened.

The texts at early reading levels were really designed to help move readers up a trajectory, not only of text complexity, but also of reading behaviors and skills. As you think about supporting your students across this developmental path, think about who is ready to move ahead and which goals and scaffolds will help them continue to move up this ladder.

Chapter 5

The Big Picture of the School Day and of a Reading Workshop

T HE SINGLE QUESTION that we receive the most from teachers is a question about time. It's no wonder—time, after all, is the most precious of our resources. Time is life. Time is actually all we have. What we do with our time is what we do with our life. Decisions about time are decisions about priority, about values, and about power.

It is not my province to tell you what to do with your whole school day—that is a decision that you and your community need to make. But I can tell you how my colleagues and I might organize a school day and invite you to respond to that schedule by bringing your own values to it.

Let me first say this. I do believe that kids profit from as much consistency as possible in your use of time. I think it is helpful for children if your morning meeting generally runs about the same amount of time each day, and the same for your writing workshop, your shared reading time, and your reading workshop. I say this because the challenge during all those times is to accomplish a lot within the time one has. It's good for children to be able to sustain reading for whatever time frame they have or to push to finish writing a story before writing time is over. And it helps if children have an internalized clock and a felt sense for how much time they have.

I also believe it helps to publicize your day's schedule, so that children know how the day will go and can stay within the planned schedule. Children need to be able to read that schedule so they know what comes next in the day. Some teachers add transitions such as "after that we will have . . . and then we will go to . . ." knowing this offers opportunities for shared reading and for developing high-frequency word knowledge.

Here is how I might schedule a day in a K–2 classroom:

8:30–8:35 morning meeting: calendar work, weather

8:35–8:45 a shared-reading song, interactive writing (news) (includes word study)

8:45–9:30 reading workshop

9:30–9:40 shared reading

9:40–10:30 writing workshop

10:30–10:50 word study

10:50–11:15 reading aloud

11:15–12:00 lunch and recess

12:00–12:10 storytelling

12:10–1:10 math

1:10–2:00 science or art or project time

2:00–2:45 choice time or science or social studies

2:45 singing or reading aloud to end the day

The schedule would vary based on the specific grade level. Both the reading and the writing workshop would be shorter in kindergarten so that shared reading and interactive writing could be longer.

WHAT ARE THE COMPONENTS OF BALANCED LITERACY?

A K–2 balanced literacy curriculum includes shared reading, reading aloud, word study, a writing workshop, and a reading workshop. Within the reading workshop itself, there is time for small-group work, including guided reading. Within social studies, science, math, and choice time, there are also opportunities to read and write.

The Units of Study for Teaching Reading books provide support for shared reading, reading aloud, and the reading workshop. Presumably, these would be accompanied by phonics instruction/word study and a writing workshop, such as that outlined in Units of Study in Opinion, Information, and Narrative Writing.

WHAT ARE THE STRUCTURES WITHIN A READING WORKSHOP?

The reading workshop, like the writing workshop, has a characteristic structure. Workshops are deliberately kept simple and predictable, like an art studio or a researcher's laboratory or a scholar's library, because it is the work itself that is ever-changing and complex. Students can approach any day's reading

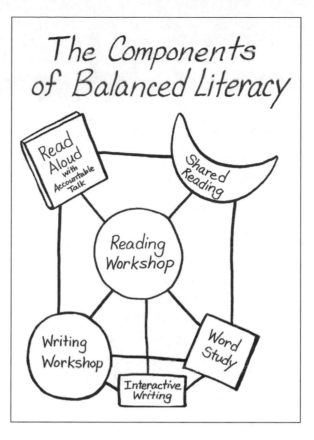

workshop as artists approach a studio or researchers approach a laboratory, planning to continue with their important ongoing work.

For the bulk of time during each reading workshop, students carry on with their reading. As they do so, they draw upon a growing repertoire of skills, tools, strategies, and habits. The whole-class instruction adds to that repertoire of skills and strategies, and the units of study organize the larger projects that give direction to students' reading. In every unit of study, the bulk of students' time during the reading workshop is spent reading, in the fullest sense of the word: reading, imagining, thinking, performing, questioning, talking, reviewing, comparing, and reading some more. If you have taught within a writing workshop structure, the reading workshop structure will be very familiar to you.

Teachers teach and assess students during the reading workshop. You lead minilessons, confer with students, assess students' reading progress using running records and other assessments, and lead small groups of all sorts, including guided reading groups.

As I describe it, you'll see how the structure upholds the tenets we know are necessary to teach children to read. You'll find brief descriptions below, as well as separate chapters in this book, about each of the major components of a reading workshop.

A CURRICULUM INVOLVING A SEQUENCE OF GRADE-SPECIFIC UNITS OF STUDY

Although the structure of the reading workshop remains largely the same throughout the year (and across years), in reading, as in writing, the actual work that kids do and the instruction you provide varies as the year unfolds. The cohort of teachers at a grade level draw upon the four unit books, as well as *If . . . Then . . . Curriculum: Assessment-Based Instruction, Grades K–2* to plan a yearlong sequence of units of study, each lasting four to six weeks. Perhaps the sequence of units in first grade might be as follows:

- *Building Good Reading Habits*
- "Word Detectives Use All They Know to Solve Words"
- *Learning About the World: Reading Nonfiction*
- *Readers Have Big Jobs to Do: Fluency, Phonics, and Comprehension*
- "Readers Get to Know Characters by Performing Their Books"
- *Meeting Characters and Learning Lessons: A Study of Story Elements*
- "Reading Nonfiction Cover to Cover: Nonfiction Book Clubs"

While units may focus on different topics (e.g., bigger books, bigger muscles, or reading nonfiction), each builds upon a set of basic reading skills that are explicitly developed throughout the units and across the grades, such as monitoring for sense, cross-checking, and reading with phrasing. Specific skills may be highlighted more in some units than in others, but all will be reinforced multiple times in a variety of contexts. As you plan your course of study for the year, make sure that your units and your reading skill learning progressions and assessments are aligned.

We suggest planning for a roughly equal division of fiction and nonfiction units, although a number of units straddle those categories. For example, during most foundational units, children are reading a mix of both fiction

and nonfiction just-right texts. Further, some units support students working in partnerships, while others support thinking and talking across loosely connected books with a reading club. When a unit supports partnerships, this usually means that the reading workshop shifts midway through the workshop to allow for partners to read and talk together. Often there are also partner conversations during the minilesson or during a mid-workshop teaching point. During units that support clubs, readers meet to read and talk in groups of four rather than in pairs.

MINILESSONS AND INDEPENDENT WORK TIME

The reading workshop opens with a minilesson in which you give a quick demonstration of a powerful reading strategy. The minilesson is meant to equip learners with a strategy they can use not only that day, but whenever

they need it. Each unit of study book contains seventeen to twenty-two mini-lessons, written in the words that a coauthor or I have used to actually teach that lesson. In most reading units of study, there are a few books threaded through the sequence of the unit. You could decide to substitute another book for any of the suggested demonstration texts, but the first time you teach a unit, staying with the books we recommend can make it easier.

After the ten-minute minilesson, you say those all-important words, "Off you go!" and then students turn to their ongoing reading work. In the primary reading workshop, that means that readers get their self-chosen, just-right books out of their book baggies or their table tubs, and they settle down to read.

Every reader has work to do, and that work grows out of assessments, coaching, and the cumulative impact of minilessons. Imagine you are teaching a unit of study on characters, and children are reading fiction. It's the spring of first grade, and students are reading level E/F, G/H/I/J, or K/L books. Some have been working on fluency since the start of the year and are continuing that work while also thinking about characters' feelings to read with appropriate expression. Others have been challenged to think about how a character's feelings change, if they do, across a book. Some readers have been coached to pause often to retell what's happened so far in the story and to predict what might happen next, as a way to hold onto progressively longer stories. Some children might be conscious that, as they read, they need to respond with ideas and questions, jotting them down in preparation for a conversation about their books.

CHILDREN ENGAGE IN ONGOING READING WORK

When children disperse from the minilesson, they bring with them bins or baggies containing the books they are reading and the ones they'll start reading soon. Your classroom library will likely contain many books that have been leveled with colored dots to help readers find accessible books. (See Chapter 8 on management systems for more about classroom libraries.) Once a week, children will shop for approximately ten books. (Early readers may select more books, and transitional readers may select fewer.) Children will fill their baggies with these books, which means that, when they finish one book and are ready to start another, they need not head to the library for fifteen minutes of roaming about. They can simply turn to the next book without missing a

beat. Most teachers send books home every night; sometimes children have separate take-home baggies. Throughout the week, children read and reread their collection of books. Reading volume is key, and it's important to supply children with enough reading materials, including not just books, but also copies of shared reading texts, word wall words, and so on, to keep early readers going across longer stretches of time, both in school and at home.

Later in the year, children will often read books with fellow members of an ability-based book club, drawing from text sets that contain multiple copies of a title or titles within a series, such as Magic Tree House or Pinky and Rex, or collected books on topics such as underwater animals or transportation.

CONFERENCES AND SMALL GROUPS

The simplicity and predictability of the workshop frees you from constant logistical management, allowing you time to observe, listen, assess, and teach into each student's zone of proximal development. While your students are nose-deep in their books during reading time, you circulate. You pull close to observe, mull over what is and is not working for a child, and intervene to coach, demonstrate, encourage, and celebrate with individuals and small groups. The teaching in these conferences or small-group lessons may reinforce the minilesson, or it might address the unique needs and goals of a child

or a group of children. The teaching in a conference or a small group, like the teaching within minilessons, aims to support not just a given day's work, but also children's reading from that point forward.

Both conferences and small groups are essential in both reading and writing workshops, because they allow you to tailor your instruction to the needs and goals of individual learners. By conferring with individual students, you develop the knowledge, insight, and methods you need to reach learners where they are and help them progress. A teacher-student reading conference often provides the material for the small-group strategy lessons and the minilessons you teach later.

In addition to conferences, you will likely lead several small groups during reading time. Some of these will be guided reading groups, and others will be small groups of other sorts, such as shared reading or interactive writing. The ideal situation is to be able to select the method for small-group work that best suits the learners and the moment. Both conferences and small-group instruction are important enough that I devote an entire chapter to each later in this guide.

MID-WORKSHOP TEACHING

Mid-workshop teaching can be a way to peel kids' attention from their books for just a minute while you make a relevant teaching point that has wide implications. There is nothing essential about mid-workshop teaching. Sometimes you'll forego these, and sometimes you'll stop the class more than once for mid-workshop teaching. This, of course, is exactly the same as in a writing workshop.

PARTNERSHIPS AND CLUBS

Across most K–2 units, children will work in ability-based partnerships. For other units, children will work in groups of about four students to form a reading club, each reading a title within a given series or connected to a particular topic. In kindergarten and first grade, as children are working to build their reading stamina, the teacher will transition students from independent reading to partner reading midway through the workshop each day. Partner time is designed to give young readers a second wind, renewing their energy

to continue on, allowing for more time dedicated to eyes on print, this time with the company of a peer.

Beyond developing readers' stamina, these partnerships and clubs also provide children with an immediate audience with whom to practice strategies. For example, a child may read aloud a page using her most fluent voice to perform a scene or retell the big events in sequence with a friend.

In second grade, as students grow more able to read for longer stretches of time, partnerships tend to work together at the tail end of the workshop, during the share. Therefore, a larger percentage of the workshop is devoted to independent reading. Kindergarten and first-grade teachers will want to keep a finger on the pulse of their readers, helping to stretch them toward progressively longer periods of uninterrupted reading, moving steadily away from a fifty-fifty split between independent and partner reading toward more time for independent reading.

SHARE

The share is framed by a teeny bit of teacher talk, which sometimes takes the form of celebrating what a few readers have done in ways that apply to other readers. This may provide follow-up to the topic addressed in the day's minilesson. For example, if your minilesson demonstrated a few ways readers could figure out an unfamiliar word, during the share, you might suggest that readers share a place in their own books where they used a particular strategy, explaining what they did to help themselves figure out the word.

You might also use the share to offer students more practice with a given skill or repertoire of strategies. For instance, you might close the workshop with a shared reading of a poem or an excerpt as a way to support students' growing fluency. Similarly, you may choose interactive writing as a way to coach young readers to attend to the beginning sound of a word.

In second grade, the workshop typically ends with a small amount of time for readers to work collaboratively with partners or with a bit longer time for readers to work with clubs. The teacher will often guide partners to extend the work they're doing independently by reading and talking together. For example, if your minilesson taught readers to consider how a character is feeling across a story, you might suggest that partners continue that work together, changing their voices to match the feeling of the text as they read to perform scenes.

READ-ALOUD

The read-aloud gives a classroom its heart and soul. It is the time each day when the class laughs together, cries together, and wonders together. Nothing creates a community like the read-aloud. When you read aloud to your students, you draw them into wonderful worlds created by authors—worlds full of excitement and wonder, deep emotion and great wisdom. Your read-aloud time will reinforce the joy of being a reader, but it is also a time to show kids the strategies and higher-level thinking they can use to become more proficient readers. During read-aloud, you show your students how to talk about books, listen to ideas, and elaborate. You teach them how to connect one idea to another and extend a thought. During read-aloud time, you not only model the work of proficient, fluent, and engaged reading, but you also teach your kids how to engage in accountable talk about books. "For classroom talk to promote learning," according to Lauren Resnick and Institute for Learning colleagues, "it must be accountable to the learning community, to accurate and appropriate knowledge, and to rigorous thinking" (Michaels et al. 2010, 1). During this time, your students will discuss their thoughts and ideas about the text, either as a group or in partnerships. A great way to do this is to punctuate the read aloud with "turn-and-talks," in which students discuss their responses to a teacher prompt with a partner nearby.

When you choose your read-aloud texts, aim to include a range of levels, genres, and authors. Sometimes, your read-aloud will engage your students in texts that are well beyond anything they can read on their own. And as you'll see in the various units of study, a read-aloud text is often integral to many of the minilessons.

Reading aloud to your students provides them with a multitude of benefits, as many studies show, especially to students who may have a more limited exposure to text outside of school. Besides offering a chance to model proficient reading behaviors, read-aloud time can also expose them to new vocabulary, concepts, and text structures. This ongoing exposure to varied language and texts is essential for students as they continue to explore the world of books and build their social skills.

An example of a word wall early in the year

WORD STUDY

Word study is a daily component of balanced literacy throughout the primary grades, providing time for teaching phonics, spelling, and vocabulary. Primary teachers generally devote twenty to thirty minutes a day to a self-contained word study time and then also support phonics within interactive writing and shared reading, as well as during the reading and the writing workshops.

The TCRWP encourages the schools with which we work to adopt a program that supports phonics instruction, although that, of course, is a school's choice. In any case, you will probably use a spelling inventory to group your students and to determine what to teach each group of students about phonics. Using this data, you can decide on your whole-class course of study and also design auxiliary small-group activities (such as word sorts) that support students at various stages of development. Your word study sessions might begin with a minilesson that is applicable to most of your students, and then

you can provide time for students to work independently or in partnerships or groups.

During the independent work portion of word study, your students might work in a number of ways. They might use white boards, or they might work in small groups around word study instruction. They might make word sorts or collections, or they might take out their reading and writing materials and apply the word study instruction to their ongoing work. Your early readers may be studying phonemic awareness. Other readers might study vowel sounds and their letter representations. Still other readers might be learning prefixes and suffixes. And, of course, you'll support each group of students with appropriate instruction.

It is important for word study to transfer into students' independent reading and writing work. To facilitate this, you can coach students to draw on what they've learned during word study as they read or write on their own.

SHARED READING

Shared reading is an opportunity for you to read a text with your students, with all eyes on a shared text. The shared reading text is always one that everyone in the class (or in the small group) can see, so it may be a big book with large print, a poem printed on a chart, or a text projected with an interactive white board or a document camera. Shared reading has enough flexibility that this method can not only help readers develop the earliest reading behaviors, but also support more mature readers.

Shared reading is especially useful for teaching concepts of print, word-solving strategies, fluency, and orchestrated use of multiple sources of information. You might begin each ten-minute session by warming readers up with a text they already know well. Everyone reads it together, which offers opportunities to work on phrasing and fluency, among other things. Then you might turn students' attention to the text they will be working on that day, which may be a new text or one they've just been exposed to in the last day or two. Often, you'll spend several days on a shared reading text. When students reread texts together, they become more familiar with them. You might also give students copies of these texts to reread during independent reading time. For more information about shared reading, you can refer to the work of Don Holdaway or Brenda Parkes.

Chapter 6

Tracking Kids' Progress and Using Assessment to Support Instruction

I N CARL ANDERSON'S (2005) BOOK *Assessing Writers*, he describes how he kept a journal to document all the new things his daughter Anzia was beginning to do as a writer. He jotted down snippets from conversations with her and memories and important milestones. From stories she wrote in school to letters to Santa Claus, Carl collected notes on her development. "As I wrote about Anzia in my journal that year," says Carl, "I was composing a mental image of the kind of writer she was becoming." He writes, "In other words, I was assessing her as a writer."

So too, will you collect notes and record milestones for each of your readers. While you might not compose entire notebook entries for each one of your students' accomplishments, it's good to have routines and systems for getting to know each reader. You can collect observations, notes, and data from students' conversations, high-frequency word assessments, letter-sound ID assessments, reading logs, and observations of reading behaviors. You can conduct running records. You can look at Post-its. You can note the types of books, authors, and genres that a child is gravitating toward. All this will help you to assess your students as readers.

When you're making choices among assessment options, ask yourself what you want to know about any child in your classroom. Think about a young boy in class, one who is making great strides as a reader. I'd want to know how often he was reading, as well as how much he reads in one sitting and across a week. I'd be interested to know something about his book choices. I'd want to know how he processes text, what his reading actually sounds like. I'd want to know if he actually understood what he was reading, and what kind of thinking work he was doing. I'd want to know his grasp of comprehension skills (especially those I was about to teach), such as predicting how the book might go or inferring characters' feelings.

If I could find all that out, I could teach him more wisely. If I could find that out for every child and be aware of changes over time, all of my instruction would gain more traction. The partnerships I set up among children would be more strategic. My conferring and small-group work would be more informed. I would see the results of my teaching. If all my colleagues knew as much, we'd know how things were going for individual readers and for reading overall in our school.

Reading can feel like invisible work, but with smart assessments, you *can* know what's really going on with your readers.

CHOOSING YOUR ASSESSMENT TOOLS AND GETTING ORGANIZED

A quick guide to various types of assessments you may want to plan for across your school year follows. More detail about each assessment, including where to find it and tips on administering it, will be discussed throughout the chapter.

For emergent readers, children who are not yet reading conventionally, you'll want to find out what they know about how books work. A simple assessment you might use is concepts about print. Along with this, you'll also want to learn what each child knows about stories and storytelling. A scale of emergent reading stages will help you know where children stand regarding their ability to tell a story across the pages of a familiar book.

Emergent Readers		
Assessment	**Who is this assessment for?**	**What will you find out?**
Concepts about Print	Emergent readers (usually preschool and beginning of kindergarten)	Basic knowledge about books, letters, and words. For example, identifying the front and back of the book, moving left to right, knowing the difference between letters and words.
Emergent Storybook Reading Stages	Emergent readers (usually preschool and beginning of kindergarten)	This scale, based on the work of Elizabeth Sulzby, provides examples at each stage: early emergent reading (when children might simply point to objects in the picture and name them), to using sentences and phrases and transitional words to list the events, to fluent storytelling that sounds much like the teacher (and the many steps in between).

Once your students are beginning to read leveled books, or are beginning to make attempts at conventional writing, you'll want to learn what they know about foundational skills, especially letter-sound identification, spelling patterns, and high-frequency words. You'll also want to use running records to learn how each child is processing text.

Foundational Skills and Reading Level		
Assessment	**Who is this assessment for?**	**What will you find out?**
Letter-Sound Identification	Emergent and beginning readers, any student who does not yet know all the letters and sounds (usually mid-kindergarten to mid-first grade)	The letter names and sounds each student can identify
Spelling Inventory	All stages of readers (usually starting in mid-kindergarten and continuing through the grades)	Word knowledge, including spelling patterns, that students bring to the work of reading and writing
High-Frequency Words	Beginning readers and early transitional readers (usually mid-kindergarten to mid-second grade)	The number of high-frequency words that a student can recognize on sight
Running Records	Begin as soon as a child has a concept of story, one-to-one correspondence, some letter sounds, and high-frequency words. Then continue on a regular basis with all readers (usually starting in mid-kindergarten).	Gather details about the child's fluency, accuracy, use of sources of information for word solving, ability to retell, and ability to answer literal and inferential questions at specific text levels, along with the child's current reading level.

As children continue to grow as readers, they will begin to read for longer stretches of time, and they will begin to read more books and longer books. You may want to assess volume and stamina using a simple system of tallies or a more detailed book log, depending on the level of the reader. It's also important to assess comprehension to be sure that students understand what they are reading.

Volume, Stamina, and Comprehension		
Assessment	**Who is this assessment for?**	**What will you find out?**
Tallies or Book Logs	Informal logs (such as tallies) can be started in kindergarten and first grade. Logs that include writing the title could begin with transitional readers (early chapter books that take more than one sitting to read), usually in second grade.	Track overall reading volume, book choices, and reading rate. Look across a day, a week, or a month to see what books a child is choosing, how often he is finishing books, and how much time he is putting into reading. Reading logs let children reflect on their volume of reading, asking, "How is reading going for me?"
Writing about Reading	Begin when stopping to draw and/or write a short note or response to text will not interfere with students' comprehension of the text.	How is the child thinking about the text? What comprehension strategies is she using/not using?

There are multiple sources for all of these assessments, as will be discussed throughout the chapter. You can also refer to the online resources for a list of sources for these assessment tools.

When you start the year, it's helpful to lay out your curriculum and school calendar and to plan an assessment schedule. This will help you allocate time, match assessments to instruction, and collaborate with colleagues. Of all the assessments suggested above, you'll need to decide which apply to your classroom and when it makes sense to conduct them. Many of these are ongoing assessments that are spread out across time (e.g., running records, book logs, observations), while others might be given just a few times a year (e.g., spelling inventories and high-frequency word lists). An assessment calendar will allow you and your colleagues to plan for those predictable times when you could easily be overwhelmed. When you know a busy period is coming up, you can prepare for it.

Some schools and districts create structures for teachers to come together in vertical teams to create assessment plans across the grades. One goal of a vertical team may be to plan for consistent use of specific assessment tools from grade to grade. If a first-grade team at a school uses one brand

of running records, while the second grade uses another, it can be difficult to have cross-grade conversations about how students are doing as readers, and it creates an unnecessary layer of complication for anyone working with students across grades. Sharing assessment tools among teachers at all grade levels ensures that your assessments are aligned with another teacher's assessments. It is hard on children and on their parents if, during one school year, the child is reading level H books, and the next year, the child is directed to level F books.

The demands on your record keeping are far greater in reading than in writing workshop. You'll want to develop a portable, efficient system for carrying your assessment information with you on the run as you move among your readers. The data you gather will become a life force of sorts in your classroom, informing every instructional choice you make with your readers. As you assess each reader individually, constructing a sense of that particular reader's learning pathway, you'll also need to ensure that each reader has goals that are within his zone of proximal development, a clear sense of how to work toward those goals, and a constant stream of feedback that enables that reader to refine, extend, adjust, or accelerate his efforts.

To accomplish this, it helps to be as streamlined and organized as possible, to have access to the information you need at your fingertips. Some teachers find that having a binder for each student works quite nicely, with one easy-access shelf in the classroom set aside for the data binders. Other teachers find that a system of pocket-folders works. In some cases, it may be handy to have a container or small cabinet on wheels with folders inside that can be moved around the room (or from one room to another).

Consider your records of each child's literacy work analogous to medical records for patients in a hospital. This, of course, is not a new concept, and there are many reading researchers who have developed systems (see Myra Barrs's *Learning Records* for one impressive example). What would your "medical records for reading" contain, and how would you use them to inform and fuel your teaching?

At the front of each data binder, you might include a quick-reference sheet that contains some easily accessible facts to guide your teaching of that child:

- At-a-glance data from the reader's periodic and formative assessments, such as running records
- Date when the child needs to be reassessed with hopes of progressing to another level of text difficulty

- Next steps or goals you have for the child, most likely gleaned from ongoing research in conferences and running records

- Spelling inventory stage, if relevant

- High-frequency word data, if relevant

The rest of the binder might be dedicated to ongoing data collection throughout the year. We'd recommend keeping the dated record sheets from your conferences and small groups, with compliments, teaching points, and next steps recorded for each conference (more on various record-keeping systems for conferring and small groups below). This is also where you might keep completed running records, anecdotal records, notes about the student, spelling inventories, and the like, as well as samples of student work (e.g., Post-its from read-alouds or reading workshop, drawings, and writing about reading). The binder will become the child's literacy portrait, containing all the relevant data.

GETTING TO KNOW YOUR READERS AT THE START OF THE YEAR

At the start of the year, you need to assess readers quickly, while also launching a joyful and productive reading workshop, one that is held together with routines and rituals. You might begin to informally assess your students' reading behaviors and habits by placing baskets of books at each table and inviting kids to select books for themselves. You might say to your class, "Try to choose a book that feels just right—not too easy and not too hard." Then circulate around the room, spending a bit of time at each table, connecting briefly with many students all around the classroom, rather than becoming bogged down in one location while the other side of the room becomes disengaged.

Observations and conversations during those first few days can provide insight into students' interests and preferences as readers, as well as their habits and stamina. Informal assessment of reading levels can also take place when you ask students to read aloud to you and discuss what they've read.

Of course, assessment notes from prior years can be incredibly valuable. We recommend that schools implement a system for passing up a (small) literacy portfolio of reading data from year to year. This collection might include:

- A list of reading levels for the incoming students

- The last running record from the year

- The last letter-sound identification and/or spelling inventory and high-frequency word assessments

- An end-of-the-year sample of the student's writing, preferably an on-demand writing assessment (see *Units of Study in Opinion, Information, and Narrative Writing, K–2*)

In many schools, students bring home a baggie of just-right books at the end of the year as a starter kit for summer reading. If books are in short supply, teachers might send only one or two books home or use free or inexpensive resources for books online (such as Reading A–Z or Keep Books). In the fall, children bring their book baggies with them to their new classrooms, where their new teachers can use those books to begin evaluating their students' reading and connect the new year's reading work to the prior year's work.

As you plan your first unit, the last year's reading levels can inform instructional decisions. A useful resource for some options is *If . . . Then . . . Curriculum: Assessment-Based Instruction, Grades K–2*. For example, if an incoming group of first-graders is reading well below the benchmark level for the beginning of first grade, you might look in *If . . . Then . . . Curriculum* for the alternative unit "Readers Are Resourceful: Tackling Hard Words and Tricky Parts in Books" as an extension to Unit 1.

Information passed from one year to the next can serve as a starting point for the first few days of school until fresh assessments can be conducted. If the information passed up to you seems outdated now that an entire summer has passed, use that information in combination with your own observations to choose a place to start. The important thing is to use what is available to you in ways that help you tailor your instruction and get your year going without waiting for weeks and weeks to pass by.

USING RUNNING RECORDS TO INFORM YOUR CLASSROOM INSTRUCTION

Kindergartners, first-graders, and second-graders are growing, growing, growing. Visit a kindergarten in September and you'll see one group of kids. Return in early October and you'll see a bigger, stronger, smarter, more mature group. Return in January, and you'll see a whole different group! When you gather information with ongoing running records, you'll be able to understand and track children's growth as readers.

Running records can help you and your students know how they are processing texts and comprehending at various levels, which will help you track their progress, get the right books into their hands, and make intelligent reading plans together. In this series, we often refer to Fountas and Pinnell's guided reading levels for this work. These levels, A–Z, denote increasingly difficult levels of texts. If you ask a child to read up a ladder of increasingly difficult texts, you can, in just a few minutes, get a snapshot of how that child's fluency, accuracy, and literal and inferential comprehension change as she tackles increasingly difficult texts. We can never get an exact picture of what's happening in a child's mind, but running records provide a way to note her reading behaviors and decision making, so her reading can be analyzed and that information can be used to guide our teaching decisions. It's a simple tool, and it gives you a useful profile of a reader.

these reasons, we selected two sets of Kaeden books, levels A–K, to serve as our running record assessments at these levels. The student texts for levels L–Z can be downloaded directly from our website, free of cost.

In the end, all of these systems essentially accomplish the same task. If texts have been leveled A–Z (or 1–40), then the assessment tool extracts snippets of those leveled texts or provides briefer texts, putting these passages onto forms so that a child can hold one form and you another. On the teacher's form, you can record exactly what the child does when he reads the passage so you can reconstruct a child's reading of the passage to ascertain if a text at that level of text difficulty represents the child's independent reading level, instructional level, or hard/frustration level. You can then begin to develop some tentative theories about the child's specific strengths and about what breaks down for him at levels that are a bit too hard.

Some experts on running records do not include retelling or comprehension questions as part of the running record. For example, in *An Observation Survey of Early Literacy Achievement*, Marie Clay notes that comprehension questions present some complications. For example, according to research, a student's response to comprehension questions depends more upon the difficulty of the sentence structure of the question than on the child's reading.

However, at TCRWP we have found that comprehension questions, when chosen carefully as prompts for literal or inferential thinking, have proven useful in gleaning insight into where student's strengths and weaknesses may be. Children are invited to retell the main points of the story, and then questions are used as needed to prompt a structured conversation. Checking comprehension as part of your assessment of a child's reading level is important, because matching students to books requires being sure that students comprehend what they read.

The payoff for conducting running records becomes apparent when you use the information from this assessment to channel students toward

Selecting a Tool for Conducting Running Records

There are a variety of tools you can use for conducting running records. One such tool is the Fountas and Pinnell Benchmark Assessment System. Your school may have versions of the Developmental Reading Assessment (DRA) or Qualitative Reading Inventory (QRI) available. TCRWP makes available on our website running records that you can download (though for readers of level A–L texts, you'll need to purchase one set of books from the publisher, because you can't assess those readers well from a printed-out text). We considered many different publishers in searching for assessment texts for levels A–K. In Kaeden books, we found stories that would likely be engaging to children, illustrations that matched the text well enough for readers to use them as a source of information, as well as vocabulary and print conventions that matched each reading level's specifications (e.g., C-V-C patterned words, wrapped text, or dialogue, as appropriate for the level). For books that will help them make progress in their reading. To do this, you and the other teachers in your school may need at least a quick introduction or refresher on conducting running records.

Administering Running Records

This single chapter could never take the place of in-depth coursework and staff development on the administration and analysis of running records. The use of running records in classrooms has been built upon decades of research and scholarship. To learn the important and complex work of how to conduct running records, we recommend Marie Clay's *Running Records for Classroom Teachers*, as well as Irene Fountas and Gay Su Pinnell's book *Guided Reading: Good First Teaching for All Children*. This chapter aims to provide you with the practical nuts and bolts of doing this work in a reading workshop classroom and show you how to use the information you gather from your assessments. It is, after all, important not just that you are assessing kids, but also that you are able to use the information gathered in your assessments.

The gist of a running record is this: You give a leveled text to a child, providing a quick introduction, then ask him to read about 100 words aloud. Meanwhile, you hold a form that reproduces a portion of that leveled text. On this form, you note exactly what the child says and does as he reads the text. You note the words the child has read correctly with a check mark, as well as if the child corrects himself, omits words, or substitutes words to take the place of the words in the text. After the child finishes reading the text silently, you ask him to retell the text, considering how well he conveys key details in the text. Then you ask a few simple questions about it, assessing both literal and inferential comprehension. Using a set of criteria, you determine if the child has understood the story well enough so that you can ask him to try the same process again with a harder leveled text.

Using records from the previous year or some quick questions and observations, you should be able to start the process with a text that is slightly easy for the child to ensure he'll have success and be at ease for the assessment. It is important, though, not to stop the assessment once you find the first level at which she reads with 96% accuracy and adequate comprehension. To find a reader's just-right text level, you need to continue assessing her reading as she works with increasingly difficult texts until her comprehension of the text begins to break down—in other words, until her "ceiling level" is established. You also cannot adapt or even cut short the part of the assessment where you assess understanding. Reading is not reading if a child does not understand the passage enough to retell it and to answer a few literal and simple inferential questions.

Once you've figured out the text level that is just right for the child, you can show her how to find books at that level in the classroom, or you can offer her a stack of books to choose from. The child can then keep a short stack on hand in a bin or baggie to read in the coming week.

Conducting Running Records at the Beginning of the Year

At the start of the year, it can feel like there isn't possibly enough time to assess all of your students within the first few weeks. The effort to assess each child carefully and to create impeccable records could easily consume the majority of your time and energy. This is also the time when you need to establish a productive work environment in the classroom, develop individual relationships with children, create a culture of excellence, and launch the learning life of the community. It is possible, however, to develop systems for streamlining running records, and doing so will make the rest of your reading instruction easier at the start of the year.

To begin, you can informally assess your students' independent reading levels from the first day of school, using the baskets of books, texts from your classroom library, and the summer book baggies mentioned earlier in this chapter. These quick checks, along with a list of children's reading levels from the prior year, should make it possible to estimate each child's independent reading level, so that you need not wade through book after book to discover the child's approximate level.

Professionals other than the classroom teacher can participate in the work of conducting running records and matching readers to books. Many schools hire a reading specialist or others who have special training in reading assessment to work with children during summer school or during the final two weeks of summer, conducting assessments and matching books to children. Some schools ask that these knowledgeable professionals conduct all the assessments for children who are particularly at risk, thereby increasing the likelihood that these youngsters' time in school will be maximized, with every moment spent doing work that has been tailored to the child, and that their assessments will be as informed as possible.

Some schools ask that summer assessments be given to a random sampling of children from every classroom, because having a few already-assessed children dotting a teacher's roster provides another way for classroom teachers to align their assessments with a schoolwide standard. In this situation, the teacher will have standards of measurement right there before her eyes. She can think to herself, "If Jordan has been assessed as someone who can handle level G books, then Alexander is probably not reading level G as well, because his reading is considerably less strong." Even if a school is not able to use professionals to help during the summer, it is likely that at the very start of the year, some of the specialist teachers will not yet have their full caseload in place. Those teachers, then, can be brought into the work of assessing readers.

Conducting Running Records as a Regular Part of Your Reading Workshop

We recommend that you incorporate running records into your regular routines and plans for reading workshop, continuously conducting running records with several children a week, so that at any point, you are up to date on children's reading behaviors and habits and confident that you've matched them up to books that are just right for them. Then, when it's time to report students' reading levels, you can simply report your most recent assessment.

You don't have to always do a formal assessment. If you know the level of the book the child is reading, you can do running records on-the-run constantly, using any piece of paper to record words correct and errors on any book. You can ask the child to read a little bit aloud to you, retell, and answer some literal and inferential questions. To guide this work, you can find an "In-Book Assessment" form on the TCRWP website and in the online resources that accompany this series.

When you first start conducting running records, they have the potential to be intimidating. You may feel paralyzed by the thought that you have to catch *everything* the child does. But don't let that distract you from the main purpose of the running record, which is to get a quick snapshot of how the child is processing text. In the beginning, you'll miss some of what the child did. But your accuracy and efficiency will improve over time. Remind yourself that imperfect data is better than nothing, and pull up beside your readers for on-the-run running records whenever you can.

You can also practice these with colleagues, norm expectations, and get to know your tools well so you can do the work quickly. Your running record needs to be sufficient for others to reconstruct what the reader did as he read. This way, any teacher can retrieve running records from an earlier time

and, if necessary, reconsider the conclusions that were drawn based on those running records.

If your school or district requires a particular window for administering running records, you'll find that you'll be able to conduct them much more quickly when you've been incorporating them into your regular work with children. There are many ways you can make the administration of running records more manageable. Prepare your materials in bulk, with a long-lasting supply of forms at each level, to avoid time-consuming interruptions when you run out of forms. Create a station at a table or desk in your classroom for conducting running records, where all your materials are organized and ready to go—copies of forms organized by level, benchmark books that students will read from, teacher guides and resources, extra paper for recording student comprehension responses, binders for completed running records, and sharpened pencils.

To get as many running records done as efficiently as possible, you may want to call two, or even three or four, students at a time. Have one student sit with you, and the others nearby, with their chairs turned around so that they can read from their independent book baggies while you conduct a running record. As soon as you finish working with one student, you can move immediately to another with everything ready to go. If you work with one student after another reading the same book, you can save a little time because you have the story fresh in your own mind when you analyze the retelling and comprehension work.

Often, you'll need to complete a series of two, three, or more running records. You'll start with texts the child can easily read with accuracy, fluency, and comprehension and continue up a level or so at a time until you determine the child's ceiling (the hard/frustration level). At times, you may question the results of a running record, especially when a child is just on the cusp of being able to read a text independently. Perhaps the child had just one error too many, or her fluency started out great but then faded, or her response to a comprehension question was not terrible but not exactly on point either. When in doubt, the answer is quite simple: try another text. The more information you have about the reader, the better you will be able to determine if the child's reading behavior was a one-time fluke or part of a pattern. Many teachers save a set of trade books from their classroom libraries to use as back-up texts for running records. You may use alternative running record materials that are available in your building. Perhaps your school currently uses Fountas and Pinnell running records, but there are old DRA kits hiding somewhere (or vice versa), or you can download running records available online, such as the TCRWP Running Records Assessment. The important thing is that you can confirm the accuracy of the level of the text you are using, making sure that it is representative of the text level you hope to assess.

Here's a summary of tips for conducting running records:

- Prepare your materials in bulk ahead of time.

- Create a running records station in your classroom.

- Have kids sit nearby, so you can progress immediately from one student to the next.

- Work on the same text with several kids so the story is fresh in your mind.

- Avoid doing two running records in a row with one child.

- When in doubt, conduct another running record.

Try to avoid the frenzy that occurs when an assessment window approaches and running records haven't been done for months on end. In many schools, during the windows for data collection, teachers enter their latest results from running records that may have been administered within a week or even a month of the data entry window. The important thing is that you know for sure what books each one of your students can read with accuracy, comprehension, and fluency at all times—not just three times a year.

Assessing Children's Nonfiction Reading Levels

Your initial running records will use fiction texts and will give you a baseline for children's reading levels, as well as a wealth of information about each reader. But what about their nonfiction levels?

If you have lots of time for assessment and plenty to spend on assessment tools, you could assess kids as both fiction and as nonfiction readers, using parallel running record assessments. (The Fountas and Pinnell Benchmark Assessment System includes both fiction and nonfiction texts at each level.) You could even assess children using both assessments at the same time, which would let you know which children read nonfiction at lower levels than fiction, which read at the same level, and so on. You might find that their patterns of fluency and accuracy are not always similar or that their ability to

do inferential thinking differs across text types. If your school is doing deeply calibrated, parallel assessments like that, please let us know, because we would love to study the data to see if patterns emerge.

However, all of that requires an enormous amount of time, and therein lies the rub. You only have so much time with the children, and it can start to feel as if you are spending time on assessment that needs to be spent on instruction. It can seem like you spend so much time collecting data that you have no time to teach in response to it, to apply it. It is also not good if you have time to give running records but no time left for performance assessments of higher-level thinking skills.

Ultimately, we decided it was good enough to assess children's fiction levels and then start with those as their most likely/nearly right/good-enough-to-start-with levels for nonfiction, with the intention of watching kids and moving them down a level in nonfiction if they seem to struggle, which happens fairly often. Children's nonfiction levels often lag a bit behind their fiction levels, but after they have been studying nonfiction for a while, you should be able to move them back up so they are reading the same level in nonfiction as in fiction. That's our best advice to you.

You'll note that we do not supply leveled nonfiction texts on our website, and that is only partially because we felt that conducting running records in both fiction and nonfiction seems excessively time-consuming and difficult. Also, the difficulty a child experiences reading a nonfiction text relates very directly to the knowledge the child brings to that text. Although this is partly true for fiction texts, too—knowing something about mystery or fantasy will help a reader with a mystery or fantasy story—the importance of background knowledge is more significant when children are reading nonfiction. Knowing a lot about dinosaurs dramatically helps a child read a text about Tyrannosaurus rex. The fact that the child comes to that text already knowing about the concepts of carnivores and herbivores, about scavengers and predators, makes a huge difference! So the level at which a child reads nonfiction about highly familiar topics may not represent the level at which that child reads nonfiction texts on unfamiliar topics.

Different Types of Information from Running Records

The data gleaned from a running record reaches beyond matching the child to a reading level. It can tell you what sources of information your readers do and do not rely upon when reading. When reading, children need to practice

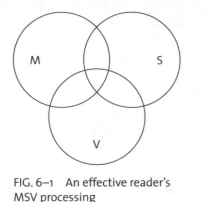

FIG. 6–1   An effective reader's MSV processing

using all available sources of information in an integrated, reciprocal way—the meaning (semantic), structure (syntactic), and visual (graphophonic) systems. If a child neglects to use or overuses one source of information, you need to teach her to integrate the one(s) not being used more effectively. A successful reader draws upon all three sources of information.

When you study running records, look for the processing children do in their reading, especially what they do when faced with a challenge. You'll need to study what students do when reading at an instructional or even a frustration level to discover this information. A running record without errors gives you nothing to study!

It is only when the child begins to make errors or when comprehension breaks down that you'll be able to see what information sources a particular reader does and does not rely upon. For example, if a child ignores the picture more than once in favor of sounding out a word, letter by letter, that suggests a particular approach when encountering unfamiliar words. This child may not be likely to use the pictures or what is happening in the story to help figure out the meaning of the words she is working so hard to decode. This also lets you know that she is focusing on letter-by-letter decoding (which is not very efficient) rather than looking for letter clusters, spelling patterns, or parts of the word.

Imagine that another child, a transitional reader, pauses at a word, studies the picture, and substitutes a word that makes sense for the picture but doesn't sound right in the sentence. A sentence reads, "Henry was swinging high to the sky," and the child substitutes *swing* for *swinging*. The child does this several more times, substituting words that essentially make sense but aren't fitting the syntax of the sentences in the book. This lets you know that the student needs support with both using syntax as a source of information for solving words, and cross-checking meaning (the pictures) with the visual information (the print) on the page. This student might be encouraged to check by reading to the end of the word.

Perhaps another child points to every word as she reads, which was a helpful strategy as a beginning reader, but now that she is reading levels G and H, it is interfering with her fluency. She reads too slowly and choppily to fully understand what's going on in the story.

Another student might read quickly, making a series of errors that all seem to make sense in the context of the story but don't match the print. He seems to understand the text, and you imagine he's predicting the words that likely come next. Though errors that draw on all three sources of information appropriately can be insignificant, a pattern of this behavior can be problematic. These errors can affect shades of meaning or academic vocabulary important to a topic. Slowing down and drawing this child's attention to the visual information on the page will help him avoid plowing right past errors that *will* change the meaning. You can reinforce his self-correction of errors and support more sophisticated skills, such as vocabulary acquisition and noticing author's craft and intention.

As you analyze the errors in your students' reading, remember to approach the work with a sense of curiosity. Unlike writing, where we can study what a child has put on the page, reading is an invisible process; the child's thinking is tucked inside the mind and out of reach. Analyzing a running record or listening to a child read is your chance to make this process visible, to peek inside her mind and try to figure out how she is making sense of one of the most complex things children will ever learn to do!

As you read running records, ask yourself:

- What are my students doing when they encounter trouble?
- Do they make attempts?
- Do they check their attempts?
- Do they make multiple attempts?
- What sources of information do they use?
- Do they use meaning, structure, and visual information equally, or do they lean more heavily on one information source?
- How effectively do they use sources of information?

As you do this work, remember to work from a strength-based model, notice what each child *can* do, and then think about what their next steps might be. Often we are so eager to decide what to teach next that we skip right over what it is children are already doing. Take time to notice their strengths and use this as a jumping-off point for your next teaching and coaching.

As your readers continue to grow and change, fluency will play an increasingly important role. Your emergent and beginning readers will need to point crisply to one word at a time, often reading in a choppy, staccato fashion until the book becomes more familiar on subsequent rereadings. For these readers, fluency is something to work on in familiar, easy texts. As kids move into levels F, G, and beyond, you can begin to expect they'll read more smoothly on their first reading of a text. Take notes in the margins of your running record forms. Can the child read without pointing? This will help develop fluency. Does she pause before each word to solve it, with little or no automaticity? This will make reading fluently difficult. Are there signs of phrasing—two or three words grouped together—instead of reading one word at a time? Beginning at level J, the TCRWP and Fountas and Pinnell running records include a fluency scale that helps you determine if the child's fluency on a first reading indicates that the level is a good match for that reader. In general, once children are reading at about level J, even the first reading should include the three hallmarks of strong fluency (Rasinski 2010): accuracy, automaticity, and prosody (or expression). Reading should sound natural and expressive, with appropriate reading rate, emphasis on particular words, and overall tone.

Assessing reading isn't only about accuracy and fluency, but is also about comprehension. For many students, it's not the words that are a problem, but the general comprehension of the text. The child's retelling of the text, as well as her responses to inferential questions about the text, provide a small, but important glimpse into how well she will be able to understand other texts at the same level of difficulty. Suppose a student reads a level I running record text with 100% accuracy and is very fluent, with expressive and dramatic reading. However, when asked to talk about the story, it is clear that (in the words of Cris Tovani) she "read it, but didn't get it." She tries reading another level I, and this happens again—and again. If this is a pattern for the child at level I, that means level I cannot be her independent reading level; she'll need to work on comprehension first. It is never enough for a child to simply say the words correctly. Without comprehension, it's simply word calling, not *reading*.

A Sample Running Record

Here is an example of a set of running records a teacher conducted with one student (see Figure 6–2). You'll see that she recorded the child's accurate reading, omissions, substitutions, self-corrections, and other reading behaviors using conventional coding for running records. She also recorded the student's retelling and responses to the comprehension questions, rather than just checking off the questions. This provides better, more accurate information.

The teacher used forms she downloaded from the Teachers College Reading and Writing Project website, and you could use these, too, if you are not already using another assessment system. Or you can simply make a photocopy of the leveled text you are about to give the child so that you can have something on which to mark the child's reading as a record of the assessment you are conducting.

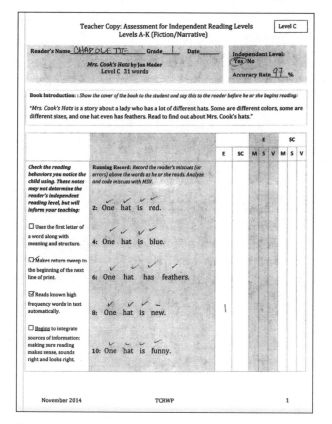

FIG. 6–2 See the online resources for the full running record.

You'll notice that in the example shown in Figure 6–2, the student read with high accuracy and understood the text well. This is an indication that she could read other texts at this level with success. But what about the next level up? What strategies might this reader rely on when reading gets more challenging? Notice that she skipped the word *new*. This is only one error, so more information is needed to develop a theory about this reader.

In the second example (see Figure 6–3), there is evidence that the student is beginning to face some challenges as a reader. A pattern begins to form. When she encounters unfamiliar or tricky words, she simply skips them, not making any attempt to substitute a word or to use the print to figure it out. Look, for example, at the word *backyard*. Notice how the reader did not use meaning (the story or the picture) to help her solve the word. Since she did not continue reading, the teacher told her the word (coded with "T"). She did

this again at the words *chest*, *shoulder*, *stomach*, and *scored*. You might begin to form a theory about this child as a reader. When she encounters tricky words, she either skips over them or waits to be prompted by the teacher. Even faced with these challenges, the student still reads fairly successfully, with 91% accuracy and strong comprehension. She may be able to do this work even at level E or F or G—or not. More information is needed to find out where her ceiling is.

Now in the third example (see Figure 6–4), there are enough errors to paint a more complete picture of this child as a reader. Not only does she skip words when the going gets tough, but she also has a tendency to use only the first part of a word, often with disregard for sentence structure (*Squirrel/Squirrel's*, *fly/flew*). The hard work involved in trying to figure out all those tricky words leaves little energy for thinking about the story, and her

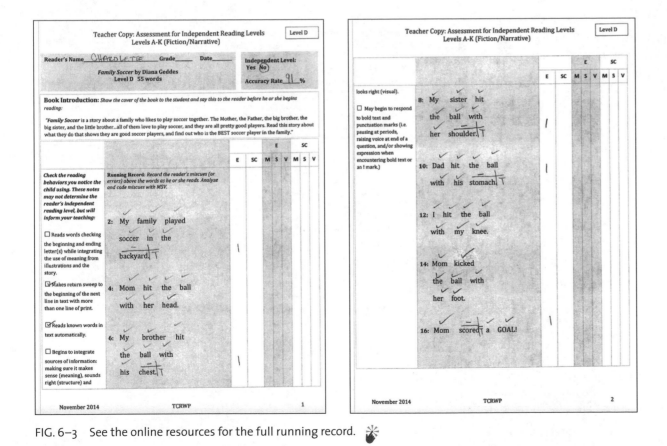

FIG. 6–3   See the online resources for the full running record.

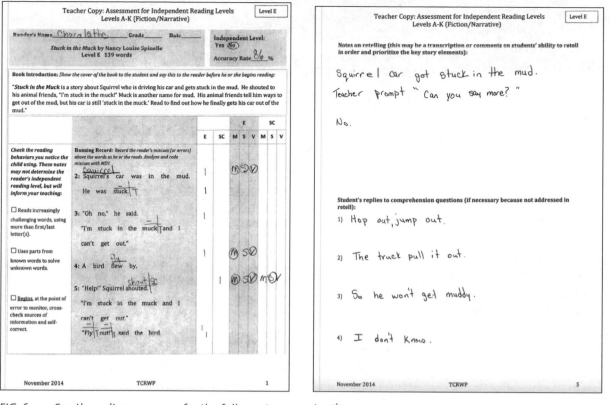

FIG. 6–4   See the online resources for the full running record.

comprehension suffers in the end, leaving her unable to see that Squirrel goes from being mildly worried to very worried to finally being relieved when the tow truck pulls him out.

As evident from her lack of attempts to solve unknown words, the level E text was Charlotte's ceiling. As text becomes increasingly complex, the reader has to learn how to strategically use meaning, structure, and visual information to help with problem solving on-the-run. Charlotte needs to learn how to look at the visual print in meaningful parts (initial letter, letter clusters, word parts, onset, rime, inflectional endings) as she holds on to the meaning of the story. She will also have to learn how to use structure (what would sound right) to help her solve with the visual and meaning information. She must learn how to integrate these sources to help her problem solve, self-monitor, cross-check information, and self-correct.

Your completed running records can provide a wealth of information about each student. When looking closely at a set of running records, it is often hard to know where to start. One important piece of advice to keep in mind is to be on the lookout for patterns rather than individual errors or one-time exceptions. Look at each child's set of running records as a researcher, trying to develop a theory about the reader. Ask yourself, "What kind of reader is this child? What patterns do I see that are supporting this child? What patterns do I see that are unhelpful for this child? What are this child's next steps? What are her goals as a reader?"

As you can see from the example above, it's most helpful to look at the instructional, as well as the challenging or hard level running records to gather data and determine the student's needs, because there will be multiple errors with the more challenging texts and multiple opportunities to analyze the types of errors students make. The more running records you have for a child, the clearer the picture will be. If you are looking at only one short level C running record, chances are, you have only a handful of errors to form your theory. If you can look across two running records, or even three running records gathered over time, you'll have more information.

When Readers Are Ready for a New Level

When a child achieves above 96% accuracy with adequate fluency and comprehension, this is one indicator that he is able to read independently at that level. We recommend that you put scaffolds in place to support the student in strengthening the behaviors and comprehension work required at the independent level, and you will want to teach your children to select carefully from the wide range of books that will be available in any given level. There will be a big difference, for example, between an "easy level D" and a "hard level D," and this is made all the more complicated by the fact that each child's vocabulary and prior knowledge will play an important role in how easy or hard the book will be.

Students who are approaching readiness to read at a higher independent level may be introduced to some of the work required for that next level through conferring and small-group work. This is commonly known as a child's "instructional" or "challenge" level—texts that children can read with 90–95% accuracy, fluency, and comprehension. These texts are almost "just right" but not quite. Guided reading, shared reading, strategy lessons, partner reading, and other supports are suggested for instructional texts throughout the units of study. Marie Clay suggests "cautiously increasing" the level of text difficulty, building in repetition and "massive practice" with new skills and strategies to help readers handle new work. The more children practice, the more independent the work becomes as they build a self-extending system for processing text. Massive practice with texts that are high-success texts and that are just a bit challenging will help children read with success.

Establishing Benchmarks that Correlate to Assessment Windows for Running Records

You may want to establish normed benchmarks as targets for each of your assessment windows. In Figure 6–5, you will note the TCRWP benchmarks, based on our data from almost 60,000 children over many years. Our

<table>
<tr><th colspan="5">Teachers College Reading and Writing Project
Benchmark Reading Levels and Marking Period Assessments</th></tr>
<tr><th>SEPTEMBER</th><th>NOVEMBER</th><th>JANUARY</th><th>MARCH</th><th>JUNE</th></tr>
<tr>
<td>Kindergarten
Emergent Story Books
Shared Reading</td>
<td>Kindergarten
Emergent Story Books
Shared Reading
A/B (with book intro)</td>
<td>Kindergarten
B/C (with book intro)</td>
<td>Kindergarten
1=Early Emergent
2=A/B (with book intro)
3=C (with book intro)
4=D/E</td>
<td>Kindergarten
1=B or below
2=C (with book intro)
3=D/E
4=F or above</td>
</tr>
<tr>
<td>Grade 1:
1=B or below
2=C
3=D/E
4=F or above</td>
<td>Grade 1:
1=C or below
2=D/E
3=F/G
4=H or above</td>
<td>Grade 1:
1=D or below
2=E/F
3=G/H
4=I or above</td>
<td>Grade 1:
1=E or below
2=F/G
3=H/I/J
4=K or above</td>
<td>Grade 1:
1=G or below
2=H
3=I/J/K
4=L or above</td>
</tr>
<tr>
<td>Grade 2:
1=F or below
2=G/H
3=I/J/K
4=L or above</td>
<td>Grade 2:
1=G or below
2=H/I
3=J/K/L
4=M or above</td>
<td>Grade 2:
1=H or below
2=I/J
3=K/L
4=M or above</td>
<td>Grade 2:
1=I or below
2=J/K
3=L/M
4=N or above</td>
<td>Grade 2:
1=J or below
2=K/L
3=M
4=N or above</td>
</tr>
<tr>
<td>Grade 3:
1=K or below (avg. H)
2=L
3=M
4=N or above</td>
<td>Grade 3:
1=K or below (avg. I)
2=L/M (avg. L)
3=N
4=O or above</td>
<td>Grade 3:
1=L or below
2=M/N
3=O
4=P or above</td>
<td>Grade 3:
1=M or below (avg. J)
2=N
3=O
4=P or above</td>
<td>Grade 3:
1=N or below (avg. K)
2=O
3=P
4=Q or above</td>
</tr>
</table>

FIG. 6–5 Benchmark chart

benchmarks come from a correlation between the level of text complexity at which a student can read with fluency, comprehension, and 96% accuracy and that student's scores on high-stakes texts that year, and for younger children, several years later. That is, it was the children who were reading at level D/E in June of kindergarten who scored a 3 on the high-stakes test years later, when they were in third grade. The correlation between rising levels of text complexity and rising scores has been extremely strong—so much so that when it is not strong, we know that is a signal that the school is probably misleveling readers and needs intensive help immediately in conducting running records. These correlations also allow administrators, educators, and parents to know when to raise red flags regarding a student's potential achievement, and to do so early enough in the year to actually change students' rate of growth.

There are interesting things to note about this data. First, the correlation between the level of text complexity with which a student read and the scores on high-stakes tests existed despite the fact that the context for collecting these running records was far from ideal. The people doing the assessing were K–6 teachers from New York City's crowded classrooms; during the early years of data collection, many of these teachers had just learned how to conduct running records. And yet, levels were still predictive of scores. Problems abounded. And yet there has nevertheless been alignment between the level of text difficulty that readers seemed to be able to handle and scores on the standardized tests. We have also found alignment between our benchmarks and other major reading assessment systems' grade-level expectations.

To a remarkable degree, students' reading levels, as measured by their ability to read at a level with accuracy, fluency, and basic comprehension, predicted the scores that they received on high-stakes tests. This suggests that teachers seeking to support students' testing success would be wise to work toward moving students up reading levels. Giving book introductions to kick-start students into a new level, getting students into book clubs to practice higher-level comprehension, tracking students' reading growth, and getting children involved in goal-setting—all of these and other ways of fostering reading level growth are likely to prove as powerful as (and certainly more engaging than!) mere test preparation.

Analyzing a Class Set of Data

While there are seemingly endless possibilities for the information you could glean from a single set of running records, there are particular behaviors and strategies that are especially helpful to consider. Look at each child's ceiling (hard level, beyond instructional) to consider the biggest challenges facing your students:

- Reading behaviors, especially monitoring for sense
- Use of sources of information: meaning, visual, syntax
- Fluency
- Literal comprehension
- Inferential comprehension

These challenges can become instructional goals for each of your students. As you meet with each student, you might keep a running list of basic assessment information, such as independent reading level, and each child's overall biggest goals as readers.

When you analyze your students' running records, look for patterns throughout the class at the individual, small-group, and whole-class level. For example, you may notice that there are several students who need support with keeping track of the story, retelling, and holding on to meaning. When this happens, you can plan to meet with these students and provide instruction that particularly focuses on practicing the work they need most.

Although these students may be reading at different levels, they all share a similar need.

You may also notice whole-class trends in the data. If most of the class needs support in self-monitoring and cross-checking, using meaning, syntax, and visual sources of information, for example, be sure to tailor your unit of study and other whole-class teaching (shared reading, read-aloud, word work, and other components) to address trends you see in your assessment data.

Gathering Notes During Conferring and Small-Group Work

By the time several weeks have passed, you will likely have completed at least one or two running records with nearly all your students, and they'll be able to sustain independent work for longer stretches of time. You can then begin conferring with individuals and teaching small groups.

Across the year, notes from individual conferences and small-group work (including guided reading) can provide invaluable data on student progress. Looking across a month's worth of notes, patterns will emerge that other forms of assessment may not capture. "Wow," you might think, "At the start of the year, all my conferences with this student were about retelling and summarizing—literal comprehension. Now my notes are more about inferring how the character feels and noticing character change." That's progress.

Conferring notes should take no longer than a moment to jot down—just a few words and abbreviations. These notes are individual to each teacher, and there is no single perfect system. But you'll know that your notes are working when they help you to have better conversations with your students about their reading. Each time you sit down to confer with a student you should be able to say, "Last time we met, we talked about . . ." Your notes should allow you to pick up where you left off, making your work an ongoing string of connected lessons, rather than a series of one-shot deals with little follow-up. If you find it difficult to have a conversation with a student about the work you've been teaching, that's a sign that you need to change your strategy for note-taking.

Many teachers find it helpful to have a form to help organize their thinking and provide reminders for parts of the conference they want to be sure to address. For example, a simple three-column organizer with sections for "Research/Compliment," "Teaching Point," and "Next Steps" can be helpful.

Some find it more helpful to keep a tabbed binder with sections for each student, while other teachers prefer using a grid showing the whole class at once. Still others prefer using index cards or Post-its, collecting them across the day, and at the end of day moving them into the tabbed binders.

The important thing is to keep experimenting until you find a system that works for you. In addition to using your notes to track patterns and progress, you can use the information from your notes to plan next steps with individuals, groups, and the whole class. Looking across your "Next Steps" column or the "Needs" section of your notes for each child, you may be able to easily ascertain that more than half of your class needs support in a particular skill or that there are groups of children with similar next steps that you could pull together during reading workshop.

It is helpful to have a structure in place that supports you in using your conferring notes to plan for flexible grouping. Many teachers include planning for small groups in their routine for lesson planning each week. Perhaps

Conference and Small Group Schedule

Week: 1 – CHARACTER UNIT

	Monday	Tuesday	Wednesday	Thursday	Friday
Strategy Lessons	Monitoring — Alex, Tatiana, Hillary, Miguel, Javier	Determining Importance — Dennis, Sariah, Jose, Jordan	Monitoring — Alex, Tatiana, Hillary, Miguel, Javier	Determining Importance — Dennis, Sariah, Jose, Jordan	Making Inferences — Jaime, Alisa, Jordan, David, Brandon
Guided Reading	F — Isaiah →, Tayanna →, Quinn →	F	H — Sabrina →, Dominique →, John →, Destiny →	H	F — Isaiah, Tayanna, Quinn

Week 2 – CHARACTER UNIT

	Monday	Tuesday	Wednesday	Thursday	Friday
Strategy Lessons	Cross-checking — Isaiah →, Tayanna →, Quinn →	Cross-checking	Monitoring — Alex, Tatiana, Hillary, Miguel, Javier	Determining Importance — Dennis, Sariah, Jose, Jordan	Making Inferences — Jaime, Alisa, Jordan, David, Brandon
Guided Reading	J→K — Jaime →, Alisa →, Jordan →, David →, Brandon →	K	F — Isaiah, Tayanna, Quinn	M — Marisol →, Jasmine →, Tomas →, Peter →	M

Thursday after school is your usual time that you set aside for lesson planning. Along with deciding what minilessons to teach, you can also build a rough outline of your conferring and small-group work for the week. Review the notes for each student to plan an outline of what your week of conferring might look like. For some students, the plan might simply be to conduct a running record, while for others the plan might be to teach a guided reading session, and for others it may be a strategy lesson or shared reading or a one-to-one conference. Glancing back at your week's worth of conferring notes can help you plan strategically and make the most of your week.

USING ADDITIONAL ASSESSMENTS TO INFORM YOUR CLASSROOM INSTRUCTION

Running records and conferring notes are not the only forms of assessment you can use to inform your classroom instruction. There are a number of other useful assessments available to help you understand your students' needs, so you can give them the most effective instruction possible.

Assessing Kindergarten Readers

So far, we've laid out the beginning of the year assuming that most, if not all, of your students are reading leveled books at the start of the year. Of course, the start of the year in kindergarten is a bit different. Unlike in other grades, your students have not yet been to school! While most students in other grades are reading conventionally, yours are mostly brand new to reading. They are mostly likely emergent readers. Unlike teachers of other grades, who might have the benefit of looking at the last year's data to get things up and running, you'll be starting from scratch.

So, while teachers in other grades will put out baskets of books to encourage students to select a just-right book for themselves, your first unit will begin with putting out baskets of high-interest nonfiction books that your kids are dying to get their hands on. These children will not likely be decoding print, but they will "read" engaging books by studying the pictures and talking about what they see, one page at a time. These books may have beautiful photography and engaging text features, such as flaps and wheels and pulls. Such books are often hard to assign a Fountas and Pinnell guided reading level to and are usually housed in the unleveled part of a classroom library.

Instead of diving into assessing kindergartners' reading levels right away, you'll want to work quickly to find out what children know about general concepts about books and about print. Where is the cover of a book? Where are the pictures? Where are the words? What's the difference between a letter and a word? These are basic concepts about print and are easily and quickly assessed using a concepts about print assessment (available from many sources, including the TCRWP website).

You'll also want to find out which, if any, letter names and letter sounds each child can identify. A simple letter-sound identification assessment will give you this information (also available from many sources, including TCRWP). Then you can look across this information to decide how best to use all the parts of your day to teach these. If you see that many students are confused about the difference between letters and words, for example, you might do some work during shared reading. Counting words and counting letters might help students understand the difference between the two, or you can cut sentence strips apart first into words and then into letters.

Your emergent readers aren't yet drawing representationally or writing letters or words yet, but they will still engage in all kinds of reading work. Some of the most important work involves talking about familiar books and storytelling to go with the pictures. With young readers, there are two types of talk to observe: talking *about* books (e.g., favorite parts, questions, and other ideas about the text) and children's *storytelling* to go with the pictures across the pages.

As you prepare for teaching emergent readers, you may wonder, "How do I know if children are doing this work well?" if they aren't yet reading conventionally. Although no two children are alike, they do tend to go through predictable phases as emergent readers, and many teachers use stages of emergent storybook reading to assess student progress in this unit. You can find the emergent storybook reading stages in the online resources that accompany this series. You can use this scale, based on the work of Elizabeth Sulzby, as one of many ongoing informal formative assessments regarding children's progress. The scale provides examples at each stage: early emergent reading (when children might simply point to objects in the picture and name them), to using sentences and phrases and transitional words to list events, to fluent storytelling that sounds just like the teacher (and the many steps in between). These stages may help you think more deeply about all Common Core State Standards for Reading Literature in an integrated way.

Phonics and High-Frequency Word Assessments in Kindergarten and First and Second Grade

Children's knowledge of letter sounds, spelling patterns, and high-frequency words will play an important role in your instruction at every grade level, but especially with emergent and beginning readers. Decades ago, many teachers simply assumed children in their class came to school knowing little or nothing about reading or writing. Many teachers used to teach their whole class the same information about letter names and sounds and about spelling and high-frequency words. We now know that this way of thinking about young readers is deeply flawed. According to the National Center for Education Statistics (*Entering Kindergarten: Findings From the Condition of Education*, 2000), approximately two out of three children enter kindergarten *already* recognizing both uppercase and lowercase letters. Many children already know that print goes from left to right and can even identify the beginning sounds in words, before they've even come to school. We recommend different assessments, depending on the age and stage of your students. Though we explain these in greater depth in Chapter 11, "Word Study," it is important to note here that they are a key part of a well-rounded assessment program.

Specifically, once your students are in the beginning stages of reading or writing, it makes sense to periodically assess what they know about spelling patterns. Usually, around the middle of kindergarten is when you might first give a spelling inventory. Such an inventory looks and sounds like a traditional spelling test: you say the word, and kids write it as best they can. But when you analyze the results, you don't simply mark the words correct or incorrect. You analyze them for spelling features. Examples include the spelling inventories in *Words Their Way* (Bear et al. 2012) and the Developmental Spelling Assessment. Again, this is discussed in detail in Chapter 11.

You'll also want to know which high-frequency words children already can recognize on sight with automaticity and which ones they have not yet incorporated into their bank of sight words. Because high-frequency words occur often, they are worth knowing. Nearly 50% of the words we read and write are the same 100 high-frequency words. There are thirteen words that make up nearly 25% of what we read and write! Imagine how laborious it would be to have to stop and decode the words *the* and *and* every time you

encountered them! Usually starting in mid-kindergarten, we recommend periodically assessing this.

Many children will learn high-frequency words simply by reading a lot. The first time they encounter a word, they work hard to solve it, then the next time, and the next, they begin to recognize the word, and eventually, "snap!" they've got it. Your high-frequency word instruction will help add to this ever-increasing bank of words they know on sight. Your first step will be to find out which words each child already knows, so that you can focus on introducing new words and expanding their sight word vocabulary. A high-frequency word assessment usually consists of showing a child one word at a time to read to you. You check off the words he knows and leave blank the words he does not yet know. There are assessments with a writing option as well. Any high-frequency word assessment will do (there is one available from TCRWP, among others), as long as you are looking to see which words each child knows with automaticity. If a child still has to pause for a length of time or work to decode the word rather than recognizing it on sight, then he will benefit from more practice with the word.

There are many ways to collect and record this data, but most important is how you use it. For example, you may look at high-frequency word assessment data for your class and notice a large range in the number of words

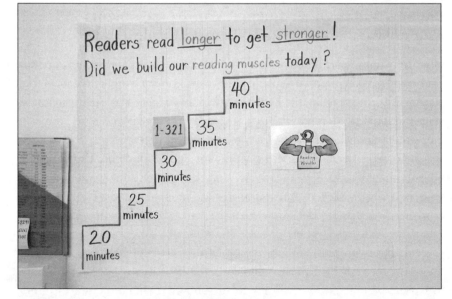

FIG. 6–6   Stamina charts for kindergarten *(left)* and second grade *(right)*

each student knows. You can use this data to support students by making an individual word ring for each student, filled with words the student needs to practice. You can then help the child practice reading those words, go on hunts for the words, find them in the child's writing, and make a personalized word wall to use during writing. Different students may each have different words they are working on, based on the words they missed in the high-frequency word assessment. You might also notice words students missed and then try to find poems and songs with those words and do some shared reading with them, so students can practice finding the words in context as well.

Assessing Reading Volume and Stamina

Of course, all the data in the world won't help much if students aren't actually reading every day. You'll want to devise ways to track how much reading your students are doing each day. This can be as simple as setting a timer at the start of reading workshop and keeping track of how many minutes the entire class reads day to day. You might track this data on a chart for the whole class to see, inviting the students to set attainable goals each day. "Wow, we read for fifteen minutes every day this week," you might point out to your students. "Thumbs up if you think we can read for twenty whole minutes tomorrow! Great! Turn and tell your partner two things you can do tomorrow to keep yourself reading even longer."

In kindergarten and first grade, you won't want to take time away from students' reading to have them copy the titles of every book they read. Remember, at beginning reading levels, it usually only takes a few minutes to read an entire book, and for many children it will take as long for them to copy the title as it would to read the entire book—twice! So instead of doing that, children can simply tally up how many books they've read each day. They might keep a Post-it in the back of each book, or in a special spot on a reading mat, or you might create a kid-friendly reading log where they can tally up how many books they've read each day. Children can then see something that would otherwise be a very abstract concept: How much reading did you do today? Children can then reflect on how much reading they did and set reasonable goals to do the same amount or even more the next day. There will, of course, be children who make a hundred tallies right away, although they haven't yet read a book. You can foster their love of books and desire to read by saying, "I am so glad to see you are the kind of reader who *wants* to read your books a hundred times! Let's get started doing that right now!"

Once children are fluent enough as writers to jot down the title of a book quickly, then you might introduce a book log (usually by the start of second grade). Book logs also make more sense when children are reading books that take more than one sitting to complete. A log will help them keep track of how many pages they read each day and how long it took to do it.

Reading logs provide a wealth of information that you can use in conferences and small groups. You could collect all the book logs from your students

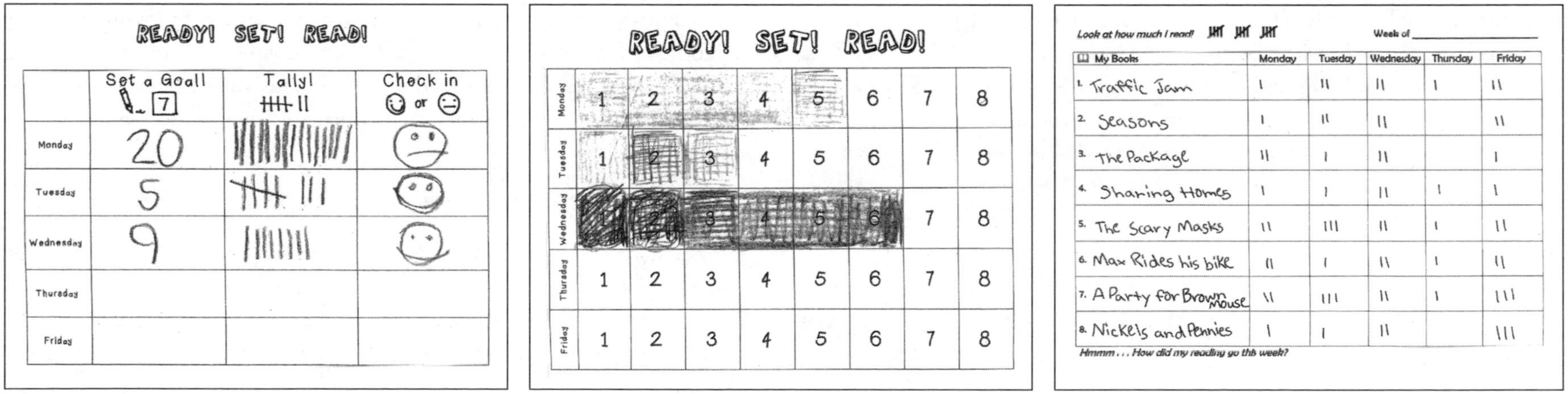

FIG. 6–7   Examples of tally book logs

from time to time, study them, and come back prepared with a list of strategies to teach. However, you might find it more helpful to incorporate book logs into your day-to-day conferring and research, looking from the book log to the latest running record to what the child is saying about his books, and fitting all that you know about that student together to form a theory about the child as a reader. In a conference, you can look at a book log together with a student, noting times when reading was high-volume and times when reading was low volume for him. You might notice patterns in the child's reading. Maybe he reads quickly through realistic fiction, while fantasy reading seems to take forever.

There will be students who exaggerate the page numbers and the number of minutes read, in hopes of pleasing you. It is important that book logs are used only for information to fuel conversations and instruction, not as an inducement to speed through books or to accumulate points or rewards. Donalyn Miller, in *Reading in the Wild*, suggests instituting book logs at the start of the year to establish baseline goals and expectations for reading volume and stamina, and then scaling back the emphasis on book logs as the year goes on to avoid fueling an obsession with reading too quickly or fibbing on book logs just to get them done. Book logs can be brought back from time to time for the purpose of reflecting on how long and how much each student is reading currently and tracking growth.

Assessing Book Talk and Writing about Reading

You'll also need to attend to your readers' developing abilities to comprehend texts deeply. You'll learn this best by listening closely to book talks, by hearing what children say and do with partners, and by listening to children's retelling of their independent reading books. Although we do not have a scale with which to measure this, the truth is that there is little that is more important. You may want each child to keep a reading portfolio that includes artifacts that represent the child's growing abilities to comprehend.

Children who are not yet transitional readers (meaning they are reading below levels H/I) will not be doing a lot of writing about reading during independent reading. You won't want to take time away from reading to ask them to write very much, but you might build some informal assessments into your read-aloud time. For example, you might read aloud a short picture book, and at preset places in the text, ask each child either to turn and talk (as you record their responses) or stop and jot (or sketch) in response to the prompt

"What do you think will happen next?" or "How does the character feel, and why?" or "What is this nonfiction book mostly teaching us?" You could date the children's responses and keep them, plus the text, from September and from several subsequent months. You might also include a rubric that analyzes what that child does and does not do when asked to predict. Or you may ask students to stop and jot during a read-aloud and then collect and analyze these responses. Similar records could be kept for any other comprehension skill, and we strongly suggest you select a few skills and make a point of keeping this sort of record. There is a saying about assessment: "We inspect what we respect."

If you teach second-graders, or very fluent first-graders, you may also invite kids to stop and sketch or stop and jot a quick response to their reading during reading workshop, as long as it doesn't take much time away from reading their books. In the midst of independent reading time you might say, "Everybody, right now, what exactly is your character thinking or feeling? Make a quick sketch, or jot a word or two on a Post-it and leave it on the corner of your desk for me. Put your initials on the back." You can then quickly skim the Post-its, looking for overall patterns, and divide them into groups: kids who drew or wrote evidence of characters' actions rather than feelings, kids who drew or wrote something related to character feelings or thoughts, and kids who thought outside the box, doing something unexpected. These quick, informal checks are not very precise, but they can certainly help you decide which students to follow up with.

Your assessment of children's day-to-day responses to text can include bits of transcribed conversations, sample Post-its from their book baggies, and observations during read-aloud and shared reading. Watch closely as children talk with their reading partners, dramatizing bits of stories and teaching each other information from their nonfiction reading. All of this will help you determine how to focus your read-aloud work, as well as your whole-class, small-group, and individual instruction during reading workshop.

Setting Assessment-Based Goals with Students

A principal recently asked me, "What do you think students would say is the most important thing about reading conferences?" I thought for a moment, and replied, "Well, I hope they would say that a conference is when the teacher helps them set their goals, so they know what to work on and practice. It sets up their reading work." The principal was surprised. "Really? I would

think that kids would say that it's all about getting to read with the teacher." My response was, "Well, yes. But no." Kids do say that sometimes—and why wouldn't they? Teachers are great! But our aim, as teachers of young children, should be to foster independence, so that kids read for their *own* purposes and goals.

We have to be careful that reading workshop doesn't become a time when kids simply wait their turn to read with the teacher, not doing much reading work or thinking deeply about what they read until the teacher comes along, and then kicking it into high gear. When kids have crystal clear goals and plans that they are working toward, they feel themselves improving as readers. Reading becomes the reward itself, rather than reading with the teacher (though that will always be important as well).

It helps to make goals visible. Talk explicitly about goals with kids, giving names to the work they are doing. Structure time into your workshop for kids to reflect on their goals and set new ones. During a share session, for example, you might point to each item on an anchor chart and ask students to give a thumbs up if they tried each strategy that day. "If you didn't use this strategy today, and you think it might have helped, make it your goal for tomorrow that you'll practice this. You can look at all our charts every day to remember all that you've learned and set goals for yourself as a reader." This is a form of self-assessment and goal-setting that is simple to incorporate into your existing workshop structure.

Reading Goals:
- Making sure I read every word on the page.
- Retelling—and rereading when I can't.
- Thinking and talking about characters' feelings.
- Reading with a smooth voice.

In your conferring and small-group work with kids, be sure that every kid leaves with a very clear goal and purpose. The selected goal should be based on the wealth of assessment data described previously in this chapter. It makes a world of difference that kids are doing work that is selected based on their needs as readers, rather than work that is randomly selected because it's the next thing on a checklist or the next lesson in a book. You might make it a routine to leave a reminder or a tool with each kid when you confer or teach small groups. Children will need to be able to recall what you and others have

taught them to do in conferences and small groups. If the readers in your class are going to be accountable for actually living up to the goals that are settled upon, it is important that those goals are recorded and made visible. Students need a record-keeping system of their own to keep track of all of this valuable information.

One way that some teachers set up such a system is to provide a resource in each child's reading folder or book baggie titled "Goals, Plans, and Reflections." This might be series of pages in sheet protectors in the center of a pocket folder or a ring of cards with reminders or a bookmark with picture clues that remind students of strategies to be working on.

You might decide to make goals public, creating a chart that helps students see who else has similar long-term goals. A pocket chart works well for creating flexible groups of students with similar goals, because student names can easily be moved around as they grow and change as readers from week to week and month to month.

WORKING TOGETHER WITH COLLEAGUES

In John Goodlad's book *A Place Called School*, he describes the old traditional model of most schools as being like an egg-crate. Each teacher kept to her own classroom, so that if you were to look at a school hallway from above, it would have appeared like an egg-crate, each classroom a separate compartment, with little or no interaction or connection to other classrooms next door or across the hall.

It's best to avoid locking yourself in an egg-crate cell. Instead, keep an open-door policy, even if you are the lone soldier, and no one else is on board with you quite yet. Seek out your colleagues and invite them in. Plan together when you can; watch each other teach; share resources. Have honest conversations and even debates with one another. Do anything and everything you can to support one another. As engaging and rich and authentic and important as teaching reading may be, it is not simple. It takes a lifetime to learn this work, and it certainly cannot be done alone.

In terms of assessment, you'll need to work together at the very least to decide on an assessment calendar, as discussed earlier in this chapter, and to decide on what data to pass up from one grade to another. You'll also need to gather colleagues to norm how you assess, so that your data will be meaningful to each other, to children, and to parents. You'll certainly want to do this for running records and perhaps for other assessments as well. I caution you

1st Grade   **Interim Reading Assessment**

Student Name: Assessment for: March 2015 Class: 103

Dear Families,

Spring is a time for watching things grow. We're writing to you because we have been watching your child grow as a reader, and wanted to tell you what we have seen.

Most of us measure whether a child has grown inches taller by using a measuring stick that shows the child's growth in inches, and shows also what the expected height is for children at that age. Some children grow slowly and then spurt up, so it is not a huge worry when a child is not the exact height that one expects, but it is good to keep an eye on this.

In the same way, we measure your child's reading growth above all by noticing whether the books that your child can read now are harder than those he or she could read in the fall. As you know, there is a general way of measuring book difficulty from A through Z.

At this time in your child's grade-level, children are "at standards" if they are reading these levels for these grades:

First grade: H/I/J

Your child is in 1st grade, and is, in fact, reading books at level I. When we are asked to put your child's reading on a scale, the book level that your child can handle suggests that out of a 1–4 scale, your child is at a level of 3—Meets Standards.

There is one important way for children to progress from the book level they can read to the next level and it is this: the child must read lots and lots and lots of books at his or her level. The child will do best if he or she can talk about those books with someone who loves reading—and loves the child—and who makes reading into a great pleasure.

Here are a few books at your child's current reading level:

Big Dog, Little Dog (Eastman)

Hattie and the Fox (Fox)

Henny Penny (Galdone)

PJ Funnybunny Camps Out (Sadler)

There's a Nightmare in My Closet (Mayer)

We assess other aspects of reading too, such as your child's understanding of phonics (which relates to spelling) and the speed at which your child reads. Most of all, we assess your child's comprehension, and we do this by listening to your child talk about the books he or she has read. We also assess your child's progress as a writer. Some of those assessments give us numbers on a chart, and some don't. We would be happy to tell you about any of those assessments.

Most of all, we hope that you and the school can work together to make it likely that your child is reading, reading, reading, and that your child knows that you love reading too.

Sincerely,

Teachers College Reading and Writing Project
Benchmark Reading Levels and Marking Period Assessments

SEPTEMBER	NOVEMBER	JANUARY	MARCH	JUNE
Kindergarten	**Kindergarten**	**Kindergarten**	**Kindergarten**	**Kindergarten**
Emergent Story Books	Emergent Story Books	B/C (with book intro)	1=Early Emergent	1=B or below
Shared Reading	Shared Reading		2=A/B (with book intro)	2=C (with book intro)
	A/B (with book intro)		3=C (with book intro)	3=D/E
			4=D/E	4=F or above
Grade 1:	**Grade 1:**	**Grade 1:**	**Grade 1:**	**Grade 1:**
1=B or below	1=C or below	1=D or below	1=E or below	1=G or below
2=C	2=D/E	2=E/F	2=F/G	2=H
3=D/E	3=F/G	3=G/H	3=H/I/J	3=I/J/K
4=F or above	4=H or above	4=I or above	4=K or above	4=L or above
Grade 2:	**Grade 2:**	**Grade 2:**	**Grade 2:**	**Grade 2:**
1=F or below	1=G or below	1=H or below	1=I or below	1=J or below
2=G/H	2=H/I	2=I/J	2=J/K	2=K/L
3=I/J/K	3=J/K/L	3=K/L	3=L/M	3=M
4=L or above	4=M or above	4=M or above	4=N or above	4=N or above
Grade 3:	**Grade 3:**	**Grade 3:**	**Grade 3:**	**Grade 3:**
1=K or below (avg. H)	1=K or below (avg. I)	1=L or below	1=M or below (avg. J)	1=N or below (avg. K)
2=L	2=L/M (avg. L)	2=M/N	2=N	2=O
3=M	3=N	3=O	3=O	3=P
4=N or above	4=O or above	4=P or above	4=P or above	4=Q or above

FIG. 6–8   Letter to parents with Benchmark Reading Levels and Marking Period Assessment chart

to remember that selecting a schoolwide tool for assessing readers does not mean that your school community's assessments are in alignment. Instead, this requires shared, ongoing conversations about assessments.

For running records, you might bring a child into a faculty meeting and ask all the teachers in the school to record running records of the child's reading while one teacher works with the child in a fishbowl. The important part of this exercise is for each teacher to analyze the running record separately and then to spend time comparing and contrasting conclusions as part of an effort to norm expectations and to align methods for analyzing running records and assessing retellings and answers to comprehension questions. What constitutes a just-right retelling or an acceptable answer to recall questions? You'll discover dramatic differences in judgment, and you'll need to come to a place of consensus. It's also interesting to assess a few children at different grade levels who read at the same reading level. Listening to a second-grade reader who reads at level L, for instance, will be quite different than listening to a fifth-grader reading level L. That kind of pairing helps you pay attention not just to the level, but to what you can find out about the reader.

You can also work together with colleagues to develop a shared understanding about comprehension skills. What do weaker predictions look like compared to stronger predictions? What about character traits? What do we agree on as strong character trait work versus work that shows a need for support? Take any unit and name two or three of the biggest goals for comprehension, and then work together to collect or create examples of student work (or transcripts of student talk) that represent the expectations for that work.

By working together with your colleagues in this way, by having these conversations about assessments, you'll come to a shared understanding about the meaning of the assessments you undertake. But not only that—you'll also be supporting each other in the challenging, rich, and rewarding practice of teaching reading.

COMMUNICATING WITH FAMILIES

Teaching reading is complex work, and communicating with families is no easy task. How do you convey to a parent, who is not a teacher, what "level D" actually means?

The Teachers College Reading and Writing Project and participating schools have drafted letters that you can use to communicate with parents and other caregivers, so these adults know the levels of text difficulty that are "standard" for that child's grade level at a given time of the year and they know how the child in their care is doing in relation to those expectations. Included in each letter is a list of book recommendations for the child, based on his current level.

The data binders that you created at the start of the year will be incredibly helpful to have at your side as you talk with parents about the progress of their children. With your data binder in hand, you'll be able not only to provide generalizations, such as "He's having trouble with comprehension," but also specific examples. You might say, for example, "See here on this running record, his responses here, here, and here let me know that he's thinking only about the actions of the characters and not about their thoughts or feelings. In this same book, paying attention to characters' thoughts and feelings might sound like this . . . We call that making inferences, and your son is working on that."

MAKING READING PROGRESS VISIBLE

We all know that the work of reading is largely invisible. Unlike in writing workshop, it can be hard in reading workshop to know what's really going on with your students—unless you use smart assessments. With the right assessment tools, you can get a clearer picture of where your students are, and you can make thoughtful decisions about how to help them move along the pathway toward greater proficiency as readers. We offer a number of resources to help you, both in the online resources and on the TCWRP website. Try them out, see what fits your needs, and trust your judgment.

Chapter 7

The Architecture (and the Principles) that Inform Minilessons

WHEN I WAS A BRAND-NEW TEACHER, my colleagues and I had a time in our day that we referred to as DEAR time—Drop Everything and Read. For fifteen minutes, we and the kids would all get out our books and settle down to read, read, read. There was a big emphasis on us, as teachers, reading during this time, so I'd settle down alongside the kids and sink into my novel. It was a peaceful time, a lovely interlude in the midst of a busy day. The room had a campy Kumbaya feeling to it. Sometimes, today, I'll try to explain the reading workshop to a teacher from my generation and her eyes will light up and she'll say, "Oh! I got it! So it's sort of like DEAR time, is that it?"

That's a sign to me that I have a lot more explaining to do, because there are important differences between the DEAR times of yesteryear and today's reading workshop. And the biggest difference is that, although it is crucially important that we, as teachers, live in our classroom as richly literate adults, carrying our books and our love of reading with us, we've come to realize that children need not only large stretches of time to read books of their own choice, but also explicit direct instruction in the skills, strategies, and habits of proficient readers. That instruction happens during every minute of the reading workshop, from the first to the last minute, but it starts with the minilesson.

Just as the art instructor pulls students together to learn how to mix colors, just as the football coach and his team huddle over a new play, just as a writing workshop teacher convenes kids to show them techniques for writing story leads, so too, the teacher of reading pulls children together for a minilesson, which opens the day's reading workshop and drives the curriculum.

Because children gather in and disperse from the meeting area at the start of every day's reading workshop (and then again at the start of every day's writing workshop), most teachers that I know well have found it worthwhile to take a bit of time at the start of the year to make sure that children can move to and from the meeting area efficiently and calmly. They teach children to walk directly from their work spots to the meeting area, to sit in their assigned spot, on their bottoms, instead of kneeling and blocking other children's

consistent, whether you are teaching writing or reading. The architecture of a minilesson (as we have taken to calling the design) is easy to learn, and it provides enduring structural support for any minilesson you might write.

SAMPLE MINILESSON

Minilessons are only ten minutes long, yet within those fleeting minutes, there are four component parts. The minilesson that follows illustrates the major components of most minilessons. Let's read a sample minilesson and then discuss its component parts.

view. In some classrooms, teachers ask children to bring the same materials to each day's workshop, so they are sure to have whatever they need on hand. In other classrooms, when the teacher says, "Let's gather for our reading minilesson," she gestures toward the white board that lists that day's materials.

No one way of managing a reading workshop is more correct than another, but it is important to take seriously the challenge of managing workshop instruction, bearing in mind that this method of teaching calls for learners to do more self-management than they may have been asked to do before. I write in some detail about management in Chapter 8 of this book.

Usually, children sit in the meeting area alongside a long-term partner, clustered as close to the teacher as possible. This is not ordinarily a time for children to sit in a circle, because conversations are minimal. This is a time for you to teach as efficiently and explicitly as possible, so children sit alongside a partner, facing you. Partners need to be able to read the same books, because children typically read alone for a while—as long as they can—and then reread those same books with a partner.

Although the teachers with whom I teach often worry over the *content* of their minilessons, your first priority should probably be to master the *methods* of teaching minilessons. While the content of minilessons changes from day to day, the architecture of minilessons remains largely the same, and it remains

MINILESSON

Readers Can Read Snap Words with Endings

CONNECTION

Tell a story about not recognizing someone very familiar to you because the person wore something new. This will be a metaphor for ways that word endings can disguise familiar words.

"Readers, let me tell you a story." With wide eyes, and in my best storyteller's voice, I began my tale. "Yesterday, I walked up to my apartment, and there, standing outside my door, was a stranger! I didn't know who she was or what she was doing there. She had on a dark coat and a hat. I was nervous. What did this stranger want at my house?

"At first I didn't want to go near her, but then I thought, Hey, this is *my* house! So I walked a little closer, and guess what?" I paused briefly to let the children's thoughts about the story run wild.

"It was my *mom*, in a *hat*." I clutched my forehead and shook my head to show just how silly I'd been, and the children laughed. "I didn't recognize *my mom*, a person I know by heart!

"I realized that the reason I didn't recognize this person who I know by heart is that she'd put on a hat, she'd changed things. I'm not used to seeing her in a hat, so I didn't recognize her."

❖ Name the teaching point.

"And *this* is what I want to teach you, readers. There are words that you know by heart in your books—your snap words. But you don't always recognize them, because authors sometimes change them around a bit. When you see a word that looks like a stranger to you—look again. You can ask yourself, 'Does this look like another word that I know?' It might be a familiar snap word, wearing not a new hat, but a new ending."

TEACHING

Demonstrate finding a known word inside an unknown word and then reading the new word.

"I'll show you what I mean. But first, turn on your snap word machine." I flicked an imaginary switch. "And give it *extra strength*!" I twisted an imaginary dial. I watched as the children did the same.

"Okay, ready? If I get to a word that seems like a stranger has come into the story, watch as I ask myself, 'Does this look like a word that I *do* know?'"

I revealed the first page of the book under the document camera. "This is a true story called 'Hide and Seek,' by Lila, a first-grade writer across the hall. Let me read the first page on my own, okay? I'm going to pretend to be a kindergarten reader and use my extra-strength snap word power." I pointed under the words as I read the title and the first two words. I stopped at *playing*.

> *I was playing*
>
> *hide and seek*
>
> *with Dad.*

"Oh, hmm, . . . Gosh, this is a long word. Wait! Does this look like a word that I know? Don't tell me. I want to strengthen my own snap word power. It does! I see the word *play* at the beginning, and I know just *play* wouldn't sound right

there. 'I was play.' No. What would sound right? *Play-ing*! Thumbs up if you thought *playing* too!" Thumbs and smiles popped up all around.

Name the strategy and demonstrate once again.

"Readers, did you see how, when I got to a challenging word, I used my extra-strength snap word power to read a snap word with its ending? You did? Okay, keep watching, because I'll practice that work again." I kept reading and stopped again at *comes*.

> *"Here he comes!"*
>
> *I said.*

I pointed to *comes*. "Hmm, . . . does this look like a word I know?" I waited a moment for children to think to themselves and then answered my own question. "Yes, I recognize *come* at the beginning, and I can move my eyes to the end. *Comes*. Yes! 'Here he comes!' That makes sense in this story! And it sounds right, too." I continued reading to the end of the page.

ACTIVE ENGAGEMENT

Give children the opportunity to read high-frequency words with inflected endings.

"You look ready to try this out, graduates! All right, here is page 3 of the story. Read it with your partner and find out what happens to the girl in the story. And remember, if you get to a word that you don't know, use your extra-strength snap word power! Ask yourself, 'Does it look like a word that I *do* know? Is it just a snap word with an ending on it?'"

> *Dad looked and looked.*
>
> *"I got you!" Dad said.*

I listened in as partners read, and coached them to recognize the high-frequency words in continuous text and to make meaning of the story.

"Eyes on me, readers!" I called them back. "Well, your snap word power certainly did gain extra strength! I heard some of you say that *looked* was tough, but when you recognized *look*, you read the word to the end in a snap!"

LINK

Remind readers that they can always be on the lookout for familiar words when they face a reading challenge.

"Show me your extra-strength snap word power again, readers." The children obliged, turning their imaginary dials. As they did this, I added another extra-strength icon next to *snap word power* on our chart.

"You are going to need that extra strength, because your regular snap word power may not be enough to meet the challenges in your books. Remember, if you get to a word you do not know, you can always ask yourself, 'Do I know a word that looks like this word?' You might recognize a snap word there with an ending.

"Off you go!" They moved to their reading spots, twisting the imaginary dials on their snap word machines.

COMPONENTS OF A MINILESSON

Each minilesson has the same predictable structure and is designed to be completed in ten minutes. The minilesson consists of the following components:

- **Connection:** Contextualizes the day's teaching by connecting it to work students have already been doing
- **Teaching point:** Crystallizes what you plan to teach in that day's minilesson
- **Teaching:** Teaches a particular strategy, using one of several teaching methods
- **Active engagement:** Provides students with guided practice as they try out what they learned in the teaching
- **Link:** Restates what children have learned, doing so in a way that is transferable to another day and another text

I invite you to continue reading as I provide more details about each of these components in the sections below.

CONNECTION: Contextualize the Learning of the Day

During the first two or three minutes of a minilesson, I try to connect the content of the day's teaching with the work the class has been doing, so that this new bit of instruction does not come out of thin air but is instead contextualized. Recalling what children have already been learning also reminds children of the whole repertoire of strategies that they've learned, so that at the end of the upcoming minilesson, children leave, not just with one strategy in hand, but rather, with an expanded repertoire at the ready.

Although minilessons are a form of whole-class instruction, when taught well, they have an intimacy and immediacy, and that tone is established in the connection. "Come close," we say. "I've been thinking and thinking about what the one most important tip I can give you might be, and it is this." Alternatively, I might say, "Readers, can I tell you a secret? I want to let you in on something that I do, something I haven't really told too many people about." I might say, "Last night, I couldn't sleep. I kept thinking about your work and thinking, thinking, thinking about what I could say today that might help. Suddenly, in the middle of the night, an idea came to me. I got out of bed and wrote it on a Post-it. Ready to hear my idea? This is it." Or I might say, "Last night, I was telling my family all about the cool stuff you've been doing. I told them . . . Then as we talked about you, my sister said, 'Hey, Lucy, why don't you show them . . .'" In these and other ways, I try to let children know that my teaching is personalized, tailored to them.

Over the years, I've developed a handful of ways to help children connect with the work we're doing. Perhaps the most common thing I do is use the connection to recruit students to recall what they have already learned—strategies they may draw upon that day—so that I can then add to this repertoire. I sometimes recruit them to do this recalling by saying, "You all have learned so many things about . . . Right now, will you list three things you've learned about . . . ?" Then I say, "Turn and tell the person near you what you have learned!" and the room erupts into conversation. I listen for a minute or two and then say, "Wow! You have learned a lot! Then I name the things I either heard or wish I had heard. In my teaching point, I am then apt to say, "Today I want to teach you one more way readers . . ." and add to the children's repertoire.

I can easily vary my methods for accomplishing the job of surfacing what children already know related to the day's teaching point. For example, I might again suggest that kids have learned a lot, and then say, "Let's reread our anchor chart. As I read a strategy, signal with a thumbs up if it's something you do a lot, a thumbs down if you have never tried it, and a thumbs in between if you have used the strategy once in a while." If I want to be creative, I might create a scenario. "Imagine that a reporter heard about the brilliant work you have been doing, and the reporter came to interview you to learn all that you do as a reader of series books. Will Partner 1 be the reporter, and will you interview Partner 2? Partner 1, hold an imaginary microphone," I made one with my fist, "and pass it to the subject of your interview."

In all of these examples, I am recruiting kids to do a little bit of talking during the connection. It's critical that that invitation to talk doesn't swamp the minilesson. You are setting kids up to talk to a partner, and to talk for just a minute or two. Be sure to limit the talk, and remember, there are other possible ways to start a minilesson.

For example, I sometimes start a minilesson by sharing brief examples of student work. I'm always playing Johnny Appleseed as I teach, finding one youngster who does something that can nourish other readers' imaginations, showing them what's possible. But I also keep a file of work from previous years and, frankly, from other people's classes. Kids are interested in other kids, even if I need to preface my story by saying, "Can I tell you about something that one of last year's readers did?" I save work that is funny, especially, and that represents problems many people encounter. I find it can be effective to show children some of this work, rallying the class to provide ideas that could help that reader.

When I talk about children, I know that what I say will be interesting to other kids if I'm detailed, so I zoom in on a few specifics. In one minilesson, I told children that the day before, Joel had given me a lecture on penguins. "Did you know that all the boys are called king penguins?" he said. "All you gotta do is be a boy, and you're called king penguin." I knew that detail would connect with listeners in a minilesson because it is a fascinating bit of penguin trivia, and also because I told the story using direct address. Chances are good I did not actually remember the exact words that Joel said to me, but I know from my work in the writing workshop that when characters talk, the text tends to be livelier. This may seem unimportant, but actually minilessons are much better if we tell stories fairly well, and including the actual words that a person said and thought usually ramps up the liveliness of a minilesson.

It is not at all unusual for me to launch into a minilesson by telling a story that will seem to the kids to have nothing to do with reading but that, in the end, will become a metaphor for whatever I want to say. For example,

in one of the minilessons in the first-grade unit, *Bigger Books, Bigger Reading Muscles,* I talk about how I took my bike to get fixed. The man at the shop did several checks on my bike to make sure that all of the things he fixed were working. "Well, isn't this just like reading?" I asked the kids. "When we read, we also need to check that what we fix up works right. Sometimes we need to triple-check it!"

When I tell stories, whether it is a true story from my life or a story about something a student said or did, I rely on what I know about writing compelling personal narratives to make my stories engaging. It generally works to tell a story bit by bit, letting it unfold chronologically. Listen, for example, to the start of this story, and you will see that I'm telling my story very much as I would write it if I were in a writing workshop, working to write a strong personal narrative. "Yesterday I watched a tiny ant as he made his way across my paper. To see what he'd do, I laid my pencil across his path. I thought he'd climb over it, like one of those monster tractor toys that climb up and go over a hurdle. Instead, the ant turned left, walking patiently along the length of the pencil. My pencil felt so high to the ant that he didn't even consider climbing over it . . ." Of course, before that story ended, I'd shown students that it had a lot to do with reading. For now, I'll let you guess that connection!

When watching teachers work with the K–8 Units of Study in Opinion/Argument, Information, and Narrative Writing series, I find myself wishing I could gather those teachers in a huddle and offer a few tips about minilessons. What I'd want to say to teachers is that we do mean it when we say that minilessons should be ten minutes in length. For that to happen, you must move briskly. If the minilesson connection suggests that you tell students to tell a partner three things they have learned so far, know that you don't *actually* give students time enough to tell each other three things they've learned. They think of those things and begin talking about them, but by then, you are saying, "I heard you say . . ." You won't actually have enough time to continue listening to hear a whole collection of wise comments to repeat to the class. Listen to a student or two and then ask for the class's attention, and as they are looking toward you, start saying, "I heard you say that . . ." Perhaps they might well have said some of what you repeat, but you didn't get a chance to hear it. There are countless little ways to shave minutes off your minilesson, and you absolutely need to do that, because it's important to get kids applying the new strategy in their own reading as soon as possible.

There are predictable problems that you will encounter if you author your own minilessons. Some teachers have been taught that it is better to elicit information from kids than to say anything to them in a straightforward way. The result is that sometimes the connection to a minilesson is filled with a barrage of questions. "Class, during the last session we talked about . . . what, class?" the teacher will ask. "And you were having trouble with . . . what, class?" she'll ask. You may notice in the connections we described that some of them do recruit bits of input from students, but on the whole, for minilessons to be only ten minutes long, those bits of input need to be very brief. The most valuable place for student participation is later in the minilesson, once you have shown kids how to do something and now want to give them a chance to try that new work out, with support. I suggest, therefore, that you avoid launching minilessons with questions, and, above all, avoid asking known-answer questions in which you're looking for a particular response. It's just not an effective use of time, and you'll get frustrated because kids can't read your mind, so their answers will tend to take you off in different directions, turning a minilesson into a conversational swamp. You have the floor. Try to speak in clear and interesting ways.

TEACHING POINT: Crystallize the Day's Teaching

This is actually a subordinate part of the connection. In the teaching point, we crystallize what it is we hope to teach in that day's minilesson. I work hard to make the teaching point crystal clear and, when possible, memorable and worth remembering. Here are a few examples of teaching points:

> "Today I want to teach you that readers don't just whip through a book, then toss it to the side and say, 'I'm done!' No way! Readers (like writers) have a saying: 'When you are done, you've just begun!' When readers finish a book, they think, 'Let me try that again,' and then they reread the book. *Reread* means to read again."

> "Today I want to teach you that when you talk about a nonfiction book, it's really important not *just* to say, 'Look!' 'Wow!' 'Huh?' 'Why?' Those are great thought starters. But above all, nonfiction readers need to explain what they have learned to others and share that learning. And to do that, it helps to use the fancy words that go with the topic."

> "Today I want to teach you that it's important to practice reading with your eyes, instead of your finger, so you can read more quickly, scooping up more words at a time, reading in phrases instead of word by word."

> "Today I want to teach you that when you read stories, you're not just tagging along behind the character. You're also looking ahead and imagining

what's next. You think about what's already happened to predict what might happen next."

> "Today I want to teach you that one of the best things about books is that even after you take a sneak peek and you anticipate what the book will probably teach you, there will be surprises. Usually, the places where books surprise you are the places where they teach you the most, so be glad for the surprises."

> "Today I want to teach you *another* tool readers use to get their job done. They listen carefully as they read to consider what word might come next. They think 'What would sound right? What kind of word would fit here?'"

An effective teaching point conveys what readers often try to do, and also how we go about doing it. The teaching point frequently starts with a sentence or two about a goal that a reader might take on, and then the teaching point conveys the step-by-step procedure the reader might go through to accomplish those goals. Notice, for example, the goal in the teaching point above: "Today I want to teach you *another* tool readers use to get their job done. They listen carefully as they read to consider what word might come next." And then note the strategy for reaching that goal: "They think, 'What would sound right? What kind of word would fit here?'"

I wouldn't feel that my teaching point had earned its keep if it went like this: "Today I am going to teach you how to solve tricky words." Such a teaching point wouldn't be worth posting as a bullet on a chart or reiterating several times within the minilesson. That is, a teaching point doesn't simply name the terrain that the minilesson will cover. It actually crystallizes the most important lesson from the day.

I want to point out that there is a huge difference between teaching a minilesson and giving an assignment. Sometimes teachers will angle their teaching points in ways that sound more like assignments than replicable teaching points. For example, if a teacher prefaces what she thinks is a teaching point by saying, "Today I want you to . . ." or "Today you will . . . ," I'm immediately wary that instead of giving a minilesson, the teacher is probably laying out an assignment. A teaching point is a tip that learners can draw on often, whenever they read or write. So again—be wary of any teaching point that sounds like this: "Today I want you to retell your book when you are finished," or "Today I want you to find the sight words in your books." Those are assignments, not teaching points.

How different the message is if you say instead, "Today I want to teach you that to get really smart about your topic, you don't just read a book—you also have little chats about that book. You read the words on the page, and then you use your *own* words and your *own* ideas to talk about the book (or the page) with yourself or with a friend." The difference is not just a matter of words. It's a difference of intent. In a teaching point, you crystallize a technique that you expect your students can draw upon repeatedly, perhaps today and certainly for the rest of their lives. Once the transferable technique or strategy is clearly identified in the teaching point, you'll set students up with tasks that help them apply and practice the technique.

Seymour Sarason, a scholar who has written on school change, points out that very often in schools today, people take revolutionary new ideas and stretch, chop, splice, and twist those ideas so they fit into the ongoing assumptions and norms of their teaching. He suggests that it is for this reason that American schools are characterized by a constant frenzy of change and by an underlying sense that the more things change, the more they remain the same. "New math," Sarason writes, "ended up as very much like old math." Your reading workshops can end up as very much like traditional whole-class instruction if you don't guard against your teaching points becoming one-day assignments.

TEACHING: Provide Concrete Instruction Using One of Many Methods

When teaching reading, you'll need to demonstrate the skills and strategies that you teach by bringing books into your minilessons and other whole-class instruction. It is helpful to children if you return to books that they already know. This means they'll be able to focus on the particular skill or strategy that you are spotlighting. Each unit, therefore, incorporates a few books that are used often, and later units reference books from earlier units.

Obviously, the texts you choose as your touchstones need to be ones that allow you to demonstrate the work you want to teach. If you are teaching kids to solve multisyllabic words, you'll need to use a book with lots of multisyllabic words. Generally, if the text that threads through your minilesson is leveled to match what most kids in the room are reading, it will work.

There will be times when you decide to read the entire text to the class outside of the reading workshop so that you can simply reference parts of the text in the minilesson. If you are trying to teach a specific word-solving

strategy, but students are all focused on what happens next to Frog, it will be difficult for them to focus on the strategy you are teaching.

Once I have decided generally what I will teach and chosen the text into which I'll embed my teaching, I need to decide on the method I'll use to teach. As far as I can figure out, there are only four main methods available to any of us, so I'm going to teach using one of those four methods. Those methods are demonstration, guided practice, explicitly telling and showing an example, and inquiry. To help teachers grasp what it means to teach using those four methods, I often ask them to get into pairs, and I then ask one teacher to teach the other how to put on his shoes, and to do this bit of instruction using a specific teaching method. (I don't discuss what those methods might be just yet. I simply suggest teachers use a specific teaching method, not naming it to their student.) After two minutes, I stop the group and suggest that the student and teacher reverse roles, and now the new teacher plan a way to teach his student how to put on shoes, but this time, I ask the teacher to use a different teaching method. I continue this until people have had four opportunities to teach that one putting-on-your-shoes lesson, and then I ask teachers to list the methods they used.

As mentioned earlier, I have come to believe we have only four options. One person may name one of those options differently than another person does, but if we discount the various names people ascribe to a method, I think it is fair to say that when asked to teach someone how to put on his shoes, the teacher will probably rely first on the method of demonstration. This method involves the teacher starting off by removing her shoe and then proceeding to narrate the step-by-step process of putting that shoe on and tucking in little pointers. That is, at one point the teacher adds the tip, "Sometimes you need to wiggle your foot from right to left a bit to get it into the shoe. Don't step down too hard on the heel of your shoe, or it might fold in on you." Later, the teacher may add another tip.

Then again, a teacher can decide to walk her students through the process. If the teacher ascribes to the method of guided practice, the teacher's shoes can stay securely on her feet, and attention shifts to the learner. "Okay," the teacher says. "Start by pointing your toe." Then the teacher waits for the sock-footed learner to do that action. "That's it. Now stick that pointed toe right into the shoe, all the way to the far end of it." That's guided practice.

Another method that can be used involves giving a little lecture, complete with illustrations, on the topic of inserting a foot into a shoe. The teacher following such a method could even use PowerPoint to illustrate the four stages of foot insertion. That's the method I call "explicitly telling and showing an example."

Finally, a teacher could simply say, "How do you think I got this shoe on my foot? You figure it out." And that's inquiry.

Each of those methods can be used to teach readers in a minilesson.

Let's go back to the minilesson we have been studying and consider the teaching point:

> "And *this* is what I want to teach you, readers. There are words that you know by heart in your books—your snap words. But you don't always recognize them because authors sometimes change them around a bit. When you see a word that looks like a stranger to you—look again. You can ask yourself, does this look like another word that I know? It might be a familiar snap word, wearing not a new hat, but a new ending."

Ninety percent of our reading and writing minilessons rely upon demonstration as the method of choice, so let's devise a minilesson that uses demonstration to teach this. I do not recommend that you simply summarize what you want to tell people, like this:

> "Readers, I notice when snap words like these have endings that make them look different."

That's not teaching by demonstration. That's teaching by leaving one's shoe on and simply looking back to explain (and perhaps showing an example). No, if I want to demonstrate, the first thing I need to do is to take off my shoe, to un-do the reading work I have already done so that I can put my shoe on (that is, read the passage and encounter the character acting out of character) in front of the learners. Now I also do not want to demonstrate the entire process of reading. Rather, I want to demonstrate how I first read along, following the text just fine, and then was stopped in my tracks by a word that looked unfamiliar. Then I realized that, in fact, the word was a familiar one with an ending on it, as you'll see in this part of the minilesson.

Demonstrate finding a known word inside an unknown word and then reading the new word.

"I'll show you what I mean. But first, turn on your snap word machine." I flicked an imaginary switch, "and give it *extra strength*!" I twisted an imaginary dial. I watched as the children did the same.

"Okay, ready? If I get to a word that seems like a stranger has come into the story, watch as I ask myself, 'Does this look like a word that I *do* know?'"

I revealed the first page of the book under the document camera. "This is a true story called 'Hide and Seek,' by Lila, a first-grade writer across the hall. Let me read the first page on my own, okay? I'm going to pretend to be a kindergarten reader and use my extra-strength snap word power." I pointed under the words as I read the title and the first two words. I stopped at *playing*.

> *I was playing*
>
> *hide and seek*
>
> *with Dad.*

"Oh, hmm, . . . Gosh, this is a long word. Wait! Does this look like a word that I know? Don't tell me, I want to strengthen my own snap word power. It does! I see the word *play* at the beginning, and I know just *play* wouldn't sound right there. 'I was play.' No. What would sound right? *Play-ing*! Thumbs up if you thought *playing* too!" Thumbs and smiles popped up all around.

Name the strategy and demonstrate once again.

"Readers, did you see how, when I got to a challenging word, I used my extra-strength snap word power to read a snap word with its ending? You did? Okay, keep watching, because I'll practice that work again." I kept reading and stopped again at *comes*.

> *"Here he comes!"*
>
> *I said.*

I pointed to *comes*. "Hmm, . . . does this look like a word I know?" I waited a moment for children to think to themselves and then answered my own question. "Yes, I recognize *come* at the beginning, and I can move my eyes to the end. *Comes*. Yes! 'Here he comes!' That makes sense in this story! And it sounds right, too." I continued reading to the end of the page.

This is beginning to be an effective bit of teaching. I want to point out that although I wanted to do this work without children calling out the answers, I did try to do everything possible to ensure they were doing the work with me as I did it. Kids will learn more if they see themselves doing what you are trying to do. Brian Cambourne, the great Australian educator, once told me that people fly hang gliders on the field outside his office. On many days, he can look out his office window and see the people strapping themselves into harnesses and running pell-mell toward a cliff, whereupon they throw themselves over the cliff, into the air. Brian pointed out that although he has watched this perhaps several hundred times, those hang gliders aren't functioning as mentors to him because he does not watch them as one would watch a mentor. He has absolutely no intention of ever strapping those machines onto his back and racing toward the cliff, so he does not vicariously experience what those hang gliding people are doing, nor does he learn from their actions. You don't want students to watch you working away at the front of the room in the same detached manner with which Cambourne watches those hang gliders out his window. You want them to be ready to glide.

ACTIVE ENGAGEMENT: Give Students a Chance to Try Out Their New Learning

This is the time to say to students, "Now you try it," and provide them with just a little bit of guided practice. In this minilesson, I used another page of the book and asked students to try another example of solving a snap word with a new ending. We used the word *looked*. This created an active engagement section very similar to the teaching section, but with the kids doing 95% of the work. I set them up to do this work by saying, "You look ready to try this out, readers! All right, here is page 3 of the story. Read it with your partner and find out what happens to the girl in the game! And remember, if you get to a word that you don't know, use your extra-strength snap word power! Ask yourself, 'Does it look like a word that I *do* know? Is it just a snap word with an ending on it?'"

After setting students up to try out the strategy themselves, I listened to partnerships and coached them to recognize the high-frequency words in continuous text and to make meaning of the story.

The important thing to realize is that in this example I provided kids with lots of assistance and that is the intent during this section of the minilesson. I first modeled solving a snap word with a new ending twice. I selected a part to read together that contains snap words with new endings. I channeled children to work in the supportive safe harbor of a partnership. And, of course, after children had done the work, I read the whole word again to the class.

In this example, the activity that children participated in was that of talking with a partner (referred to as "turn and talk"). I could instead have set children up to "stop and jot" or to "list across your fingers" or to be active in other small ways. And this example involved children with a continuation of the text used in the previous section of the minilesson. I could, instead, have asked children to find a snap word with a new ending in their own independent reading book.

There are a few principles to remember when constructing the active engagement sections of a minilesson. First, aim to give children a two- or three-minute interval to practice what you've just taught in your teaching point and in your teaching component of the minilesson. This will only be possible if you take some time to set them up to have success quickly. For example, although theoretically, I could have asked children to use their independent reading books as a place to practice the strategy of solving a snap word with a new ending, that would have taken more time, and their books may not have had snap words with new endings. So in this instance, the only way to provide readers with a really brief chance to experience the content of the minilesson was to do so in a shared text, where I had preselected a passage that would allow students to try the strategy.

There are other ways to scaffold learning, and as you read through this series, you might collect a list of possible ways to do so. You may find that you use the same scaffolds in the active engagement sections of a minilesson and in conferences and small groups. For example, one scaffold you can use in all these instances is that once you've set kids up to do the work, you can sometimes also set a few up to simultaneously do the work aloud, publicly, on chart paper. That way, if anyone is stumped, that person can shift from doing the work to watching another person do it. Then again, while readers are working, you can call out brief prompts to remind them of what you want them to do, or of the next steps. Sometimes your prompts provide the actual words you think they might think or write to get themselves started. For example, you might call out, "I used to think Rob was . . . but now I'm realizing that maybe he's . . . ." If you wanted to do so, you could leave a bit of time and then call out, in a voiceover as children worked, "I think this because A, because B."

It's also helpful to remember that kids are ravenous learners, and you can usually tuck some helpful tips into either your teaching or your active engagement. For example, if you are helping readers solve for tricky words, you might tuck in the tip "Remember to think about what is happening in the story." In addition or alternatively, you could say, "If you are looking for the right word, read the sentence from the beginning and think if it sounds right."

Finally, all your readers should be actively involved during this section of the minilesson. I had all students try to solve for the word together and share with their partners. I could have had two or three members of the class do the work while others looked on, but then not every member of the class would have had a chance to participate.

The active engagement section of a minilesson generally ends just like the teaching section ends, with you summarizing what you hope students have learned in ways that are transferable to another text, another day. If you scan minilessons throughout the series, you will see bold headings that say, "Debrief in ways that are transferable to another day, another text," or some variation on that. If you read half a dozen examples of the text that follows, you'll quickly learn how to do this important work.

When restating what you hope children have learned that applies to another day and another text, you'll often restate the teaching point. I find it helpful to look back at the exact wording of the original teaching point and use those same words again. The goal is to make the minilesson and the teaching point stick, and one way to do this is through making the key words of the teaching point into almost a mantra.

LINK: Reminds Kids that Today's Learning is Transferable

The minilesson ends with you restating what you hope children have learned, doing so in a way that is transferable to another day and another text. "You are going to need that extra strength, because your regular snap word power may not be enough to meet the challenges in your books. Remember, if you get to a word you do not know, you can always ask yourself, 'Do I know a word that looks like this word?' You might recognize a snap word there with an ending."

Often at this point, the teaching point gets added to a class chart—an anchor chart—that compiles what you have been teaching across a number of sessions, so the children are reminded of the repertoire of strategies they have been studying.

Usually before sending children off to do their reading, you'll also recall other things you have been teaching that you hope they are doing today, perhaps gesturing to the same chart. You might say something like "So, readers, you've been learning so many things about what it means not only to read stories, but to read characters. You've learned to do A, you've learned to do B, and today, I hope you have learned to do C. Today as you read, I can't wait to see you do all of these things."

Sometimes you'll also add on instructions: "If you find snap words with new endings you may want to put a Post-it on them, so during partner time you can show your partner the ones you found," or "I put some highlighter tape on the table so you can highlight snap words with new endings if you find them to show your partner."

Chapter 8

Management Systems

T O TEACH within a reading workshop, you need to establish the structures and expectations that ensure all students will work with engagement and tenacity at their own important reading projects. Otherwise, all your attention will be focused on keeping kids working, and therefore, you won't be able to devote yourself to the important work of assessing, coaching, scaffolding, and teaching. Yet teaching young people to work with independence is no small feat!

It is important to give careful thought to the systems and expectations that will help your students sustain rigorous reading work without your micromanaging their every move. That is, as you approach a new school year with your students, be mindful that the minilessons—the words that you say for ten minutes at the start of reading time—will go nowhere without structures in place that shape the work your students do.

The good news is that the reading workshop, like the writing workshop, is deliberately kept simple and predictable, like an art studio or a researcher's laboratory or a scholar's library, because it is the work itself that is ever-changing and complex. Students can approach any day's reading workshop as artists approach a studio, planning to continue with their important, ongoing work. Each day's teaching in a workshop does not set up a new hoop for all the students to jump through in sync on that day. Instead, for the bulk of time during each day, students carry on with their work. As they do so, they draw upon a growing repertoire of skills, tools, strategies, and habits. But the bulk of students' time during the reading workshop is spent reading, in the fullest sense of the word—reading, imagining, thinking, recalling, questioning, talking, writing, reviewing, comparing, researching, and reading some more.

Workshops, by definition, are places in which teachers are engaged in continual assessment. The simplicity and predictability of the workshop frees teachers from constant choreographing, allowing them time to observe, listen, and teach into each student's zone of proximal development. Like an artist in a pottery studio or a physicist in a physics lab, the teacher circulates. She pulls close to observe, mulls over what is and is not working, and intervenes to coach, demonstrate, encourage, and celebrate. In short, the teacher teaches.

But this sort of teaching is only possible if your workshop hums along without your micromanaging everything. Thankfully, thousands of teachers have worked for years to devise management structures and systems that make it possible for children to carry on as readers and as writers working productively with independence and rigor. When you institute simple and predictable structures and systems, you will be freed from constant choreography so you are able to teach.

THE IMPORTANCE OF STRUCTURES AND SYSTEMS

Why do so many people assume that classroom management is a concern for novice and struggling teachers but not for master teachers? Is there really a good teacher anywhere who doesn't think hard about methods for maximizing students' productivity, for inspiring the highest possible work ethic, and for holding every learner accountable for doing her best? I get frustrated when I hear some people say with disdain, "She has trouble with classroom management."

Who doesn't have trouble with classroom management? How could it *not* be tricky to build an environment in which twenty or thirty youngsters each pursue their own important projects as readers, working within the confines of a small room, each needing his own mix of silence and discussion, time and deadlines, resources and collaboration?

Corporate management is considered an executive skill, and high-level executives are often coached in methods for maximizing productivity. Directors, managers, and executives attend seminars on developing accountability systems, on providing feedback, and on organizing time, space, and personnel to maximize productivity. If the people working under your direction were grown-ups instead of children, the job of managing

the workers would be regarded as highly demanding leadership work. But all too often in schools, classroom management is treated as a task akin to doing the laundry. That's wrong.

As a classroom teacher, you absolutely need to give careful attention to methods of managing young people so they sustain high levels of purposeful work. You and your colleagues would be wise to assume from the start that classroom management will be a challenge and to give careful thought to instituting systems that channel your students to do their best work.

LEARNING CLASSROOM MANAGEMENT SYSTEMS AND STRATEGIES

I recently visited the classroom of a first-year teacher. This teacher was teaching a writing workshop, but he could just as well have been leading a reading workshop; his methods were largely transferable. "Students," Manuel said, "in a moment, I'd like you to bring your writing folder and your pen to the meeting area. Put everything else away and show me you are ready." As he counted ("Five, four, three, two, one."), children hurried to clear off their workspaces of everything but the materials they would need during the upcoming hour. "Table 2," Manuel signaled, "let's gather." Soon Manuel had signaled four other tables as well, and each time he gestured, his students stood, pushed in their chairs, walked swiftly and directly to the meeting area, and sat cross-legged, shoulder to shoulder with their writing partners. Manuel had soon taken his place in a chair at the front of the meeting area.

"Can I have your focus?" he said, touching his eyes to signal that he wanted children's eyes on him. Almost every child turned in his direction. Manuel then began a ten-minute minilesson in which he named a strategy, demonstrated that strategy, gave the children a few minutes of guided practice with the strategy, and invited his students to add that strategy to their repertoire. Soon the children had dispersed to their work spots, each hard at work on her ongoing work. None of them required Manuel to come to their side and provide a personalized jump start.

As I watched all this, I marveled that Manuel, a novice teacher, was teaching in such efficient and effective ways. I remembered with a pang my first years as a teacher. "How did he get to be so good?" I wondered, but then I knew. Manuel is the teacher he is because, although he is new to the profession, his methods are not new. His methods have gone through hundreds of drafts and have benefited from the legacy of experienced teachers. This is how it should be!

The best way I know to learn classroom management strategies is to visit well-established reading and writing workshops to study the infrastructure that underlies this kind of teaching. Both reading and writing workshops are structured in such predictable, consistent ways that the infrastructure of most workshops remains almost the same throughout the year and throughout a student's elementary school experience. This means that when you visit one hour of a workshop, you peek in on not only today's, but also tomorrow's teaching. In this chapter, you and I will visit a few primary-school reading workshops when they're in full swing, and we'll pay special attention to the nitty-gritty of classroom management. I'll be at your side on this tour, commenting on what we see together. We'll pay special attention to the management of each component of the reading workshop:

- Managing the minilesson: the beginning of each day's reading instruction

- Managing reading time: the heart and soul of the reading workshop

- Managing conferring and small-group instruction

- Managing mid-workshop, partner time, and share session: workshop closure

- Managing books, libraries, and other materials

MANAGING THE MINILESSON: THE BEGINNING OF EACH DAY'S READING INSTRUCTION
Convening the Class for the Minilesson

Before gathering at the carpet for the minilesson, most teachers have the class set up for reading workshop. Teachers often refer to this as their setup routine, and it involves readers gathering their reading materials and getting their reading space prepared for private reading. I think of this routine as an opportunity to set everyone up for success.

Children get out the books they plan to read and then stack those books in the order they plan to read them. If they are reading longer chapter books, they might take out their reading logs and Post-its. Each pair of partners turns their chairs back to back to set up for reading time. Readers also take out any personal charts or goal cards from their book baggies or bins. Setting up for the reading workshop in this way saves precious minutes of reading time. When the minilesson is over, children head straight to their reading spots, and everything is ready for them to begin reading immediately. When the transition from minilesson to reading time is seamless—when children don't get derailed locating books, moving chairs, or searching for pencils—it is far more likely that they will remember the minilesson once they settle down to read.

Many teachers find it helpful to circulate around the room five minutes before the workshop begins, saying, "Five more minutes until we gather on the carpet," or something similar. This gives students time to finish up whatever they are doing and to make sure that their reading work is set up and ready. The workshop itself begins when you use an attention-getting signal to secure students' attention and then ask them to convene. It is remarkably

Students gather their reading bins before the minilesson.

important for you to develop such a signal and to teach children that it is a meaningful one. The signal can be obvious. Most teachers simply stand in the midst of the hubbub and say, in a voice one notch louder than usual, "Readers." Once students have given you their full attention—and don't hesitate to wait until they literally stop what they were doing and look at you—then you'll convene them. Experienced workshop teachers know that attention to procedures early in the year pays off, so they are apt to start the year by demonstrating—acting out—their hopes for how students will gather

for minilessons. To do this, show children that you expect them to push in their chairs, to make a beeline for their spot on the meeting area rug, to sit (rather than hover), to handle materials however you expect them to be handled, and to begin rereading the anchor charts containing teaching points from previous days.

Some people use a countdown as a scaffold to move students expeditiously along. "Let's take the count of four to gather for a minilesson. Four: I love that you are getting your books out of your book bins." If there are some materials that you want brought to the meeting area, you might hold those materials up, creating a Technicolor illustration. Then your countdown can continue. "Three: I love that you are setting up your chairs back to back, grabbing the materials you need for the minilesson, and coming quickly. Two: I love that you are sitting on your bottoms, in your spots. One: Nice to see you opening your books ready to reread, if need be, and to see you rereading our anchor charts."

Of course, before long, this behavior becomes automatic, and you need only say, "Blue and green tables, please come to the carpet." Then, while you gesture to the next two tables, the first group of children push in their chairs, come quickly and quietly, sit in their assigned spots, open their notebooks to the first available page, and begin rereading charts from previous minilessons. This is very efficient!

You may question this detailed attention to transitions, and some teachers may prefer a more organic, easygoing approach. But for many teachers, transitions can be a source of delay and tension, and neither is advisable. A fiction writer once said, "The hardest part of writing fiction is getting characters from here to there," and this can be true for teaching as well.

If you want students' attention but don't need them to gather—which will be the case for your mid-workshop teaching points and for most of your share sessions—you can use the attention-getting device again. Most teachers simply stand in a certain part of the room and say, "Readers," with a commanding voice. After saying that (or whatever you choose as your signal), give the classroom a 360° survey, waiting for absolute silence and for all eyes to be on you before proceeding.

The important thing is that you use the signal you settle on consistently and teach children to honor it. This requires that after you say, "Readers," you wait as long as necessary until every child has put his pencil down, stopped talking, and looked at you. You may need to wait as long as three minutes before further addressing the group, although if this is a schoolwide procedure and if other teachers maintain high standards around this, then it will be easy to institute.

Some teachers are uncomfortable insisting on utter silence, and therefore they speak over still-murmuring children. I'm convinced that you do your students no favors when you collude with their tendencies to ignore your words. If your goal is to teach children that words matter, then your words, for a start, must mean something. When you ask for attention, you should expect that children will comprehend and honor your request. The same children who are Teflon listeners, regularly letting instructions roll off without getting through, tend also to be Teflon readers, regularly moving their eyes but not their minds over the words on a page, then looking up to say, "I read it, honest; I just don't remember what I read." If you regularly repeat yourself several times to be sure children take in what you've said, you are enabling your students to live as if they have comprehension problems. The first step to remedying this is to develop a way to signal for children's attention, and the second step is to resist repeating yourself.

It helps, then, for you to keep in mind that there will be times when you speak to your whole class and you do not need everyone's full attention. Your students could be deeply immersed in their reading, and you don't actually want to stop them. You just want to float a reminder across the landscape of the classroom, rather like those blimps that fly over crowded beaches with advertisements trailing behind them. Use an entirely different voice, then, if you simply want to say something like "We'll get together with our partners in five minutes. By then, make sure you have marked a few spots with notes about your character so that you can be ready to read and share together."

I find it striking that in classrooms in which the transitions are long and mired in tension, teachers often assume this is par for the course. They shrug and say, "What are you going to do?" as if they assume this is how workshops proceed in most classrooms. I've come to realize that many aspects of classroom management are shaped more by our expectations than by anything else. When teachers make a point of teaching classroom management, thirty children can come and go quite seamlessly between the meeting area and their workspaces.

Establishing Long-Term Partnerships and Reading Clubs

When children gather on the carpet, they usually sit in assigned spots beside an assigned partner. Usually teachers assign students to sit beside their reading partner during the minilesson and workshop time. Most reading partnerships pair students who are at similar reading levels. That is to say, a child is not paired with someone who is a stronger reader, but rather with another child who has similar goals and is working with similar books. This means that partners tend to have equal footing and can both give and receive help. In some cases, you may decide to expand a partnership into a triad, bringing three readers together. Whatever the configurations, be sure that all readers engage with one another and work together in a collaborative way. As readers grow and change, and as you get to know your students better, you may decide to switch partnerships. But generally, partners are long term. Children thrive when they have consistency, and working with a long-term partnership provides this.

Of course, you won't be able to establish long-term partnerships until you have used running records to assess all your students. Before having a chance to do this, many teachers channel children to work with informal reading buddies, so that children won't have to go without reading partners for the first week or two of the school year. Partnerships support engagement and stamina, and both are especially important at the start of the year.

During the workshop time, children usually sit back to back for private reading and side by side for partner reading. When children set up for reading workshop, they set up their reading spots so they will be back to back and ready for private reading. When you see this in classrooms, you will see chairs, bean bags, pillows, and cushions set up back to back. This routine makes it easy for children to transition from private to partner reading.

Partners often talk during the active engagement section of a minilesson, during the mid-workshop, and during the share session. These include brief interludes for talking, and often the teacher will give directions, such as asking for either Partner 1 or 2 to do the talking at that particular time. "Partner 1, will you teach Partner 2 what you learned from your nonfiction reading today? Remember as you do this to organize your teaching into categories and

to elaborate on a point before moving on to the next point. Reference illustrations, charts, and diagrams from your book as you teach. Go!"

In kindergarten and first grade, halfway through the workshop, teachers call, "Partner time!" and partners sit side by side and read through their stacks of books together. In schools that have adopted a workshop approach, a first-grade teacher generally will not need to reteach children how to work in partnerships; that should be in place from kindergarten. But it is helpful for a teacher to watch, early on in the year, to see what habits need to be retaught. Do partners sit side by side with one book in the middle? Do partners make plans for how they will read and talk with each other? Do they take turns and listen to each other? Use the information you gather when observing partnerships to plan for the routines you want to set up.

Partners who are reading shorter texts (approximately below level J) will spend time reading books aloud to one another and talking to one another. They will stack their books together on their mats and try and read through bunches of books again and again. Partners who are reading longer texts (approximately above level J) will also spend time reading and talking together, but rather than reading their entire book, these partnerships will reread important parts of their books before engaging in a conversation. To support talk and conversations around books, these partnerships benefit from having some books in their baggies that are the same. You will often hear these referred to as same-book partnerships.

Some teachers organize students so they work in mixed-ability partnerships during the interactive read-aloud and matched partnerships during the reading workshop. That's a terrific idea if the logistics aren't too complicated, because research is clear that students benefit from heterogeneous pairings, when possible.

Some units support not just partnerships, but clubs. Usually a club consists of two ability-based partnerships, and usually the four readers are roughly similar in their reading abilities. This is important, because usually a club reads the same books about a familiar character or topic, meeting perhaps a few times in a week to talk about the series or topic across the texts. Often units begin with partnerships and end with clubs, and when this is the case, teachers need to know how the clubs will go because sometimes the clubs rely on prior work with partners. For example, you may want one set of partners to have read one book about a flying bug during the first bend of a unit and another set of partners to have read about a second flying bug, so that when the four readers come together, their club can begin with the members

collecting information that seems to be true of many flying insects. Similarly, at the start of a unit on series books, for example, it's important that children who will eventually come together as a series-based club each read one of the books in the series. So that means there would be four Pinky and Rex readers coming together into The Pinky and Rex Club, and they would each have done a bit of prior reading related to that club.

Club conversations can take place during the share time at the end of a workshop; they usually last a bit longer than the typical time for partner sharing. You can gather readers for this time by saying something like "Club time! Let's start our clubs by gathering in the meeting area. As always, bring your books, Post-its, and pens! It's time to share in your clubs. You'll share with your clubs in the same ways that you share with your partner."

Management during the Minilesson

The biggest challenge you'll encounter when teaching a minilesson is achieving that magical balance wherein children are wide-awake, active participants—and yet their involvement does not turn a tight, economical bit of explicit instruction into a free-for-all, with chitchat and commentary, questions, and free associations overwhelming lines of thought. Over the years, my colleagues and I have recommended different ways to walk this delicate balance, and

frankly, you'll need to do some self-assessment to decide on a plan that works for you and your students.

For years, we suggested that the best way to keep minilessons streamlined was to essentially convey to kids, "For ten minutes at the start of most reading workshops, I'll pull you together here on the carpet, and I'll teach you a strategy that you can use to make your reading better. For most of the minilesson, this is my time to talk and your time to listen. I'll tell you what I want to teach and show you how to do it. Then you'll have time to talk to a partner as you try what I've taught."

in your demonstration, it's helpful to get them started trying to do the same thing that you will soon demonstrate. Start the demonstration with some guided practice. "How would you do this?" you might ask, getting children started doing the work in their minds. Then, just when they are beginning to do something, you can say, "Watch me for a sec," and pull ahead of their actions to show them how you would do that particular thing.

For your performance to function as a demonstration, the learner needs to be about to do the same thing, so he is primed to notice how you do things differently. This requires a keen level

I still believe that many teachers would be wise to convey that message and to teach minilessons in which children are essentially seen and not heard until midway into the minilesson. I say this not because I think it is the perfect solution, but because I think the perfect solution is hard for mortal men (and women) to achieve. It is a real trick to allow for more active involvement while still modulating—limiting—that involvement.

But in this series, we go for the gold. We send a more nuanced message to youngsters. We say, "I'll often channel you to talk, and then, before you finish talking, I'll ask you to hold that thought and to listen up while I make a quick point. This means you'll need to watch my signals. There will be times to talk to the group, times to talk with a partner, times to talk to yourself silently, and times to be quiet. All of this is by design, and it's intended to help all of you learn."

Thus, the minilessons in this series offer many more ways for students to be actively involved in the frontal teaching than there were before. In the chapter on minilessons, I described ways some teachers involve kids in the connection of the minilesson, and also ways you can recruit kids to actively participate in your demonstrations. The challenge is to demonstrate something that youngsters are also imagining themselves doing, or doing in their own minds, so that, as they watch you, they notice how you do things differently— better—in ways that inform their practices. To recruit students to be engaged

of engagement by the learner, which you can get if you recruit kids to be on the edge of doing something, and then, instead, you take the lead, pointing out what you hope they'll notice in your demonstration. You'll need to be accustomed to signaling to students, saying, "Watch and see if the way I do this matches what you were doing as well."

There are some management issues to work out with your whole class. For example, children need to know what to do if a partner is absent (join a nearby partnership, without asking you to problem solve). When you want them to talk to their partners in a minilesson, show them how to make a fast transition from facing forward and listening to facing their partner and talking. They can't spend five minutes getting themselves off the starting block for a turn-and-talk (or a stop-and-jot), because the entire interval of that interlude usually lasts no more than three minutes!

All of these things are worth explicitly teaching. I've watched teachers practice the transition from listening to talking to a partner by saying, "What did you eat for breakfast this morning? Turn and talk," and then, after a minute, saying, "Back to me." If you take just a minute or two to coach the behaviors you want and then remember to hold to those expectations later, you'll find this all pays off in giant ways.

All in all, make sure that your minilesson pacing is quick and upbeat. This has an impact on how engaged your students stay. Use concise and precise language, move between parts seamlessly (and do not belabor any one point), and check in quickly to make sure that your students are with you (e.g., thumbs up, turn and talk, raise a finger or two). Pacing, along with engagement, will contribute to better management as well.

MANAGING READING TIME: THE HEART AND SOUL OF THE READING WORKSHOP

While the minilesson sets the tone for the workshop and provides students with another teaching point to add to their repertoire, the main work of the day happens during reading time, when students are bent intently over their work, pages turning, or are alternating between reading, jotting, rereading. It is during reading time that you are free to support, scaffold, and foster students' growth as readers in whatever ways seem most important for each individual. In this section, I'll provide an overview of the structures to consider so that your students are not distracted during reading time, including how to effectively send them off to work, the nature of their work, and how to teach and organize for a collaborative work environment.

Sending Students Off to Work: The Transition from Minilesson to Work Time

Just as you explicitly teach children how to gather for a minilesson, you'll also teach them how to disperse after the minilesson and get started on their work. Students need to learn how to go from the minilesson to their workspaces and then to get right into the work they had set up before the minilesson—to open up their books, to decide what they are going to do, and to get started doing it. If you don't teach them otherwise, some children will sit idly by until you make your way to that table and give them each a personalized jump start. It's worthwhile to directly teach children how to get themselves started reading. Sometimes you'll disperse one cluster of students at a time. While one cluster goes off to work, you may say to those still sitting on the carpet, "Let's watch and see if they zoom to their reading spots and get started right away!" Sometimes you might speak in a stage whisper, "Oh, look, Toni has her reading log out and is filling in the time and her page number. That's so smart! I wonder if the others will do that? Oh, look. Jose is getting his log out too!" This reminds both the dispersing and the observing youngsters what you hope they will do.

Your students are apt to just read, and the hope is that they are deliberately working on goals as they read. The way you send readers off to work can make it more likely that they are deliberately trying new strategies, working toward goals they take on as important. Sometimes you'll find it helpful to ask children first to tell each other the new reading work they plan to be doing that day. You might even ask them to envision how they will go about doing that work. "Picture yourself leaving the meeting area. Where will you go, exactly? What will you do first? Thumbs up if you can picture yourself leaving and getting started," you might say, signaling to the children who seem ready that they can go back to their seats and get started.

Sometimes you may disperse children by saying, "If you are going to be doing (one kind of work), get going. If you are going to be doing (another kind of work), get going. If you are not certain what goals you can work toward today and what strategies you can try using and need some help, stay here and I'll work with you." Soon you'll be leading a small group of children who've identified themselves as needing more direction.

Other times you'll say, "Get started doing that right here in the meeting area," and then you'll watch to see when a student is engaged in the work, tapping that student on the shoulder and gesturing to say, "Go to your work

Partners turn and talk during a minilesson.

spot and keep reading." Again, this allows you to end up with a group on the carpet who need some help.

Transitions are smoother if children always know where they'll sit during reading time. You might give your students assigned spots. However, try to avoid making it a habit not only to tell children where to sit, but also to tell them what to do. This may surprise you. You may think, doesn't the teacher tell students what to do during the minilesson? Isn't that really the role of the minilesson?

Those are very important questions, and it is true that in traditional instruction, the teacher would use the whole-class instruction at the start of the lesson as the time to show everyone what he is expected to do that day. In traditional instruction, during the whole-class instruction at the start of work time, the teacher would assign the day's work, perhaps demonstrate it, and then youngsters could practice that work in the minilesson, with support, before being sent off to do that same thing with more independence during work time. But during a workshop, your whole-class instruction aims to add to students' repertoire, teaching them how to use strategies that they will then draw on over and over as they read. So you'll generally end your minilesson by saying something like "So when you are ready to work on . . . , remember this tip . . ." or "So remember that today, one of your options is to do (whatever you've just taught). But you can also draw on all you've learned to do prior to now." That is, fairly often students will leave the minilesson and still need to reflect on their progress, consider their goals, reread their books, and choose a way of proceeding. The minilesson offers a strategy to practice and use when needed rather than a global, time-constrained assignment.

The Nature of Children's Work during the Reading Workshop

The rule during a reading workshop is that during reading time, everyone reads for the entire time, so there is no such thing as being "done." If a reader completes one text, then she begins the next text. You should expect that as your young readers progress through their sequence of work, some of them will come to places in their reading where they feel stymied. "I'm stuck," they will say.

When a youngster feels stuck, his first instinct is usually to find the teacher and ask, "What should I do next?" Approach those interactions by being clear that your job can't be to dole out all the little things that every reader is to do.

A big part of being a skilled reader is noticing the work that a text demands of you, reviewing possible strategies for doing that work, monitoring and assessing how that effort works, and so on. Don't remove that responsibility from your students' shoulders by allowing them to make you decider-in-chief. Almost always, you should respond to requests for assistance by helping students problem solve—either turning them back to their own resources or by teaching them to assess and to identify goals, and then teaching them several possible strategies they might draw on to reach those goals.

If youngsters seem overly reliant on you for direction, you'll probably want to teach them how to help each other. "Readers, can I stop all of you? Would you look at all the people following me! I feel like a pied piper. Today I want to teach you that there is not just one reading teacher in this classroom. Each one of you can be a reading teacher. And you need to become reading teachers for each other, because this is how we learn to become reading teachers for ourselves. In the end, every reader needs to be his or her own reading teacher. So, right now, let me teach you what reading teachers do for each other. Then those of you in this line behind me can help each other."

In the early childhood classroom, it is important to remember that students will often forget the things they have been taught. A cycle of learning, forgetting, and learning again seems to be part and parcel of how things go

Kids in reading spots

in early childhood classrooms! Young children are also still just developing their executive function. If you find yourself needing to remind children of things you have already taught, try not to take it personally and not to be frustrated by this. Primary classrooms will need multiple voiceover reminders. Learn to give directions in lean, quick, clear ways. Voiceovers are a wonderful tool to use to keep youngsters heading in fruitful directions.

For example, you'll find that as children make the transition into partnership time, it helps to smooth the transition by saying something such as "Partners, will you start by reading Partner 2's stack of books today?" You might give added tips, perhaps by saying, "Don't forget to choose *how* to read your book before you start."

A quick table conference to engage readers

MANAGING CONFERRING AND SMALL-GROUP WORK: MAKING ONE-TO-ONE CONFERENCES AND SMALL-GROUP INSTRUCTION POSSIBLE

When conferring, you'll probably find it works best to move among children, talking with them at their workplaces, dotting the room with your presence. Although you won't come close to reaching every child every day, you can hold individual conferences with three children a day (four or five minutes per conference) and also lead several small groups, allowing you to be a presence in every section of the room. Your presence matters more because, when talking with one child, you can encourage nearby children to listen in. For most of a conference, you might deliberately ignore those listeners, looking intently into the face of the one child, which often spurs listeners to eavesdrop all the more intently. As your conference ends, you can extend it to the others who've listened in. "Do any of the rest of you want to try that, too?" you might ask. "Great! Do it! I can't wait to see."

If it seems that children are not able to sustain work long enough for you to do much conferring, you can first congratulate yourself for identifying and naming this as a problem. You are far closer to a solution once you have looked this in the eye and said, "This is important."

The next step is to think about ways you can scaffold children's independent work. Your conferences themselves can be angled so that you are teaching children how to carry on with independence another time. For example, you can be sure that some conferences will begin with a reader coming to you and saying, "I'm stuck." In those instances, your first job will be to learn what the reader has already done and to turn the reader back to her own resources. Then you can help the reader extend her work in ways that make her more self-reliant in the future. I might say, "When I'm not sure of a good book to read next, what I do is I think about people I know who like the same books as I do, and I go to them and ask them what they've enjoyed reading lately. You could try that instead of coming to me for help."

Table conferences—conferences with a whole table full of readers—provide another helpful management structure to engage more readers in their work and allow you to work with more students. Often I see a group of kids reading alongside each other, and for a minute, I observe what they are doing. I look for trends and patterns of behaviors. Maybe I see many students starting their books without setting themselves up, or readers who are skipping hard words or not slowing down to study the pictures on the page. Whatever the observable behavior might be, I may just stop all the students at once and say, "One of the things I notice you're doing as readers is . . ." Then I give the group a quick teaching point. Then as the students continue reading, I circulate among them, coaching one after another on that teaching point.

Sometimes, as I finish an individual conference, I may decide to share that conference with the group of students sitting at that table. I simply extend my teaching point to everyone and rally the group all to try that strategy at that moment in their books. I then circulate and coach each student briefly.

Extending conferences into quick, on the run, small groups is another way not only to provide more support to your readers, but also to keep more students engaged in their reading work. You may decide that after spending five minutes conferring with a student, you can invite a few other students into the conversation. Look at your conference notes and decide who might benefit from similar support, and then call the others over and tell them about your conference, asking if they'd be willing to try the same work. As they get started, you can coach into their work for a few minutes. This way, you're using time efficiently to reach more students with common needs.

One of the decisions you'll need to make about conferring is with whom you'll meet. Teachers develop their own idiosyncratic systems here. Some teachers enter a reading workshop with a little list in hand of readers they plan to see. The list may come from studying assessments or conferring/small-group records and noticing which children haven't been worked with for a while or which previous conferences and small-group work need follow-up. Alternatively, the list may come from thinking about children's assessment data and deciding which children especially need help.

Personally, although I do enter a workshop with a list of the children with whom I hope to confer, I find it important to be able to improvise based on the signals children give me. So, if youngsters at one table seem unsettled, I'm apt to confer with a child at that table, knowing that my presence can channel the entire group to work rather than socialize. Then, too, if one child is especially persistent about needing help, I generally assume he needs to be a priority, unless he is always at my elbow, in which case I'll respond differently.

I tell children that if they need my help, they should get out of their seats and follow me as I confer. I find this keeps the child who feels stymied from derailing her companions as well. In addition, children can learn from eavesdropping on conferences. The line that forms behind me also provides me with a very tangible reminder of how many children feel confused or stuck at any moment, and this keeps me on my toes. If I have six children in tow, I'm not likely to overlook them for long.

You'll want to record your conferences and small-group work and to develop a system for doing so that fits intimately into the rhythms of your own teaching. This record of your teaching must help you teach better and help your students learn better. This record keeping needs to be attuned to your teaching, reflecting, and planning. You may go through a sequence of systems before settling, temporarily, on one. Trying five or six systems is common among teachers with whom I work.

Some teachers keep a page on a clipboard that looks like a month-at-a-glance calendar but is, instead, the class-at-a-glance. For the period of time this page represents (which might be two weeks), the teacher records the compliment (c) and teaching point (tp) of any conference she holds. Sometimes the grid has light lines dividing each child's square into several parallel slots, with alternate slots labeled "c" and "tp." Alternatively, some teachers create a record-keeping sheet that culls some key goals from the list of behaviors and skills that students need to move up to a new level of text complexity. This can be quite useful, because it keeps readers' goals in your mind as you work with them and helps to give you a focus as you teach.

Some teachers have notebooks divided into sections, one for each child, and record their conferences and small-group instruction with each child that way. Others do a variation of this, recording the conferences and small-group sessions on large sticky notes and later moving the notes to the appropriate sections of their notebook. Some teachers create an enlarged version, posting their conference notes on a wall-sized grid, which reminds every child what he has agreed to do and serves as a visible record of which children have received this form of intense instruction.

MANAGING THE SHARE SESSION: WORKSHOP CLOSURE

There might be a handful of ways that share time generally goes in your classroom, and children should be inducted into those traditions right from the start. When it is almost time for the class to stop work for the share session, a child might circle the room, letting the other children know it is time to finish up. Alternatively, you could intervene to announce, "Three more minutes." In any case, readers will need a bit of time to finish what they are doing. Then you can decide whether, for this share, you want to bring children to the meeting area or work with them while they are in their reading spots.

Either way, you'll probably begin the share by talking with children for a minute or two. You may plan to share one child's work, either by giving an example of how that child put a strategy into practice in a specific book or by asking the child to share her work. Afterward, there is usually time for children to talk with their partners or their clubs.

Don't underestimate the power of the share. Research indicates that it matters what you read or think about right before you go to sleep, for it is the final thing your brain remembers and processes. That research has always made sense to me, for I know, from decades of studying professional development, that the ending of keynotes and workshops matter as much as the beginning. No matter how busy and rewarding a workshop has been, if it ends with a rushed sense of "Oh, my gosh, it's time to go," that ending diminishes the force of the prior hour. Tom Corcoran, a leader with CPRE (Consortium for Policy and Research in Education at Teachers College), studies science classrooms around the globe, and he has often spoken to me about how important the last few moments of a science class are. He laments that instead of engaging in reflection, classes are often engaged in cleaning and packing up.

Your share should give students an opportunity to reflect on what they've learned and/or take that learning a step farther. You'll see in these units of study that in a share, for instance, a partnership might demonstrate how to read and talk together, while the rest of the class studies and tries to name what they can do better in their own partnerships. Or all the students might reflect on their reading work, using an anchor chart to think about what work they might do next. The share is the true ending of reading workshop, and it's important to be prepared for those final few minutes so they give coherence and increased power to the work.

MANAGING THE CLASSROOM LIBRARY

In your reading workshops, one of the most important pathways to helping young readers grow into lifelong readers is to ensure that your students read books they can read with accuracy, fluency, and comprehension and that they have books that challenge them yet are within reach. The setup of your classroom library can support your students when they are selecting books to maximize engagement, independence, and reading volume.

Make It Easy to Find Just-Right Books

Children who self-select the books they want to read will read with more engagement, and you'll be free to support and instruct into that reading. It is important that students have access to a well-stocked classroom library and

are able to navigate the organizational system to easily locate books that are just right (or within reach) and interesting for them. Students need direct physical access to the library, and the organizational system can expand students' interests and support their decision making. Many teachers find it helps if part of their classroom library includes leveled books grouped together and another part is organized to support the curriculum and children's interests. For example, you might decide to organize some books by topics, popular series, familiar authors, student-recommended books, teacher-recommended books, or class favorites.

If you level a portion of your library, those levels need to represent the range of reading levels in your classroom. It is also helpful if the bins and books are clearly labeled in a systematic way that is easy for children to understand. Your library will change across the year to support various units of study. Reorganizing books periodically can breathe new energy into your classroom library and expose students to books they might not otherwise have discovered. Be sure to orient students to each new organizational system so they know how to navigate it to find books that are most suited for them.

If you have many readers at a particular level, it's important to have multiple bins for that level. Because there is a range of difficulty within most any text level, you might consider organizing your books in different baskets with the progression of difficulty in mind, to help children find just-right books more efficiently. For example, you might comb through your baskets containing level C books and reorganize them so that one basket holds books that are more highly patterned and usually easier, and another has books with a story structure, which are often more difficult. You could then find a visual way to direct children to the basket that best matches them as readers.

Generally, a child's book baggie holds about a week's worth of books, with book levels playing a role in the number of books per baggie. For example, level A–E books typically only take a few minutes to read, so children reading these levels will need many books in their book baggies to keep them engaged during reading time. Supplying each child with ten to fourteen books at these levels is usually sufficient and will still mean that the children reread that stack of books many times across the week. Some schools have an abundance of books, so this is manageable. If you don't have enough books at these levels, however, you might consider the following recommendations:

- Look at the books you've kept in your cupboard or book room, and consider getting those books out to children. If you have four to six copies of fifteen books within a rough band of text complexity, couldn't you consider dispersing some of those books?

- Instead of using a system of individual book baggies, you may need to devise an alternative way to get books to kids. You might put the books at a certain level in a basket that sits at the center of a table, and have four readers read from that one basket. During private and partner reading time, the readers reading those books would sit side by side, reading one book at a time and then putting it back in the basket.

As you organize your books, picture your favorite bookstore and think about what makes it inviting. Try not to clutter the library with items that don't belong. Make sure books are right side up and book covers or spines are facing out. Match bin sizes to the size and number of books they will contain.

Your classroom library holds a lot of power. It sends a strong message to the readers in your classroom, and it should convey that reading is important and that books are to be celebrated, treasured, and enjoyed.

Create a System for Book Shopping

Often, children will "shop" for books in the classroom library each week to replenish their personal supply of books for the reading workshop. You might create and introduce a book shopping schedule with a bit of fanfare, providing yet another sign that children can make their own decisions as readers. Both the contents of students' book baggies and how they shop for books will depend on their reading levels. For example, a child who can read level I books independently (with accuracy, fluency, and comprehension) in a character unit might shop for six to eight character books. This reader would also have in her baggie any books that were introduced during small-group instruction, so she might have one or two level J books if they were part of a guided reading group. At the beginning of the year in kindergarten, children will likely read books from table bins until you are ready to introduce them to book shopping independently from the classroom library.

Gather Enough Just-Right Books

Many companies publish leveled texts to support classroom libraries, but it's good to be selective to fill your library with high-quality books that are engaging for the readers in your classroom. When purchasing books, consider the reading levels that are typical for your grade level and when lots of kids might be reading at certain levels simultaneously, as well as the units of study you plan to teach throughout the year. It is common for classroom libraries to include a balance of fiction and nonfiction texts and popular series and character books (especially for levels H/I and above). The online resources provided with this series include book lists and additional information about classroom libraries.

Chapter 9

Small-Group Work
Developing a Richer Repertoire of Methods

W HEN I WAS A YOUNG PROFESSIONAL, fresh on the scene, I was invited to be one of ten young women featured in a "Young Women to Watch" article in *Ladies' Home Journal*. I was asked to appear at a certain address downtown to have my photo taken. I spruced myself up—clean hair, new pink suit—and arrived at the appointed address, a New York City loft, my first time ever in one.

"Come, come, sit here," the people told me, and I sat in a chair, expecting to say "Cheeeese" and to be on my way. To my surprise, the chair on which I sat was suddenly cranked backward, and I found myself leaning so that my head was positioned over a sink, with a team of people surrounding me, one sending a stream of water over my already clean hair, another massaging shampoo into it. Once that process was completed, a man arrived with a suitcase. I wondered if it held a new outfit to replace my new pink suit, but no, the entire suitcase was filled with makeup. A full hour later, I was standing against a wall of cascading, shiny white fabric, one foot slightly in front of the next, face cocked upward and turned to the side, chin up an inch—no, less. That's it. As I held that position, I felt someone's hands fumbling at my back, around the waistline of my skirt, and realized he was releasing the top button of my skirt so that it would ride a bit lower on my hips, then adding clothes pins to alter the drape of the skirt just so. "Head up again, eyes here," the photographer called. And then he said, "Just relax, be yourself."

There was, of course, no way under the sun I was going to just relax after having been subjected to these intensive efforts to remake me. Here's the point of my story: I think that many teachers have been subjected to equally intensive efforts to remake our small-group instruction so that it is just so. There have been so many books written on how to lead small groups in the precisely right ways that too many teachers approach a little hub of readers, gripped by anxiety over doing this The Right Way. Meanwhile, the whole point is to be personal, to be responsive, and to channel kids to do some work while you observe and coach.

TO BE RESPONSIVE, THERE CAN'T BE JUST ONE WAY TO LEAD SMALL GROUPS

When I talk with teachers about leading reading workshops, there are always two topics around which anxiety runs especially high: time and small-group work. Often I sense that teachers have been schooled to lead one specific kind of small-group work (usually their district's version of guided reading), and they want to be sure that they can fit that small group work into their reading workshop. Of course, my response to this question is that by all means they can do that. But I also encourage teachers to know that over time and with practice, they'll probably develop a more expansive repertoire of ways of working with small groups.

Some native Alaskans, lore has it, have twenty-six words for snow. They're such experts on snow that they don't think of all that white stuff as just one monolithic thing. And I'm convinced that with increasing expertise, teachers, too, come to realize that all our small-group work need not fit into one template or bear a single label.

To start, I suggest you think about all the various ways in which you teach reading to your whole class, and consider whether each of those couldn't be done through small groups. Presumably, you spend a chunk of whole-class time reading aloud and engaging kids in accountable talk. That instruction will have special payoffs for students who could use intensive personalized doses of this sort of instruction. You'll also, no doubt, devote time to word study—which may center on phonemic awareness and graphophonics or, depending on the ability levels of your readers, on vocabulary work. Again, clearly, some students would profit from intensive intervention in those areas—and a little of this might give the whole-class work more sticking power for them. Shared reading is a potent way to support your whole class—so why not also use it with a small group? My point is not to pressure you to do it all, because there will never be enough time for everything, but instead, to loosen your grip on just one way of leading small groups and to imagine a wider repertoire of possibilities. If these ways of working with texts are powerful enough to use with a whole class, imagine how powerful they will be in the context of small groups.

Of course, there are many other ways that small groups could go—ways that are uniquely suited to that formation. I describe a few of these alternatives in the chart shown here. Each of these formats for small-group work could be adjusted to support development of a wide array of skills.

Kinds of Small Groups

One thing we know for certain about young readers is they are not all the same! At a conference at Teachers College, reading researcher Richard Allington recently reported that most teachers who lead small groups have only one format for how those tend to go. The irony is that the biggest reason to work with small groups instead of the whole class is precisely so that we can tailor our teaching to our students. So what would be the reason for anyone thinking that The Right Way to lead small groups is to do the same thing in every small group? There are abundant ways you can work with small groups, and this is especially true because in this format, you will sometimes work in out-of-the-box ways, trying something bold that you have never tried before,

Key Features of Small Group Instruction

1. Engagement is high!

2. They are brief.

3. They are heavy with kid work and low on adult talk.

4. The kids move, the work sticks!

just on the off chance that it might help. After all, your small-group instruction will be your forum for working with students for whom in-the-box sorts of teaching may not have done the job. No matter which types of small group you choose, all share some basic features: (1) engagement is high, (2) they are brief, (3) they are heavy with kid work and low on adult talk, and (4) the kids move and the work sticks.

Guided Reading

During reading time, you will often lead guided reading groups. The term *guided reading* means remarkably different things to different people. Generally, when my colleagues and I lead guided reading groups, we gather four or sometimes six children (usually two or three partnerships) and select a text that we believe will provide a few but not too many challenges for those readers. Usually these texts are at children's instructional levels, offering a bit more challenge than texts they can read independently. Then we provide a book introduction that prepares readers for these challenges. We include some of the same words—especially domain-specific terms—and related concepts that are in the book. This way, when a child who knows very little about sled dogs reaches a page with the word *husky*, she will have already heard that word in the book introduction and will be able to draw from that knowledge. We also use some of the language structures from the book, especially ones that may be unusual or unlike the spoken language structures with which kids are more familiar. By using language structures from the book, such as "Where oh where . . ." or "Down came the . . . ," we can expose kids to the way the book "talks" prior to reading it. In these ways, the introduction supports what we anticipate will be tricky aspects of the book.

On the other hand, it is important to avoid providing so much support in a book introduction that kids breeze through the text without any hiccups.

Leave a few places where students need to struggle productively and use all they know to solve problems. For that reason, the book you select for a guided reading group will usually be at the children's instructional level.

As you give a book introduction, children are usually each holding a copy of the book. During the introduction, you might have children point to or find or read aloud one or two of the tricky parts, because even just this tiny bit of activity highlights that item. Again, this depends on your children. If you find that students begin reading the book and not attending to the book introduction, you might keep the copies of the book and have one child demonstrate how to read the tricky part from the book you are holding.

Then each child reads to herself (even if the children are reading aloud, they do not chime along, in sync with each other) as you move from one reader to the next. You can listen to a child read aloud to assess how he is moving through the text, problem solving tricky words or parts. You can also coach in with lean prompts to remind the child of strategies to try. If a child finishes reading the selection before the others, you might signal for her to reread or to find a favorite page or a tricky part. When everyone has finished, after no more than ten minutes, engage the children in the briefest of conversations and then select a skill or strategy to teach, drawing on a shared challenge you saw. Sometimes children will not complete the book before

Teacher leading a guided reading lesson

you stop the guided reading. Often in the tiny postreading discussion, after you quickly teach something, children practice what you taught, sometimes on the white board and sometimes by returning to the text.

You will find examples of guided reading lessons throughout the series. For example, in *Readers Have Big Jobs to Do*, Liz Dunford Franco and I describe a guided reading session that Liz did during her professional development work with half a dozen teachers. Before Liz began working with children, she pointed out to the teachers observing her that it is important to use simple and consistent language prompts when coaching into children's reading, so that students internalize the prompts and end up almost prompting themselves. In one instance during that group, a child read, "He got a gold medal," when the text said, "He got a golden medal." At that moment, Liz prompted, "Check it! Look across the whole word," directing the reader to use more visual information to fix this error efficiently.

The group of observing teachers and Liz later talked about the fact that if Liz had found herself coaching several children that way, then she would have had an indication of work she needed to do with the entire small group or even with the whole class.

In that particular guided reading group, when Liz tried to engage children in a discussion about the text, it became clear that many had been so focused on decoding that they had lost hold of meaning. Therefore, the guided reading group ended with Liz pointing out to the kids what she'd noticed and teaching them that readers *always* keep track of what's going on as they read. She modeled that it helps to stop after part of the text to retell what is happening, to predict what might happen next, and then to read on. Then, she sent the group off to read, asking them to first practice that strategy with their own copies of the text.

Aim to finish your guided reading group in ten minutes and to send children off with the books in hand so they can reread them, adding them to their book baggies. In this way, you'll give kids access to instructional-level books, gently stretching them to a new level. After a second or third time reading these books, they should be easy for children to read independently.

Guided reading is an especially powerful method to use in certain situations. For readers who are moving up a notch in text complexity, guided reading can help them grasp the main storyline of a text and the dominant language structures so that they don't get bogged down with visual demands without the support of meaning. Guided reading can help ELLs, because it is one way to scaffold their comprehension and introduce vocabulary. Book introductions also increase the likelihood that children who tend to respond to

reading trouble by relying only on letters and sounds in isolation will draw not only on phonics, but also on meaning when they encounter difficulty.

Small-Group Strategy Lesson

A strategy lesson generally includes a minute or two of strategy teaching, followed by time for guided practice. Usually children in a strategy lesson are not reading the same book but are instead working on the same strategy. Often, they are reading books that are roughly the same level of text complexity. For example, you might gather a small group of children who need support paying closer attention to monitoring for meaning as they read. Or you may gather children who need to work on pulling together parts of a text, seeing that clusters of pages all go together. Each of these groups will last for five to ten minutes as you help students work on the strategy within their own just-right books.

In the second-grade unit *Becoming Experts: Reading Nonfiction*, Celena Larkey wrote about a recent time in her professional development work when she led a small-group strategy lesson to support readers' understanding of information books. Before she began, she said to the observing teachers, "This is my first strategy lesson with this group, so I'll offer more support today than I will next time I work with these same kids. Today I'll ask the kids to practice the strategy with a partner, and next time, I'll challenge them to do this on their own, removing that scaffold."

When Celena pulled four second-graders together to start the group, she said, "As you are reading, don't let the details of the text fly by you. Really think about what you are reading. Remember that you can ask a question, think about what the text is teaching you, or look at the picture and think about what is happening. Let's do that in our own books with a partner. First, Partner 1 will read, and then both of you can talk about the details on the page. You can try any of these things to help you." She showed them a list of ways to think about the text.

"I will listen in and help you say more about what you see, notice, and think," Celena added. Then she listened in to each partnership, prompting students, giving tips, and restating the teaching point for the strategy lesson. She nudged the group to try the work several times in their books.

After this group finished, Celena and the teachers debriefed, and Celena pointed out that the teachers could work with the same group of readers the next day, providing less scaffolding.

You might gather another strategy group focused on teaching students that their predictions need to be based on the details of what they have already read. You could begin by rereading the last bit of the book you'd read aloud to the class, and then explain that when students predict, they need to draw on details from earlier in the text. You might demonstrate this quickly, before asking kids to practice the strategy with the same book. Then you could channel readers to read on in their own books until they reach a spot where they can predict, remembering to do what you just demonstrated. As students do this, move from one to another, coaching into their work.

Chapter 4 of this book will assist you in another way of pulling students together for a strategy lesson. When you examine that chapter, you will notice that groups of book difficulty levels are put together with bulleted lists of things readers should accomplish and learn while reading books from those levels: A/B, C/D, E/F/G, H/I. Children who are reading levels A, B, and C are still working on one-to-one matching, pointing under each word as they read it. You could pull students reading different level books (one reading level A, two reading level B, and one reading level C) and teach for this print recognition strategy.

What's important is that your strategy groups provide an explicit teaching point that targets a particular need you have ascertained from your work across individual conferences. Just like when you work one-on-one with a child, the strategy lesson should provide the personalized support and feedback each student in the group requires to tackle particular challenges a text presents. These groupings are flexible; you'll need to consider not only who is in each group, but also why you're placing them together and what and how you'll teach them.

Small-Group Shared Reading

One important alternative to guided reading is small-group shared reading. To lead this sort of a group, pull together a group of readers who are working at the same level of text complexity. Instead of focusing all your attention on a new text, start these readers off by working with a familiar text. You may or may not progress to also work with an unfamiliar text. Before inviting the group to join you in a choral reading of that familiar text—in which you and the students read the text aloud in unison—you may want to remind the students of a strategy or two that they have been working on independently, so that while they make their way through the text together, you can also coach to support that strategy.

For example, in the kindergarten unit *Super Powers: Reading with Print Strategies and Sight Word Power*, Amanda Hartman noticed a few below-benchmark students who were still having difficulty with one-to-one matching. She pulled a group of six kindergartners together on the rug and said to them, "Readers, we have been reading this book, *Brown Bear, Brown Bear*." She held up the book. "I put dots under each word to help us keep track of the words. Brian, your name starts with the same beginning sound as /br/own in 'Brown Bear.' Why don't you use the pointer and go first?"

Note that Amanda put dots under each word for only the first few pages in the familiar text. Once the student's pointer landed on the big black dot under the first word, *Brown*, Amanda invited the group to chime in as they

Small-group shared reading

read the book together. She said, "Everyone read along with Brian. If you have trouble reading the words, that's okay! Be sure to keep your eyes on the word that the pointer is under as we read." She gave each child a chance to do the work of pointing as the group read in choral fashion.

Amanda ended the lesson by reminding students that this new strategy could be used in other books. "Readers, I have made a copy of the words from *The Carrot Seed* for you to keep in your baggie. Notice that there are dots under the words in this book just like in *Brown Bear, Brown Bear*. Remember, if you ever feel like you are having trouble keeping track of the words in the books and poems you're reading, power up your pointer power by practicing with one of these books. The dots will help you to point under each word as you read."

When Amanda debriefed with the teachers who were with her that day, she suggested they might plan for two or three more opportunities to bring those readers together to practice one-to-one matching, making sure that over those subsequent meetings, they lightened the scaffold of the dots under the words. For example, she suggested that readers could read duplicated copies of the same texts as those she had dotted, only this time, they could read without the dots but could instead be given magic markers and guided to make their own small dots under each word. While the kids worked at that, teachers might tuck in a reminder that a "kryptonite word"—a multisyllabic word—only receives one dot.

Of course, had Amanda been with that group a few days later, she would have removed the scaffold completely, releasing the kids to greater independence. This time, she could have encouraged students to choose their own

familiar text from their baggie. She could have said, "Readers, your pointer power is becoming very strong! The dots have helped you. But now, I don't think you need the dots anymore! Let's just *imagine* the dots under the words in books." She could then have supported students as they began reading their books privately, observing their ability to use one-to-one matching with greater consistency.

Small-group shared reading can also be used to support the needs of readers at higher levels of text complexity, such as students who are struggling to notice and understand literary language. Lauren Kolbeck describes this work in the second-grade unit *Bigger Books Mean Amping Up Reading Power*. To support students this way, Lauren selected a text for shared reading that offered multiple opportunities to experience literary language. Songs and poems such as *Chicken Soup with Rice*, written by Maurice Sendak and sung by Carole King, work well for this work. As Lauren read with a small group, she gave students pieces of highlighter tape to cover confusing phrases they noticed. After they read for a bit, she supported the children in rereading and puzzling over the highlighted passages. She voiced over to the observing teachers, saying, "Remember, don't do the work for the kids! Participating in the struggle together is more fun and effective and makes the work accessible."

Natalie Louis suggests yet another way this might go. To prepare a shared reading text, Natalie masked the words across some of the initial pages of a level D text, inviting the group to search for meaning and syntax, using the picture and thinking about how the sentence might go on the page. Natalie prompted, "Look closely at the picture. What do you notice? How do you think this page will go? How might this book talk?" As the group called out possibilities for what to write, Natalie chose one sentence to record on Post-its in the book: "Penguins have flat wings." She wrote each word on a separate Post-it that covered the actual word in the text. Then, Natalie prompted students to cross-check with visual information, peeling away each Post-it to match it against the actual words on the page. She said, "Wait! I see that some of the words are the same, like *penguins* and *have*. But some of the words don't look right. What might this word say?" In this way, Natalie helped the children search and cross-check multiple sources of information (MSV). She coached kids to rely first on meaning, by searching the picture and thinking about what was happening, and then to decode the print. She continued moving through this process on subsequent pages of the shared text, assessing how children called upon the syntax and meaning on previous pages to support their new predictions. This work is especially powerful for supporting English language learners' growing understanding of language structure and for helping them connect that to the words on the page.

Small-Group Interactive Writing

You may decide to support readers through small-group interactive writing—a time when the group co-constructs a piece of shared writing on chart paper, and the teacher names the transferable strategies that students can use that time and other times. Interactive writing is one of several ways you can capitalize on the power of linking reading and writing. For example, you may find that although children stretch words to record the sounds they hear at the beginning, middle, and end of words when they *write*, they do not yet attend to sounds in all those places within a word when they *read*. You could devise interactive writing that channels students to do this as they read. Interactive writing can also build students' growing sight word knowledge.

During an interactive writing lesson, you share the pen with children, prompting them to record a feature of a word (an initial or final consonant or blend, a vowel or cluster, and so on) or a whole word or punctuation. Typically, the group co-creates a text. That text needs to be short—a banner for the classroom, a sign, a letter, or a class book, say, about a class trip. You will typically record words or parts of words that are way outside of students' zones of proximal development and then ask children to participate—to share the pen—for parts that represent a good level of challenge for them. Another rule of thumb is to correct mistakes on the spot, while of course celebrating the child's approximation and addressing the confusion to capture a teachable moment.

In the kindergarten unit *Bigger Books, Bigger Reading Muscles*, we tell about Rebecca Cronin's work with a group of children who could read level B texts independently and were ready for instruction in level C books. Because she didn't want those students to linger in level B texts,

Rebecca made plans to support the readers using interactive writing. She thought about the characteristics of texts at their instructional level before convening the group, focusing on level C texts. She decided that her aim for the group would be to write a text containing a complex pattern, longer sentences, and more than two lines of print on each page. She knew that one page might say something like "Look at Keegan with his car. His car is little and red."

To increase kids' engagement during small-group interactive writing, it can help to use the names of the children who are in the small group. In her session, Rebecca wrote about each of the children in that small group and the child's favorite toy. She titled the book "Our Favorite Toys!" She began the group by saying something like, "Today I'm hoping you will help me finish writing a book that I started writing. After we finish it, I'll give each of you a copy for your book baggie. This is a book about you and your favorite toys from our classroom. Let's read the title and the first two pages together. Then you can help me write the other pages." Rebecca worked with the group to compose a few pages, sharing the pen with kids to record initial and final consonants and blends, the children's names, sight words, and so forth. Rebecca wrote some of the words that were beyond the grasp of the group members. After the group had added a few pages, Rebecca led the group in a shared reading of the cowritten text. To end the group, she reminded kids to use all they knew about letters and sounds and snap words to help them read longer sentences and trickier patterns. In this way, she helped children make important reading-writing connections, using what they knew as writers to encode, and to decode as readers.

Imagine one more possibility. You might use writing to support reading by bringing students' writing folders into the reading workshop, suggesting that instead of reading books from the library shelves, they read the books they have authored or the books their friends have authored. Over a couple of days, you might lead a short interactive writing group to help students develop their knowledge of letters and sounds by labeling, hearing all the sounds in a word, and recording a letter for each sound. Do that work for several words and channel students to practice rereading the shared piece, sliding a finger under the word, and reading the word first slowly and then with one touch under the word. Then students could do the same work with their own writing pieces.

Small-Group Word Study inside Reading Workshop

You will, no doubt, lead word study work daily, but you may find that children are not transferring their knowledge of letters and words to reading. Students need not only isolated practice, but also practice applying these principles in context, in both reading and writing. You can group students who have similar needs, such as recognizing words from the word wall in continuous text, or flexibility with vowel sounds.

If you decide to lead a small group to support your spellers who are at the late letter-name stage, remember that these kids are starting to understand how blends and digraphs, as well as short vowels, work. In your small group, some of them might "warm up" for reading by looking over a blends chart or a vowels chart (or ring of cards) before they begin to read their books. This way, the blends and digraphs that they are just starting to master will be fresh in their minds, and they will be less likely to revert to sounding out words letter by letter, which is a very inefficient strategy in most cases.

Of course, the warm-up activities would be different for spellers at different levels. Youngsters who are in the early within-word pattern stage will be familiar with some long vowel patterns, so they may benefit from going on a vowel pattern hunt before they read. After some warm-up work, students can shift into reading while you coach them to use what they have practiced on the run as they read.

Many beginning readers will recognize high-frequency words out of context, on the word wall and on a word ring, but then become stumped by those same words in context in their books. You might decide to pull a small group of these readers, using shared reading to instruct. You could say to them, "One way to get ready to read is to look at the pictures and think about what's happening, *and then* search the book for words you know. First, go on a picture walk. Second, read the word wall. Third, go on a word hunt in your book to get ready to read." You could then give each student a copy of the book and a personalized word wall or ring of word cards to do this work while sitting with

you. Before students leave you, you could set them up to do this with another book. Over the upcoming days, you might find two to three more times to bring these readers together and continue to practice this work.

To help students transfer word study principles to the context of reading, you might use other word study tools as well, such as familiar alphabet charts or dry erase materials to manipulate letters and words in isolation, before returning to the book and supporting transfer with work on decoding similar words. You might return to your demonstration text and hunt for these vowels, discovering the different sounds each makes in different words. Partners might go on "vowel sound hunts" as they reread familiar texts, thinking about which vowels they see and what sound each one makes in a given word.

The chapter on word study has many more suggestions for small-group word work. For now, my point is that this work can be done in small groups during reading time, when it seems to be what children need most.

PRINCIPLES TO GUIDE YOUR SMALL-GROUP WORK

Small-group teaching needs to be responsive, and for that to be the case, you need to outgrow any feeling that there is a single way every small group proceeds. *Some* small groups begin with a text introduction, followed by a period when children each read while you circle among them, listening and coaching one child's reading and then another's, and end with a teensy book talk followed by a little teaching point. Yes, indeed, that is *one way* that small groups can go. But other teachers do very different things, both under the name of guided reading and in small groups in general. The important thing is that you draw on a repertoire of small-group methods, choosing ones that are especially engaging to your kids and that especially mobilize growth.

Consider Shorter, More Frequent Small-Group Sessions, Decreasing Scaffolding over Time

The first and most important thing to say about small-group work is this: Do it! One of the reasons to lead a well-structured, streamlined reading workshop in which readers know how to carry on independently is that this provides a perfect context for you to lead flexible small groups. While your kids are immersed in within-reach books they have chosen, you can very easily pull together not just one small group, but several each day. Leading a small group should be no big deal.

In a typical day's reading workshop, you might aim toward working with two small groups and holding three or four conferences, some with individuals and some with partnerships. I can see you adding up the minutes, thinking, "Two small groups—that is thirty minutes right there, and three or four conferences . . . ," but let me jump into your thinking and point out that both conferences and small-group work can vary tremendously in length.

In general, small-group work will be more powerful if you do smaller bouts of it across time than if you have one long small-group session every few weeks. You may find it helpful to work with a particular small group for approximately ten minutes, across a week or two for three sessions, rather than just once for half an hour. Plan those sessions so that you lighten your scaffolds with each subsequent session. The extra advantage of working with a group for shorter bouts of time is that you can then ask and expect children to do some group-related work between your meetings, which will influence their reading for broader stretches of time.

In your first session with a group, you might teach through shared reading, using a carefully selected text that you have prepared, bearing in mind the

work the group needs to practice. For example, to support a group that needs help with attending to word endings, you might select a text that contains many words that provide good practice. Additionally, you might decide to mask certain words or highlight word endings in the text to prompt students to use multiple sources of information on the page and to draw attention to the work at hand. This is a perfect way to provide a scaffold for kids who are doing work that is very new or challenging.

In your next session with that group, you might teach through guided reading, focusing on a particular strategy or two. The combination of text selection, book introduction, coaching, discussion, and an explicit link to ongoing work provides substantial support for readers.

In a final session, you might skip the book introduction and go straight to naming a strategy and coaching kids to try it out right away in a new, instructional-level text that you provide. With a little bit of planning, you can create a ladder of lessons that releases scaffolds over time, allowing students to do more and more of the work on their own.

Remember that you can be flexible not only in the type of small-group instruction you choose, but also in the way that the small groups go. Just like many of you may think that all small groups need to follow the same structure, you may also think that all small groups need to meet in the same space—usually at a kidney-shaped table—and that they all need you to be present from beginning to end. These rules may make you less flexible and less able to teach lots of students. Imagine, instead, that you call a group of kids to the rug, do some quick teaching, and then say, "You stay here. Keep reading. If you need support you have each other to help you practice what you just learned!" Then you call another group of children to a spot at the back of the room and teach them something. You might say, "Why don't you get started? Help each other if you need it. I'll be back in five minutes to check in." This kind of teaching frees you up to call group after group without much movement of children around the room—movement that often creates distraction. It also allows you to coach children not just in the first few minutes that they apply a strategy, but after a bit of time reading. And perhaps most importantly, it sets children up to see each other as resources: win-win-win!

Plan with Reading Development in Mind

It is helpful to approach a small group with a sense for the developmental pathway along which readers progress when learning the skills you aim to teach. Once you know which skills and behaviors readers are working to solidify across levels of text complexity, you'll be ready to recognize signs of readiness to progress toward more complex texts. You'll also better understand which particular skills and strategies to reinforce or introduce to readers at different stages of development. For example, you'll know not to coach emergent readers (A/B) to decode the text, but instead to use the pattern and the pictures to read the words. You'll aim to solidify one-to-one correspondence, helping children consistently match spoken words with print. When you observe a child reading a level B book, let's say, and you notice that she consistently searches the picture for clues and then uses the letters in the word to produce the correct word, you'll likely gather more data to assess her readiness for level C books.

During your conferences and small groups, study children with a trained eye and ear. Look and listen for patterns and behaviors that alert you to how readers are progressing across this developmental pathway, to best support their most current needs.

Make Sure the Kids Are the Ones Who Are Doing the Most Work and Release Scaffolding When You Can

It is always important to ask yourself, "Who's working the hardest here?" and to remember that children benefit from their own hard work more than from yours! When I watch small groups that are not working, almost always what I see is that the problem is that the group is literally not working: the teacher is talking and talking and talking. Limit yourself to one and a half or two minutes of talk up front, and then mobilize kids to get started on reading work and shift into lean coaching. That coaching might involve a minute of watching, a ten-second prompt, another half minute of watching, and another ten-second prompt. That is, small groups need to provide kids time to work and you time to watch and coach.

Keep an eye on ways to release the scaffolds you provide to promote maximum growth. It's important to anticipate how you'll use the gradual release of responsibility model to help students progress from heavy to light scaffolding. The concept of scaffolded instruction was first used by Wood et al. (1976) to talk about children's language development. Referring to the temporary structures that are installed and eventually removed from around a building under construction, they suggested that with varying amounts of scaffolding, learners can be successful with tasks that they cannot yet do on their own. This is an important principle of teaching. Teachers provide learners with support for doing something that is just beyond their reach independently and then gradually remove that support so learners can function with increasing autonomy (Pearson and Gallagher 1983).

Chapter 10

Conferring with Readers
Intense, Intimate, Responsive Teaching

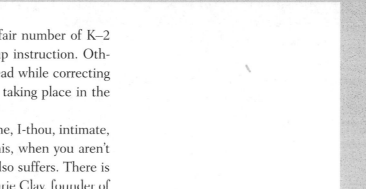

I WORRY about conferring in the primary reading workshop. A fair number of K–2 teachers have given up on conferring to rely only on small-group instruction. Others think that sitting beside a child, listening to the youngster read while correcting mess-ups, is a reading conference. In either case, less conferring is taking place in the K–2 reading classroom.

The problem with this is there is no replacement for the one-to-one, I-thou, intimate, crystal clear instruction you can give in a conference. More than this, when you aren't teaching one-to-one, not only do the kids suffer, but your teaching also suffers. There is a reason why both Don Graves, father of the writing process, and Marie Clay, founder of Reading Recovery and the most influential educator in K–2 reading, regard the relationship between one teacher and one child as being at the very heart of reading and writing instruction. That relationship is sacrosanct to two of the most important heroes the world of literacy instruction has known—and it is sacrosanct because it is through one-to-one instruction that all of us learn to teach.

I worry that when a teacher gives up on conferring to devote more time to small-group instruction, the result can be small groups that are less powerful than they can be. The best way I can describe this is to say that when teachers lose touch with one-to-one instruction, their small groups can have a tinny, mechanized feeling, because those small groups feel more like whole-class instruction delivered to a class of four students rather than one-to-one instruction given to four individuals working alongside each other.

I hope this chapter helps you confer in ways that give you a source of insight and that make all your teaching feel more alive and in touch with kids. As you muddle alongside that single reader, trying to understand the hard parts for that reader and trying to invent ways to help with those parts, you'll glean insights, ideas, methods, and scaffolds that you can bring to other readers. You'll also laugh with a reader over a part of a book, think aloud in ways the child can follow and join into, give the reader a tip that matters, and teach with the tone, intimacy, and authenticity that make a world of difference when you turn to small-group work.

THE BIG GOALS OF A CONFERENCE

One of the best ways to learn to give effective conferences to youngsters is to think, for a moment, of times when people have conferred with—or coached—you. What you want from a coach in a conference is not very different from what children want. When we want to learn to do something, we consider ourselves lucky if we can have a coach. A young swimmer who hopes to qualify for the Olympics gets herself a coach, and that coach watches her swim, noticing her needs and channeling her to work on them, and also noticing her strengths and doing everything possible to maximize those. Someday, when that swimmer makes the national team, when she walks to the Olympic pool and climbs into the water, the camera will scan to show not only her parents' faces, but her coach's face as well.

Conferring is every bit as important for readers who are working to become stronger as it is for swimmers, dieters, leaders, writers, runners, and teachers. The research is clear that providing a learner with feedback accelerates skill development. Hattie's work on this may be the best known. He reviewed 180,000 studies involving 20 to 30 million students and found that of 100 factors that contribute to student achievement, providing learners with feedback is one of the most potent ways available to support learning.

TWO KINDS OF READING CONFERENCES—EACH WITH AN ARCHITECTURE

Conferences, like minilessons, tend to follow a predictable architecture. That may sound odd—the idea that these intimate, responsive conversations have a structure or a formula to them—but actually in life, there are predictable structures undergirding many of our common interactions. For example, traditional teaching often follows a question-response-evaluate structure, with the teacher asking a known-answer question, "What is the capital of New York?", to which the child responds, "Albany," and the teacher evaluates that response, saying, "Very good." Teachers who follow this question-response-evaluate pattern of interaction may not realize they are doing so because the content of their teaching presumably changes, minute to minute, day to day. But the architecture or pattern of this teaching interaction is all-important, because as long as that pattern of interaction remains the same, the instruction itself will convey many of the same messages.

There are two kinds of conferences: research-decide-compliment-teach conferences and coaching conferences, and each kind of conference has a structure or an architecture that undergirds all interactions. So although conferences are informal in some ways, they are also highly principled teaching interactions, carefully designed to move readers and writers along skill development pathways. Of course, the teacher who is experienced at conferring will adapt the architecture as needed, but for someone learning to teach within a reading (or writing) workshop, it is important to understand the principles that underlie the design of conferences.

The Research-Decide-Compliment-Teach Conference

This kind of conference is the mainstay of the writing workshop and is critical to upper-grade reading workshops. It is important to K–2 readers as well, and especially so as those readers become more adept, but it is a bit less important

in the early stages of reading, because young readers need to get the reading process into their bones more than they need to be metacognitive about that work. Nevertheless, it is crucial to understand research-decide-compliment-teach conferences.

The Parts of a Research-Decide-Compliment-Teach Conference

- **Research:** This phase often involves listening to the reader read and either taking a quick running record or observing reading behaviors and strategies to determine the skill work the reader needs. This may involve questioning the reader or thinking back over all you know about the reader's process, goals, text level, and strategies.

- **Decide and Compliment:** This phase involves making a decision about the most helpful lesson to teach this reader, and it includes offering the reader a specific compliment that is meant to support and instruct.

- **Teach:** This phase may or may not begin with an explicit teaching point. It might, instead, begin with some coaching and then end with an explicit teaching point.

The Research Phase

When I try to help teachers learn to confer well, or help them improve their conferring, I focus on the importance of research, since that is the cornerstone of effective conferring. If you don't spend enough time trying to understand what the reader is doing and why, then what you decide to teach the student is often generic, perhaps just a recap of a minilesson or help with a tricky word. That is, when a conference doesn't begin with you taking into account what the child has done and is trying to do, then during the teaching phase of the conference, you might just reiterate teaching that has already happened, unaffected by this particular student and his work. Your conferences can be among the greatest sources of originality and power in your teaching, but the vitality, originality, and specificity that characterize powerful conferences require that you take in what the reader is understanding, doing, and working to achieve.

Think for a moment about a time you have gone to an expert for guidance, for coaching. Perhaps you have gone to your minister, your rabbi, your doctor, your hairdresser, your fitness coach, your principal, or your staff developer for assistance. When you go to that person—the person in authority—how do you want the interaction to begin? My hunch is what you want in those

instances is no different from what you want your principal to do when she does an observation of your teaching. You expect a question such as, "What have you been working on lately?" or "What sort of help could I give you?"

If a child has been working on becoming a better reader, then in the same way, it makes sense that you need to do some research before you can teach in a way that will really make a difference. So it makes sense to begin your reading conference with a basic check-in, such as "What have you been working on as a reader? Or "What strategies are helping you the most? What feels tough?" or "Tell me how your reading is going."

Listen and observe and form a theory.

Just those questions—"How's it going?" "What's feeling tough?"—can actually be very helpful. Think about a time in your life when a person you respect—perhaps someone coaching your teaching, your writing, your marriage—has said to you, "What new things have you been working on lately?" or "Can you walk me through what you have been trying to do?" If you have had the good fortune of being asked that sort of a question, you have probably found what I have found. The question alone will lead you to reflect, to dig deep, and even sometimes to have new insights about yourself.

Of course, there may also be times when someone asks, "What new things have you been working on?" and you respond with a perfunctory answer. You might do that because you sense that the person asking isn't really interested or sympathetic. We all know there are ways a person can listen, leaning in to hear more or nodding, conveying, "Say more," and signaling for us to amplify what we've said. We all know how a listener's responses—the little gasps and interjections that make us feel heard and understood—can make us want to talk. A good reading conference begins with deep listening.

That involves listening to the child actually read (more on this later). But first, let's be clear that often young readers won't find it easy to put their reading processes and strategies into words. If you ask, "What have you been working on as a reader?" many children of all ages, and especially many five-year-olds, will reply, "My book!"

You can prompt for more specific answers to that question—and some of this makes sense. Children can become skilled at talking to you about (and at thinking about) their habits and behaviors as readers. For example, they can tell you that they read, and then afterward, they talk with a partner. They can talk about trying to put their words together to read more smoothly or about pausing after a few pages to think about what they have read so far.

On the other hand, primary-aged children are not apt to be skilled at talking to you about their cognitive in-the-mind habits—nor should they be. You wouldn't expect a six-year-old to tell you that she is cross-checking meaning and syntax or trying to integrate sources of information! Much of what children do as readers is done with automaticity, inaccessible to conscious metacognitive thinking, so it will not be surprising if they are not articulate about their reading goals and strategies. As Marie Clay points out, "Most things we do as readers need to operate below the conscious level most of the time, so that fast and effective processing of the print is achieved and attention is paid to the messages rather than to the work done to get to the message" (2001, 127).

If the topic is one about which you want students to be goal-driven and articulate, and the child isn't able to tell you what she has been working on, it can sometimes help for you to observe her behaviors so you can report back what you see the child doing. You may, for example, say, "I'm noticing that when you get stuck on a word, you *stop* and try something, you don't just mumble through it or skip it. It looks like you check the picture to help you. Is that right?"

Usually, once a child has told you what he is trying to do, you can probe to understand what he means. If the child says, "I'm sounding out the words," you might say, "Oh! You're using the beginning sounds to figure out tricky words? Can you show me where that helped you?"

One way or another, part of your conference with beginning readers should usually include listening to the child read so you can see for yourself what the child is trying to do, almost doing, and not quite doing. Often as the child reads, you'll find yourself doing a super-informal, fleeting running record.

I recently asked Becky to read me a bit of her book, which happened to be an all-time favorite, *Hooray for Snail*, by John Stadler, a level F book. As she opened the book and got started, I quickly reviewed my notes on Becky; I want to bring some off-stage work to any effort to assess. I noted that she hadn't been reading level F books for long and that she was still a bit shaky on looking not only at the beginnings, but also at the ends and middles of words.

Sometimes my conferences refer back to previous conferences. For example, I might have said to Becky, "Last time we talked, you planned to pay attention to the dialogue in the story to understand the characters better. How has that been helping you?" Then I could have followed up by saying, "Can you show me a place where you practiced that on your own?"

As Becky read along, I listened for errors, because I knew that in the places where she wasn't getting the text exactly, I could see what she was doing and not doing as a reader. Those were my windows, giving me opportunities to watch the system she drew upon as she read. I was deliberate about listening for a few errors before drawing conclusions because I wanted to see the patterns in what she did.

Depending on the level of text that a child is reading, you'll likely be especially alert for different sorts of work that you hope to see the reader doing. The Units of Study series will help you do that. Because Becky was reading level F, I was especially alert for how she was able to consolidate the pages, putting them together into a story. I also wanted to know how she'd handle unfamiliar words, and I knew there would be a lot of those.

Becky read the first page: "Snail is on the . . ." And then she appealed for help. I signaled for her to work on it. She gave it a try: /B/ /B/. I noticed that she didn't try past the initial letter.

"Oh my gosh, what's going on at this point in the story?" I asked, looking with Becky at the picture. In casual conversation, we discussed that Snail wasn't playing yet, he was on the bench. After helping Becky search for meaning by using the picture and her knowledge of what was happening in the story, she said, "Oh! Snail is on the bench." and continued to read a bit more of the book. Snail gets the bat, the bat is heavy, and little Snail is sweating.

Again I asked, "So, Becky, what is going on so far in this book?'

Becky responded by telling me line for line what she had read so far, saying nothing more than the words on the page. "Snail is on the bench. Snail listens . . ." Soon she was reading on for a bit.

As Becky read, I continued to listen, while also looking briefly at the books in her baggie, checking to see if they were all roughly the same level—and whether some were a bit easier.

Decide

To an outside observer, my conference may have seemed fairly relaxed. But meanwhile, I was listening with every cell in my brain activated and thinking, thinking, thinking. Malcolm Gladwell, the author of the bestselling book *Blink: The Power of Thinking without Thinking*, talks about how an expert can thin-slice and, in the blink of an eye, make critical judgments. And as the authors of *Breakthrough* point out:

> Instruction is powerful only when it is sufficiently precise and focused to build directly on what students already know and to take them to the new level. While a teacher does and must do many things, the most critical is designing and organizing instruction so that it is focused. Without focus, instruction is inefficient, and students spend too much time completing activities that are too easy and do not involve new learning or on tasks that are too difficult. (Fullan et al. 2006, 34)

As I listened to Becky and took in all the evidence I observed and all that was available in my reading records, I was theorizing, predicting, and connecting this reader to other readers I'd known, determining priorities, imagining alternative ways to respond, and lesson planning! Meanwhile, I was smiling genially and nodding warmly enough to keep more data coming my way.

I knew I needed to avoid leaping to an instant conclusion about what I would teach. I wanted to take a minute to actually *select* the most powerful things to compliment and teach, rather than just grabbing at straws. Doing this involves not just identifying the goal on which to focus, the skill to support, but also understanding where the reader is along that learning progression. You need to decide what, precisely, the learner doesn't yet know how to do and seems ready to learn.

By this point, I had developed a theory about Becky. She was new to reading level F books, and her phonics skills weren't strong enough to rely on alone to decode the considerable number of tricky words she was encountering. She needed to rely more on meaning to give her a starting idea for what the words on a page might possibly be, and she needed to channel more time and attention into thinking about what was happening, adding what she could learn from the story to what she could learn from the words.

I was then ready to teach—I did not need to listen to Becky read the rest of the book. In fact, usually if I confer midway through a book, students can apply what they've learned as they finish reading that book.

Compliment

If you think about times when people in authority have come into your life, assessed your work, and then intervened in ways that aim to help you improve, my hunch is that some of those times were incredibly helpful, while other times felt incredibly destructive. It's important to think, "What was the difference? Why did the one interaction hurt me for life, and why did the other help in ways that still matter to me?"

I think that, mostly, the way you feel about a conferring interaction depends on whether the coach gives you the sense that you have the capacity to do the work, to rise to the occasion. If someone watches you teach or hears your ideas about a book or reads your rough draft writing or studies the records of your reading or hears about your marriage and then says, "Geez. This is a bigger problem than I realized. I don't know . . . ," then this one interaction can convince you that you are not cut out to be a teacher, a writer, a reader, a wife. Marie Clay has written extensively about the idea that sometimes, without meaning to do so, we can actually teach children that they can't solve problems, they can't help themselves, or they can't get better. Clay's classic paper "Learning to Be Learning Disabled" shows that, just as a teacher can help a child learn to be an active agent of his own learning, a teacher can also teach children to be passive victims, filled with self-doubts (Clay 1987).

When conferring, it's important to take a few moments to name what the child has already done that you hope she continues forever more, work that you hope becomes part of the child's identity. You can teach as much through finding and recognizing and celebrating good work as by issuing challenges, so that is one reason that the compliment portion of a conference is extremely important. The compliment also allows readers to sense that you have confidence in them. If you can convey this message, a reader is more likely to listen to what you have to say.

The trick is that a good compliment applies not just to today's reading, but to tomorrow's as well. So if a reader's book tells about the life cycle of a frog, and the reader has recorded keywords that name each stage on Post-its, I'm not going to say, "I love the way you recorded the stages of the frog's life cycle. You are really great at learning the stages of the frog's life cycle," because I don't really want to say, "Whenever you read a book, remember to record the stages of the animal's life cycle." But I could recast what the reader has done in a more generalized way by saying, "It's really helpful that you think about the important information you're learning about the topic and that you collect keywords, thinking about what they mean, so you can learn not just new *facts*, but also new *words*." That compliment is transferable to other reading contexts. It says, "Whenever you read a book, remember to do this."

Try to compliment work that feels as if it represents the cusp of a learner's trajectory. If the learner has just begun to do something and is still a bit shaky at this new work, and I can celebrate that brave new work, that's especially powerful. Peter Johnston has written,

> Focusing on the positive is hardly a new idea. It is just hard to remember to do it sometimes, particularly when the child's response is nowhere near what you expected . . . Much more important is noticing and helping the students notice—what they are doing well, particularly the leading edge of what is going well. This leading edge is where the student has reached beyond herself, stretching what she knows just beyond its limit, producing something that is partly correct. This is the launching for new learning. (Johnston 2004, 13)

Sometimes, when I try to notice and name what the student has done that represents the leading edge of the student's learning, I end up complimenting what the student has almost done or is just about to do. For example, I might say to the reader, "I am blown away by your decision to collect the keywords in your book as you read and learn all that you can about the topic. I know you did that so you can look back over those words and remember what they mean, so that you can use them when you talk about your topic and retell the information to your partner." I might say that, knowing full well that the

reader had no intention of pausing to look back, or of using the Post-its in that way, until I suggested it.

An Example of a Reading Compliment

When I spent a bit of time with Kobe during a unit on character, I definitely wanted to support the hard work he'd done to lift the level of his fluency. So I said to him, "Kobe, you are so persistent! I remember earlier this year you were reading word by word. Making your reading sound like talking is hard work, and some kids might have crossed their arms all discouraged and said, 'I'm not going to keep trying to make my reading smoother. It's too tough.' But you, you have been so persistent, and bit by bit, you have worked harder and harder. Now listen to you! Your reading not only sounds smoother, you have brought your whole book to life!"

Then, continuing, I said to Kobe, "To me, you are a lot like the boy in *The Carrot Seed*. Remember how he planted the carrot seed and everyone in his family said it wouldn't grow? Did that stop him? No way. Every day he watered the seed and pulled up the weeds around it, and every day, someone else told him that it wouldn't come up. But he kept taking care of the seed until one day it grew so tall, it was even taller than him! You are just the same as that boy because the two of you never give up."

Teach

After complimenting the reader, I name my teaching point and teach. This aspect of the conference feels a bit like a minilesson. The difference is that in a conference, just as in small-group work, the time spent teaching directly is less, and the time spent guiding children's active involvement is more.

My suggestion is to guard against the tendency to slip from the compliment into the teaching part of the conference because I find that often, the reader doesn't even grasp that the conference has taken a turn. For example, if I complimented Kobe on his reading voice becoming smoother, and then I wanted to teach him to be more attentive to punctuation to further support phrasing, I don't think the best way to make my point would be to go from the compliments to asking, "Do you know what a comma is? What does a comma tell a reader to do?" Instead, I'd ask permission to teach the reader a tip. "Do you mind if I give you one small, but important tip?"

Over the years, I've come to realize that, when our teaching is especially subtle, kids often miss it. If we are not explicit, the chances that they learn something they can use again another day are less likely. So, in the example above, I'd be much more apt to conduct my interview, perhaps give a compliment, and then crystallize whatever I wanted to teach into a single, straightforward teaching point.

After that you can do a tiny demonstration. You might carry the class read-aloud book with you, as well as a few texts that are on similar levels as the books your students are currently reading. If you are super-prepared for conferences, you might even have looked through those books, mining them for possible illustrations of teaching points and jotting these on Post-its so that you're able to quickly say, "For example, let's read this page of this book that we were reading last week. This is the part where . . . I'm thinking . . . Now let's read on together and see if we can . . . ." Then you can demonstrate the strategy or technique and name what you have done in the demonstration that you hope is transferable to the child's reading.

The conference then turns a bend as you say, "So try it." As the reader tries what you have just demonstrated, working either in the text you've pulled out for the occasion or in his own text, you coach into his work, giving lean pointers that help him do the work successfully.

The conference ends with a suggestion that the reader try the strategy not only right then, with that text, but often. You might give him some sort of a cue card or reminder—a bookmark, perhaps, containing a summary of what you've just gone over together, or Post-its in a special color to mark where the reader tries the strategy over the next few days, making it easy to see the traces of that work. By then, it is time to record what you've taught and learned and to scurry on to another reader, another lesson—for the child and for you.

The Coaching Conference

When you coach readers, you act rather like a running coach does, running alongside the athlete, interjecting brief bits of advice. "Today, remember to breathe from your stomach," the coach might say, just before the runner begins. Then, as the runner begins to run, the coach jogs alongside, watching. As the runner reaches a hill and begins to strain, the coach might interject,

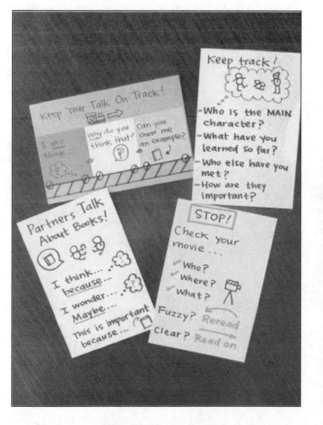

"stomach." When the runner begins to breathe faster, the coach may say, "Breathe deeply."

Similarly, when coaching a reader, you read along with the reader, watching the reader move across the terrain of the text. Your first interjection might be a bit longer than the ones that follow. You might say, "You're skipping past some words. Try to work on them a bit, word solve. You skipped that word. Keep working on it. Try to solve it." Then, as the reader reads along, you can watch. You may say, "Check it," when the reader attempts a tricky word. "Oops," you might say when the reader skips past a difficult word. Next time, you may just point at the word and say, "Stay with it. What could you try?" You may watch the reader go back and make a second try and then give a prompt to reinforce the work the reader did, saying, "You read through the whole word. Nice."

A coaching conference can begin with the same kind of observation that one uses in a research-decide-compliment-teach conference, but the assessment may have been done on another day entirely. The goal is to intervene as lightly as possible while readers continue to move through text.

One goal of coaching is to help readers develop unconscious habits. You're bypassing metacognition and trying to help build good habits into the reader's system. When coaching, you're trying to help the reader walk the walk, not talk the talk. Coaching moves are especially important when you're working with beginning readers who still need to develop an internalized sense of how to move through a text.

Often when reading alongside a young reader, you may notice that the child reads a few words and then looks up for approval. When you nod or say, "Good job," the child continues for a word or two and then looks up again. It can seem as though the child is reading your face as much as she is reading the book, and chances are she is! In fact, most teachers of young children are so in the habit of encouraging students that we let them know second to second how their reading is going by the expressions on our faces. While this is born out of good intentions, it can get in the way of reading development. When the child looks to the teacher to see if she is reading well, she is not developing the ability to know when she has made a mistake on her own. Marie Clay lets us know that part of learning to read is developing a "self-extending system," in which the reader begins to hear her own mistakes and then correct those mistakes with a variety of strategies. This cannot happen if the child is instead seeking constant feedback from the teacher. If you notice this happening in your conferences, there are two quick tips that can help.

First, sit slightly behind your reader as you listen. This will make it harder for the reader to look up at you. Second, when the child does look to you for approval or support, keep your eyes fixed on the book. Both of these actions will send the message that the answer is in the book, not on your face.

If you hang out in kindergarten or early first-grade classrooms, you'll see a preponderance of coaching conferences with kids reading books below level J. These readers often need help orchestrating their reading strategies to become more flexible and efficient with their word solving. The strategies they need to use are not new to them but need to be reinforced.

In one such coaching conference, young Jazmin had recently begun reading level E books. Even before I approached her, I recalled my most recent running records, which suggested that she was working to integrate meaning and visual information. She was using the pictures to think about what was happening on the page and then reading words in ways that made sense, but she did not rely on much visual information. She would say *mommy* for *mother*, for example. I'd brought her a new level E book—one she had not seen before—to the conference. While I might have done a coaching conference with a book from her baggie, I wanted to watch her work with an unfamiliar text.

As Jazmin began reading *A Friend for Little White Rabbit*, by Beverley Randell, I listened in to see if she was making the same types of errors she'd made in the past. I was prepared to respond with a prompt supporting her in using visual information to solve words. Jazmin began reading. "Little white lamb, little white lamb, play . . ." The word in the text was *please*.

Decide and teach.

The word *play* did make sense in the text at that point, but it didn't look right. This confirmed what I had seen in my research, so I decided to prompt Jazmin to search for more visual information. "You said *play*. That makes sense, but it doesn't look right. Reread that part and make sure to read through to the end of the word." This supported Jazmin with monitoring by confirming her use of meaning and telling her it wasn't right visually. I then prompted her to search for meaning again by rereading the sentence and integrating visual information by reading across the word. On her second reading, Jazmin correctly read *please* instead of *play*. Jazmin then continued to read and got to the word *said*. She first read it as *says* and then went back to fix it. I reinforced the work she did. "You fixed it. You made it look and sound right."

Link

At this point, I interrupted Jazmin's reading to leave her with a teaching point. I said, "Jazmin, you are the kind of reader who is working hard to use what you know is happening in the book to read words that make sense *and* also to read across the whole word. This is important for readers to do because we want to make sure we are reading the exact words the author has written. Let me show you where you did that work by yourself." I pointed out the part where Jazmin self-corrected *says* to read it as *said*. I left her, saying, "Continue to do that careful reading work, all the way across each word, when you read all of your books, Jazmin!"

Chapter 11

Word Study

THERE IS SO MUCH that early readers need to learn about letters and words and how they work. An effective word study curriculum for kindergarten, first-, and second-grade readers, according to the Common Core State Standards, covers phonemic awareness, letter-sound work, spelling patterns, high-frequency words, strategies for problem-solving words, and vocabulary. The goal in word study is to help children become efficient problem solvers of words as they are reading and writing.

We encourage you to begin your word study curriculum by assessing what children know about letters and words, both in isolation and in the context of reading. Once you have this information, you can make a plan for how to provide instruction, and you can show children how to transfer what they are learning about words to their own reading and writing. Therefore, we suggest you balance your instruction so that some of the work with words occurs in isolation and much of it occurs within the context of reading and writing. We will suggest assessment and instruction methods for kindergarten and then for first and second grade. While we describe methods for instruction and practice for whole-class teaching, any of this work would be beneficial for small-group instruction as well. Also, any activity described in either section would work well in most grades, so you might want to take a look at both sections.

ASSESSING WORD KNOWLEDGE IN KINDERGARTEN

There are three main things you need to assess early in kindergarten. The first are phonological awareness and letter-sound knowledge. Later you will assess high-frequency words.

Assessing Phonological and Phonemic Awareness

Initially, your assessment for phonological awareness can be informal. If you see signs that a child has strong phonological awareness, it's likely the child won't need individualized instruction in this area of word study. In other words, the child has an understanding of units of sound in spoken language, such as hearing and producing rhyme, as well as phonemic awareness, such as segmenting and blending phonemes in a word. You can teach the whole class and watch to make sure the child is learning. But if the child shows any trouble learning letters and sounds or gives clues that she doesn't have strong phonological awareness, you should assess this further. Without strong phonological awareness, other instruction doesn't stick.

So how do you begin assessing it? We recommend you begin with instruction, not formal assessment, and then watch to see how the instruction takes hold. Lots of kids will come to school already able to finish a rhyme or make up a variation on a rhyme, and many are able to clap and say the syllables of a word. This means those children come to school with phonological awareness, and you'll be building on their knowledge as you and the children sing, rhyme,

and read Dr. Seuss and other similar books. In this way, you are working on the first phonological awareness skills: rhyming and syllables. As you play around with language, notice whether a child can hear parts of words, such as *soft* in *softball*. If so, that child can segment by syllables. These informal observations become your initial assessments.

The next steps in developing phonemic awareness are phoneme isolation and identity, which means that the child can hear initial sounds in a word and say the initial sounds in a word, too. A child who can do this can look at a series of pictures and point to the ones that start the same way. During the writing workshop, as you teach children to stretch and hear sounds to write, you'll be supporting children's growing abilities to isolate beginning sounds. If you say "What does *ball* start with?" and the child can isolate the /b/ sound, whether or not she can match it to a letter, you can check off that she has

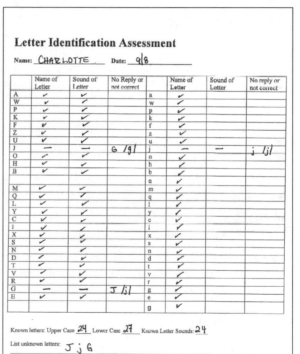

FIG. 11–1   Letter-sound assessment

a developing sense of phoneme isolation and identity. If the child can also segment a word into individual sounds, then she probably does not need a lot of phonemic awareness support. For children who are not yet doing this, you may want to continue with assessment as described below.

To assess the children in your classroom who are having trouble segmenting a word into all its phonemes (as well as blending and phonemes in general), you might carry a whole-class checklist on your clipboard with the following skills listed: rhyming, syllables, phonemic isolation and identity, blending and segmenting, and phoneme manipulation (being able to change a word by adding, deleting, or changing a phoneme). As you confer with children during reading or writing and observe them during a shared activity, such as shared reading or interactive writing, you can informally assess this list of skills.

Assessing Letter–Sound Knowledge

Assessing children's knowledge of letters and sounds will be helpful as you plan your word study instruction for your whole class. If most children are able to name many upper- and lowercase letters, then you may want to spend much of your letter and sound instruction on sounds, rather than letter names. To informally assess this at the beginning of the year, you might carry a whole-class checklist of letters with you, so that as you observe and confer with readers and writers, you can make note of letters they are able to identify and the letter sounds they know. If you are finding that particular children are not able to name many letters and their sounds, it will probably be helpful to assess them more formally, using a letter-sound identification assessment. You'll ask the child to name letters as you point to them and then say the sound for each letter. Having this information will help guide you in planning for letter-sound instruction for your whole class and for individual children.

Assessing High–Frequency Words

A month or two into the school year, it will be helpful to gather information about the high-frequency words children know how to read with automaticity. We refer to these words as "snap words" throughout most of this series, because these are words that children should be able to read "in a snap." For word lists and tips on how to assess high-frequency word knowledge, you can draw upon the resources located on the TCRWP website.

WORD STUDY INSTRUCTION IN KINDERGARTEN

While there are opportunities in reading workshop to provide explicit instruction on letters and words, the units of study are written with the assumption that children will have word study instruction and practice during a twenty-minute-a-day word study time, which is separate from reading workshop time. At the start of the year in kindergarten, the time for word study may be a bit longer, because reading and writing workshops will probably not yet be as long as they will be later in the year. At the beginning of kindergarten, children are still building their stamina for independent work.

In the following sections, we outline a possible word study plan for the entire kindergarten year. At the beginning of the year, we suggest you spend a large part of word study time studying children's names, one a day, as a way to teach a variety of word study concepts and letter knowledge, letter formation, and letter-sound correspondence. You will also teach letter-sound identification right from the start. By mid-October, you will likely have finished the name study. We suggest you shift your instruction to the explicit teaching of high-frequency words, while continuing the letter-sound instruction as needed. By mid-year, when your students no longer need such specific letter-sound teaching, you can shift your focus to more sophisticated phonics instruction, such as introducing your class to concepts such as short vowel word families. Below is a structure used in some classrooms across the year.

September–mid-October
Name study (daily)
Letter-sound instruction (daily)
Mid-October–November
High-frequency words (daily)
Letter-sound instruction (daily)
December–June
Phonics (three days a week)
High-frequency words (two days a week)

In the sections that follow, we discuss each method of word study instruction in greater detail. We also provide suggestions for how you can extend each method into other components of balanced literacy, such as shared reading, interactive writing, and writing workshop, to offer further opportunities for students to practice, solidify, and transfer the new skills they are learning.

Name Study

One of our favorite beginning structures for teaching letter-sound identification and phonological and phonemic awareness is a take on Patricia Cunningham's "star name." You set up for this practice by taking a photograph of every child in the class, pasting each photo on a sentence strip with the child's name, and placing all the names in a pocket chart, alphabetically ordered. Place the chart at kid-level in the meeting area. Then, write each child's name on a small slip of a paper and put the slips in a hat so that each day you can draw a "star name" at random.

On Day One, then, you might hold up Olivia's name on a name strip and say, "Class, whose name is this?" If most in your class shouts out, "Olivia!" you can confirm, "Yes, it is Olivia's name. Olivia's name is just one *word*, but it has many letters."

You might then circle Olivia's name with your finger or highlight it with a large piece of colored tape to visually show one word. "All our names are just one *word*, but each word is made up of different *letters*! How many letters are in Olivia's name? Let's count. One, two, three, four, five, six.

"Let's say the *names* of the letters in Olivia's name: *O-l-i-v-i-a*. How many letters are tall letters? Short letters? Straight letters? Curved? Now, we know that Olivia's name is just one word, but just as words can have a certain number of letters, a word can have a certain number of syllables, or parts. Make a fist, put it under your chin and say O-liv-i-a. Can you feel how your chin dips down for each part? Let's do it together. O-liv-i-a. Olivia's name has four parts!

"I'm going to hand out the letters in Olivia's name, and then those of you who get a letter can come up and make Olivia's name. Let's cheer as we build her name. When we cheer we can skywrite each letter together. Give me an *O*. Give me an *l*."

In just five minutes of star name work, students can practice the concepts of letter versus word, letter names, letter sounds, phonological awareness (hearing syllables), and even letter formation. When you have a better idea of the particular concepts your kindergartners need, you can highlight different concepts. If students need practice with rhyme, you can generate silly rhymes for the star name. If students need practice with letter names, you can ask them to turn and talk to compare the letters in their own name and the star name. If students already know letter names, you can highlight consonant letters and vowels and shift the inquiry to guide students to notice what sounds the letters make.

Proceed through all of the children's names through the beginning months of school. Once your name study is complete, we recommend you devote this block of time to teaching high-frequency words.

Shared Reading

Shared reading is a fruitful place to extend many kinds of word study instruction, and name study in particular. Place the star name into a familiar shared reading poem, like these:

Yum, yum, yum	Good morning to you
David likes pizza.	Good morning to you,
Yum, yum, yum.	Good morning to you,
David likes pizza.	Good morning dear Olivia,
In his tum.	Good morning to you.

You may wish to give students copies of the name poems and several students' names so that they can read them repeatedly, swapping out one name for another. Shared reading poems that can accompany a name study can be found in Irene Fountas and Gay Su Pinnell's phonics resource, *Sing a Song of Poetry* for grades K and 1 (2003).

Interactive Writing

You can connect the name study to daily interactive writing by using your class name chart as a tool to help children problem solve new words as you write together. You might point to the name chart and say, "Help me write the word *books*. Say *books*. Whose name sounds like *books* in the beginning? Say *books* and think about what sound you hear in the beginning. Skywrite the letter (or write it on a dry erase board). *Books* sounds like *Bryan* and *Billy* at the beginning. Say *books*, *Bryan*, and *Billy* as you write the letter *b*. Bryan, come write *b*." Then, fill in the rest of the word *books* so that it is conventionally spelled and the pace is quick.

Interactive writing is also powerful because it is so easy to differentiate. For instance, you can watch closely for students who are ready to listen for the ending or middle part of the word and prompt them in the same way to say the word, listen for the ending part, and think, "Do we know a friend's name that ends like *silly*? Or has a middle part that is the same?"

Another way to practice name study during interactive writing is to create a class book that features something about the star name student (e.g., what she likes to do). These texts may be copied and placed in students' reading baskets/baggies for continued reading during reading workshop. You might consider the reading levels of the class and aim to create texts at a slightly higher level than most readers, to help scaffold students into the next reading level.

Writing Workshop

Writing workshop is another place for kids to practice using what they learn during star name time. Because many children are driven to communicate a message about themselves in writing workshop, this makes that time perfect for phonics development. Imagine Jayden engaged in writing a story about his friends playing at recess. He pauses after drawing one of the friends and walks over to the name chart to find his friend Connor's name. He brings the name card back to his seat and writes Connor's name next to Connor's picture. The process of reading the name and then forming the letters will strengthen Jayden's memory for the letters.

While conferring with writers, you might also encourage them to use the name chart to write other words. For example, when conferring with a student attempting to write the word *cloud*, you might say, "Whose name starts like cloud?" Hopefully the child will recognize that *Connor* starts like *cloud*.

Phonics: Letters and Sounds

In addition to time spent on studying names, and later on high-frequency words, it's important to devote time to the teaching and practice of letters, sounds, and spelling patterns. Earlier in the year, your phonics work will probably be focused on letters and sounds, and later in the year, you'll transition to teaching early spelling patterns.

When teaching the letters and sounds, we find it helpful to teach both the letter and the sound together so that children begin to make that important connection between the sound and the print—the phonics knowledge that's important for reading and writing. It is helpful to begin instruction with consonants that many children need to learn and letters that are found in many of the children's names. This means that you will not necessarily be going in alphabetical order; you might, at first, alternate teaching a continuant sound (a sound that can be held for a prolonged time such as /m/ or /s/) with a stop sound (a short pronunciation sound such as /b/ and /t/). This way, as you introduce a new letter and sound, you can compare it to the letter and sound taught the previous day, and since the sounds will have distinct differences in how they are made in the mouth, it will be easier for children to discriminate the sounds.

You might follow a routine that combines phonemic awareness, vocabulary, letter-sound correspondence, and letter recognition and formation. If you use three of your word study blocks during the week for this letter-sound work, you'll be teaching three letters per week. To begin the word study session, you can warm up by reading the class alphabet chart. Even though the focus of the session is on one new letter and sound, it is important that children have continuous exposure to and practice with the whole alphabet. You might say, "Before we begin our letter study today, let's read our alphabet chart!" Point to the *Aa* and ask children to name the letter, the picture, and then the sound, so they might say, "A, apple, /a/." Pronunciation is important for later decoding and encoding work. For example, if children pronounce the /b/ sound "buuhh," then coach them to stop the sound as soon as it is made from their lips. This will help them later when problem-solving words. Otherwise, the blending of a word such as *bat* could turn into "buh-at."

We recommend establishing a routine for introducing the new sounds. Perhaps you always bring out two sets of objects or pictures. One set of objects (or pictures of objects) could be items that begin with the sound from the previous session, or, if it is the first session, a sound many of the children in the class know. The other set of objects would begin with the new sound you are teaching that day. You might gather children in a circle, line up the objects, and say, "Friends, I've brought us some objects to look at today. Let's name each object as I hold it up and place it in the center of our circle." Children can call out the names of the objects as you hold them up: "Bird," "Ball," "Mouse," "Monkey." After they name each object, you might warm up with a phonemic awareness song that allows for practice isolating beginning sounds.

What Is the Sound That Starts These Words?
(*to "Old MacDonald"*)

What is the sound that starts these words:
monkey, *moon*, and *map*?
/m/ is the sound that starts these words:
monkey, *moon*, and *map*
With an /m/ /m/ here,
And an /m /m/ there,
Here an /m/, there an /m/,
Everywhere an /m/ /m/.
/m/ is the sound that starts these words:
monkey, *moon*, and *map*.

Then, you can move to sorting the objects into two groups. Ask your students to figure out ways that the objects can be sorted. Channel the students to notice, if they don't do so on their own, that the objects can be sorted by their beginning sounds. Then, guide students in sorting the rest of the objects by their beginning sounds.

Next, we recommend you engage children in writing the new letter, too. They can write the letter on paper, on a white board, in the air, or on their hands with an imaginary pen. You might hold up two cards—one with an uppercase *M* and one with the lowercase *m*—and then remind students of the sound the letter makes and say, "Let's all take out our imaginary pens and

paper, our hands, and get ready to write the uppercase *M*." Then, write the letter on the white board as children pantomime writing the letter in the air.

As you write, name the verbal path of the letter. For example, you might say, "Pull down. Slant down. Slant up. Pull down. That's the uppercase *M*."

One reason naming the verbal path for forming the letter is important is so that children know the directional movement to use when writing that letter. This is important, not so much to help children write neatly, but because correctly formed letters are easier to make physically. Further, and perhaps more importantly for the purposes of phonics instruction, adding a tactile component to your teaching by asking kids to trace the letter in the air, along with an auditory component, saying the verbal path aloud, can be particularly powerful for kids who are struggling to learn letters and sounds.

Many teachers conclude the session by recruiting the kids to add a page to a picture dictionary. You might want to create a big book with a page for each letter, or simply create a chart for each letter, which hangs in the room. Turn to a blank page for the newly presented letter, and ask students to think about and then turn and tell a partner words that begin with that letter. As children talk, listen in and record as many words as you can, along with a few of your own, if you'd like. You might include some of your students' names that begin with that letter, if possible, to connect to the name study. We recommend that you sketch a picture next to each word and ask students to say each word aloud to solidify their learning before wrapping up the day's work.

Interactive Writing

As you lead interactive writing sessions, bring tools you create during word study time, such as the alphabet chart and the picture dictionary, so that the tools children are using in word study and writing workshop are also the tools the whole class uses when writing a text. While writing a class story about getting a new pet hamster named Max, for example, you might ask the children to help write the hamster's name by listening for the first sound in the name *Max* and pointing to the letter on the alphabet chart.

Writing Workshop

You can coach writers in writing workshop to use the same tools for spelling words while they are writing. We recommend that each child has an individual alphabet chart included with her writing materials. As you confer, it can be helpful to highlight the letter sounds children know on their alphabet charts so that they feel confident about using those accurately as they listen for and record sounds. Also, it is helpful for you to know which letter sounds you expect a child to record correctly and which he is still learning.

Also during writing time, an important way to practice letters and sounds is to teach children to reread their writing, even if at this point they are only writing labels with a single letter. You might also suggest that students attempt to read a partner's writing during the share at the end of writing workshop. Partners can let each other know which words they had trouble reading, encouraging the writer to check the spelling of those words. This work will help to build phonemic awareness, letter-sound correspondence, letter formation, and concepts of print such as directionality and one-to-one correspondence. That is, it helps all around!

Students reading the word wall

High-Frequency Words

We recommend you begin your instruction of high-frequency words, or snap words, by teaching two or three each week and then quickly building to three or four. It might be easiest to start with one- and two-letter words and also to choose words that look different from each other. Create a way for students to collect, store, and easily reference the words they learn, perhaps in a snap word baggie or on a ring.

We recommend you devote three days per week to teaching high-frequency words and that you teach words both in isolation and in context. To help children learn these words (and the letters in them,) we recommend you incorporate Marie Clay's (1985) "three ways of remembering." According to Clay, the teaching needs to first emphasize the *visual* (the printed word). To provide this support, make sure that as children practice the words, they are always looking at the word in print. Encourage them to describe the salient features in a particular word (*the* has three letters, two tall letters and one

short letter; or *t* is a straight line down and a line across the middle). After the visual, emphasize *movement* in your instruction. This might mean that you guide your students do some writing, to build the letters in dough or with flexible sticks, or to manipulate magnetic letters. Finally, make sure your little ones are using their *voices*. The easiest way to do this is to be sure that as they build, study, and write a word, they say each letter slowly.

When you begin a word study session emphasizing high-frequency words, you might gather children in the meeting area with a card for each word you'll study for each child. You might then introduce the word first in context, perhaps by reading a familiar poem or a few pages from a familiar book. This gives students a feel for how the word they'll be studying works in a text and grounds the word in meaning. For example, you might say, "Let's read *Dan the Flying Man* together."

Dan, Dan the flying man, catch me, catch me if you can.

Then say, "We are studying two new words this week that appear on almost every page in this book: the word *the*," hold up a card with *the* printed on it, "and the word *you*." Ask children to read the cards with you, and then to hold up a card when you come to that word as you read. For example you might say, "Dan, Dan–," and stop. "Which one of your cards matches this next word? Hold it up. Look at it, read it. Say each letter. Check *t-h-e*, and see if it matches the word *the* on the page. Let's try reading and matching the word *the* on one more page."

After this sort of introduction to the word in context, channel children to study the word by talking about what makes it special: syllables, letter features, letter names, number of letters, and so on. It may sound like this. "The words *the* and *you* are in tons of books! How many of you have ever written *the*? Thumbs up! So many of you! Sometimes the word *the* will start with a capital letter because it starts a sentence, and sometimes it will start with a lowercase letter, but it is still the same word either way." Be sure to show children a few cards that have the word written in different fonts and colors, with some starting with a lowercase letter and some with a capital. Encourage students to share what they notice about each word with a partner, including the shapes and sizes of the letters.

Skywriting is a way to use movement, voice, and visual all at once, and meanwhile, it's fun for children. You might say, "Let's stand up and skywrite the word *the*. Notice how I say each letter out loud, slowly, as we skywrite it: *t-h-e*. Let's check the word *the* while we are writing and saying it." As children do this, encourage them to use their dominant hand to hold their elbow or shoulder as they skywrite so they can feel the gross motor movement and remember it. Provide the verbal path of the letter the first time students write, saying, "The letter *t* is a straight stick down and cross in the middle."

On another day of instruction on the same high-frequency words, you might guide students to practice the words in isolation. Invite them to place one card at a time in front of them and to say each letter slowly as they make the word with magnetic letters, tiles, or flexible sticks. Encourage students to practice saying and making each word three times. If you don't have enough materials for all students at once, you can set up two or three tables with manipulatives and other tables where children trace the word on sandpaper. Students can do this work for eight minutes or so and then switch. On the third day of instruction, you might repeat a few of the methods of instruction outlined above, depending on the needs of your students.

Interactive Writing

Even though your more formal high-frequency word instruction may not begin until mid-October, you might start introducing beginning high-frequency words such as *I* and *see* through interactive writing, because this will support writers who are ready to write simple sentences.

After a few weeks of more formal high-frequency word instruction, during interactive writing, you might transfer the words students have learned back into reading and writing through a simple activity. If your classroom already contains labels such as *clock*, *table*, and *library*, you could guide your students to extend those simple labels into sentences. You might say, "Friends, you have been studying words like *you*, *can*, *see* and *the* over the past two weeks. We can use these words to create sentences about the things in our classroom.

Like maybe right here, we could write, 'You can see the library.' Let's say that, write it, and read it together." After you and the children do this writing, you can leave the new labels up so your children can read them all day long. Of course, these labels can change as children learn new high-frequency words. Soon the signs can say, "Here is our library!" and "You can read all of the books." Similar simple sentences can be written to explain science experiments or math results.

Writing Workshop

It goes without saying that during writing workshop, your children will be practicing writing high-frequency words in context. Some kindergarten teachers teach a unit in the fall, which we call "Writing Like a Scientist." During this unit, children go outside and find lots of leaves, bring them into the classroom, draw and label those leaves with great care, and then write little list-books about the leaves. When children write patterned list books, this gives them an extra intensive chance to practice their snap words. A book might sound like this: "I see a pointy leaf. I see a shiny leaf." Or "Can you see the stem? Can you see the veins?"

Encourage children to write with their snap word collection at the ready to be referenced often. Also, during partner time, partners can read their books together, making sure the spelling matches the print on their cards.

Spelling Patterns

Once the majority of the class has developed some command of letters and sounds, your phonics instruction will shift to teaching phonics principles that will help your children read and write words using their knowledge of word parts, such as short vowel families -ap, -at, and -an.

Reports from the National Reading Panel (2001) suggest that kids need both synthetic and analytic approaches to the teaching of phonics. In analytic approaches, children are taught to analyze and blend larger subunits of words, such as onsets, rimes, phonograms, or spelling patterns. Often analytic approaches to phonics channel kids to analyze the word to figure out the phonics principle the word illustrates. Meanwhile, in the synthetic approach, sounds are taught in isolation, and then children learn to blend these sounds to form words. Most children benefit from a bit of both approaches when they are learning about how words work. Sorts, for example, are mostly analytic. They are terrific, but for some kids, they are not explicit enough, and therefore if your approach to phonics is dominated by sorting, you may consider adding more explicit instruction as well.

Making words is one of several methods that combines both analytic and synthetic approaches to phonics. Patricia Cunningham and Dorothy Hall's *Month-by-Month Reading, Writing, and Phonics for Kindergarten* (2008) is an excellent resource for this approach. Many teachers do two sessions per week of making words as part of word study instruction, and then they reinforce this teaching in a session of interactive writing.

To prepare for a making words session, we recommend you gather materials and create a system for setting up for the sessions. Make or provide the letters that each child will need to make the words you'll discuss in the session. Place a pocket chart at the front of the room, and prepare index cards with the letters you'll need ahead of time.

For the purposes of sharing what this work might look like, let's imagine that the phonics principles you have decided to support are the short *a* sound and the vowel families -an and -ad. You might start by saying, "We are going to make words in the -an and -ad word families. Take out two letters from your baggie that spell -an." As children do this, invite one child up to the pocket chart in the front of the room to spell -an for the whole class.

Then, ask children to add one letter to -an to make the word *pan*. As they work, coach them to make sure the word looks right and that they are checking all parts of the word. While children are learning about the short *a* vowel

families through this activity, they are also learning to attend to final sounds and letters as they make and read the words.

Next you'll say, "Now change the first letter to make the word *man*." After making words such as *ran* and *man*, you might say, "Just as we changed the beginning part to make a new word, we can also change the ending part to make a new word. Who can change the end of *man* and make *mad*?" Next, you may want to spell more sophisticated words, such as *sand*. Children who are ready for a challenge get that practice, and others get valuable exposure to more sophisticated work, with the scaffold of being able to observe as you make the words at the front of the room.

As children work with individual phonemes and letters to make new words, they are learning using a synthetic approach. To balance this with some analytic phonics work, you could do a quick sort of the words. In the pocket chart, display all the words the class made that day and ask children to turn and talk to each other about how the words might go together. Convene the class, and point out that *pan*, *man*, and *Dan* go together because they all have the -an part at the end, and *pad*, *mad*, and *sad* go together because they have -ad at the end. You might also point out that both have the same vowel— *a*—but they have different sounds at the end. Wrap up by reminding children that when they are reading or writing, they may see or use words with similar word parts, so they can think about the words they made today to help them.

Interactive Writing

To help students transfer learning from word study time to interactive writing, we recommend you display an alphabet chart and word family charts during interactive writing. Some teachers display a separate short vowel chart as well, especially because children learn more and more word families with different short vowels.

Imagine that you've recruited the class to help you write a how-to book on getting ready for reading workshop. As a way to extend the work with spelling patterns you've studied during word study time, you might ask them to help you add labels, or, if your book already has labels, to add sentences. To give students practice with certain kinds of words, pause at words with particular characteristics, and recommend that they help you write these words.

For example, if the students are helping you write a page that says, "First, get your book bag," you could write the first four words in that first step, and then ask for help with the word *bag*. Ask students to think about the words they made during the making words session as you point to a chart with short vowel word families. Recruit one child to come forward and write the word on the chart paper, while you continue to coach the other writers to work on white boards. At the end, remind writers that when they write words during writing workshop, they can do the same type of work, listening for sounds and parts of words and using the word family chart in addition to their alphabet chart.

ASSESSING WORD KNOWLEDGE IN FIRST AND SECOND GRADE

Assessing Phonics Knowledge

Assuming that kindergarten children will have mastered letter sounds and phonological/phonemic awareness tasks, you can start first and second grade by assessing specific spelling concepts about words such as blends, vowel patterns, and inflected endings. You may do this using a formal spelling inventory assessment, such as Donald Bear's Spelling Inventory, which can be found in his book, *Words Their Way* (Bear et al. 2012). If you have students who are reading below level D, visit the kindergarten assessment section of this chapter for support in assessing letter sounds and phonological and phonemic awareness.

A spelling inventory such as Donald Bear's can be administered to the whole class. You'll ask students to spell a series of words from the grade-appropriate word list. Words in the list are designed to assess specific spelling concepts in developmental stages. The concepts might include digraphs, blends, short vowels, long vowels, inflected endings, and syllable juncture. Look to see which parts of the word are correctly or incorrectly spelled (e.g., in *hopping*, did the student correctly spell the short vowel, double the consonant, and include the inflectional ending?). Children who miss the same concept once or twice will need to review the concept, possibly in conjunction with studying another new concept. Those who make three or more errors with a concept will need explicit instruction. If the student does not even attempt the concept (e.g., only uses short vowels in words like *rain* or *feet*), that may mean she needs instruction on prior concepts first.

Sometimes you may be perplexed by a student's spelling inventory and may need more data. A child's writing from writing workshop can give you a clearer picture of what he knows about specific spelling concepts, what is confusing to him, and where to start instruction. For example, Patrick's writing might include errors such as *sally* for *silly*, *bock* for *back*, *mod* for *mud*, and *hum* for *home*. These errors suggest that he needs work with short vowels before studying long vowel patterns.

The results of the spelling inventory and your notes on students' writing samples can help you determine what word study concepts to study with the whole class. Undoubtedly, you'll probably also notice particular things that only small groups of students need. You can differentiate instruction by pulling a small group during word study time on days when students are working on activities independently and with partners. So, if on Tuesday the class is working on a sort for CVCe words, you might decide to pull together a small group of students who instead need work on *r*-controlled vowels and have them do a different sort.

Running records also provide valuable insights into students' phonics knowledge. The information provided by children's errors can go a long way toward planning both whole class and individualized instruction. For the purposes of planning a word study curriculum, pay particular attention to children's visual errors. Then, take a closer look at the kinds of errors students are making. For example, if a child substitutes *flipping* for *flopping* and *hold* for *held*, she may need explicit instruction on short vowels during word study time.

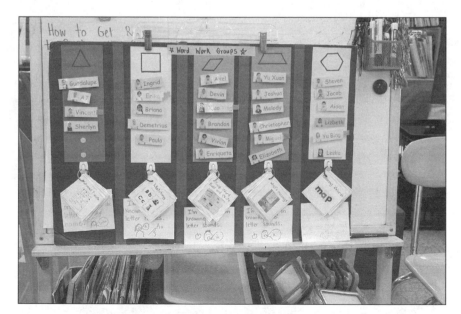

Assessing High-Frequency Words

Another component of word study that it is important to assess is high-frequency words. Informally, you may look at students' writing to see which high-frequency words are spelled accurately and which words you need to teach, practice, and reinforce. You might also look at running records and keep a running list of high-frequency words that students were unable to read with automaticity. As mentioned in the kindergarten assessment section, a formal high-frequency words assessment can be found on the TCRWP website. It contains lists of increasingly more difficult words. To know which list to give students initially, you might start with the previous year's assessments, if possible. Otherwise, look to see which list has words similar to those in the books the student is independently reading and start there.

WORD STUDY INSTRUCTION IN FIRST AND SECOND GRADE

Similar to our recommendation for kindergarten, we recommend you divide your word study time strategically. In most first- and second-grade classrooms, we recommend dividing the time between phonics and high-frequency words. Below is a sample two-week schedule. Note that you may stay with one phonics concept for a week, or, if children need more practice, extend that concept into the second week. Following this, we provide more details on each instructional method.

Week 1

Monday—High-frequency words: introduce words

Tuesday—Phonics: sorting

Wednesday—High-frequency words: *look, say, name, cover, write, check*

Thursday—Phonics: interactive editing—Game On!

Friday—High-frequency words: word hunt

Week 2

Monday—Phonics: sorting (new phonics feature or repeat from Week One)

Tuesday—High-frequency words: introduce words

Wednesday—Phonics: interactive editing—Game On!

Thursday—High-frequency words: *look, say, name, cover, write, check*

Friday—Phonics: guess the covered word

First- and second-grade students will spend much of their word study time engaged in the study of spelling patterns. Students will first study CVC patterns, or short vowel patterns followed by CVCe and CVVC or vowel teams, and last, ambiguous vowel patterns.

Phonics

There are many instructional methods for teaching phonics that can be fruitful in first- and second-grade classrooms, and many teachers have their own tried-and-true methods to which they adhere. Below, we outline some of the methods that have emerged as our favorites.

Sorting is an important kind of phonics instruction for supporting spelling pattern study. Sorting helps students uncover and notice patterns in sound and print and then apply and extend patterns to new words while reading and writing. Closed sorts are those in which the teacher provides the parameters of the sort accompanied by direct, explicit instruction. Open sorts are more inquiry-based, in which students determine how to classify the items in the sort. Both kinds lead to critical thinking and active student involvement.

To prepare for a sorting lesson, decide whether students will be sorting by sound or by visual patterns or both. If you'd like students to sort by sound, provide a group of pictures of objects with names that fall into one of the categories you'll be teaching. For example, if teaching long *a* and short *a*, provide pictures of objects such as mat, cap, cape, rake, and cake. If students will be sorting by visual patterns, provide cards with the words written on them. Of course, you might choose to have your students sort both ways, in which case you would provide both pictures and words. To encourage even deeper critical thinking, you might throw in a few words that don't fit into either category.

If you are engaging your class in a closed sort, you might present two words, such as *cap* and *cape*, and then model how you would do a sort using these words. Then you might say, "Let's say the key words and compare them. What do you notice about how they sound? When we say *cap*, you hear the short *a* sound. When you say *cape*, you hear the long *a* sound." Then, study a few words together before setting children to work in partnerships or small groups, sorting the rest of the words according to the principles you outlined.

To debrief at the end of the lesson, point out the patterns you'd like your students to notice, such as long /a/ words with an *e* at the end.

If engaging students in an open sort, you might begin by leading them to say the words aloud together, so that they all hear the sounds in each word. Then, you might ask them to work in groups to think of ways that the words fit together by sound. As with the closed sort, be sure to debrief at the end.

We recommend you channel your students to sort multiple times, with the goal of improving their speed and accuracy each time. Coach them as they work, encouraging them to recognize, recall, judge, and then apply the pattern or principle. For example, you might say, "Tell me about this column. What do you notice about these words?" or "Tell me about these words that don't seem to fit in either category."

Another phonics instruction method we've found to be particularly helpful is Dorothy Hall and Patricia Cunningham's "Guess the Covered Word" activity (Hall and Cunningham 2008). This activity supports readers in orchestrating the multiple sources of information found in text—the meaning of the text, syntax or language structure, and the visual information, or, in this case, the phonics concept.

One way to do this is to create a text based on science or social studies content you've been teaching. Let's imagine a second-grade classroom that has been studying rural, suburban, and urban communities in social studies, and in word study, the *r*-controlled spelling pattern. The teacher might write the following text with the underlined words covered up.

> People live in urban, <u>suburban</u>, and rural communities. In urban areas, which are cities, there are many buildings and little open space. You often see many people <u>board</u> buses, subways, and trains because many people get around by using public <u>transportation</u>.
>
> Suburban areas are outside cities, and people often travel to the cities for work. They have smaller <u>populations</u> than cities.
>
> Rural areas are areas with large amounts of land and fewer people than the other areas. Rural areas are usually far from urban communities. People live in forests, plains, deserts, and farms.

The teacher could then present the text to the children with the underlined words covered and say, "Today, you are going to do some reading about the different types of communities that you've been learning about in social studies. You see that I've covered up some of the words. As you read, think about what we know about the topic, and think what word might make sense and also sound right in the sentence. Then we'll peek at parts of the word to check to see if we are right. We'll be especially thinking about the *r*-controlled spelling patterns we've been studying."

Encourage the class to read along with you as you start the text, and when you get to a covered word, encourage them to use their content knowledge to guess the word that might fit there. Then, reveal the word, one part at a time. When you come to a part with the spelling pattern you'd like to emphasize, pause before revealing the word and ask students to think about how that part might be spelled. For example, if working with the word *suburban*, you might say, "Let's say the first part and then the second part, *sub-ur*. What letters do you expect to see for the /r/ sound? Turn and talk to your partner." Some children might suggest *er* and others *ur*. You might give them a hint, such as "Remember that *er* usually comes at the end of a word. We know that *suburban* still has another part—*ban*." Ideally, most children will guess that *ur* comes next. Then, reveal the remaining parts of the word to confirm their guesses.

Interactive Writing

After a session of sorting or "guess the covered word" to teach and practice a phonics concept in isolation, it is helpful to do some work with that concept in the context of writing. You may want to lead a more traditional interactive writing session, such as the one we described earlier when discussing kindergarten phonics. You could simply change the phonics concept to one you are studying with your first- or second-graders.

One variation of traditional interactive writing is interactive editing. Game On! is an engaging way to approach interactive editing with first- and second-graders. Before the session begins, we recommend studying your students' data, including their writing, to decide on the work that you want to support. You may notice that your kids need help with a particular spelling pattern. Plan to make mistakes in your interactive writing that resemble those your children are making in their writing.

You might begin a Game On! session like this: "Writers, we've been working on our 'Ladybug Life Cycle' class book. Today we'll continue to work on the book by playing Game On! Remember that we drew a diagram and wrote labels about our ladybug yesterday?" Then, channel kids to work on sentences for the first page. Ask them to turn and talk about what sentences might fit there. As they talk, listen for words that fit with the phonics concepts you'd like to highlight. Then, write a sentence or two, intentionally misspelling words that fit with the concept.

For example, if you are highlighting CVC and CVCe words, you might write:

Chapter 1: The Egg Stag

A femal ladybug lays an egg

on a leaf. It needs to be in a

saf place so other insects will

note eat it.

Then, ask children to count how many mistakes they see. After noting that many children found four mistakes, write the number four at the top of the page and announce, "Game On!" Signal for the children to turn and talk to their partners to name the mistakes. "There needs to be an *e* at the end of *stage*," one child might say to his partner. "She wrote *saf*. It's supposed to be *safe*," another might say. "She forgot the *e*!" Call the class back together and edit the spelling of the incorrect words. Finally, remind them to do this work in their own writing and to pay attention to vowels in their reading.

Writing Workshop

During writing workshop, some teachers have children do this work in their writing folders so that they are transferring the editing work to their writing. The teacher might place a Post-it on a page of the child's writing with a number on it that represents the number of words on the page that need to be fixed. This provides the child with some focused editing work.

High-Frequency Words

First- and second-grade students will still need time for explicit practice of high-frequency words in isolation and in context. Most teachers begin studying high-frequency words right away at the start of first grade, with children learning around three words a week, building to five a week. Second-graders are apt to start the year learning five words a week. We recommend making printed high-frequency word cards for each student, so that they can use them for activities in isolation and then keep them in a baggie for repeated practice. The goal is automaticity, so students will need repeated practice reading the words. We recommend that you draw upon students' high-frequency word assessments to determine which words they need to study. Students truly own a word when they use it in their writing correctly with consistency, so by looking at students' writing, you can get a sense of which words to study across the year.

A trusted activity for teaching high-frequency words is Diane Snowball and Faye Bolton's activity "look, say, spell, cover, write, check" (1999). To get this started, distribute dry erase markers and white boards in the meeting area. Ask students to pick up a card and first *look* at the word, studying it by noticing how many letters it has, saying each letter in order, and so on. You might tell kids to take a mental picture, like a detective such as Cam Jansen would, and then close their eyes and try to see the word in their minds. If they can picture the word, they should continue; if not, they should stay at *look* and study the word a bit longer. Next, ask students to *say* the name of the word out loud and then *spell* it by saying or even chanting each letter. Besides just saying the letters, you may want the students to trace over the actual letter with their fingers. Tracing slows the process down and incorporates movement, voice, and visual, thus increasing the chances of remembering. Next, ask students to *cover* the word (or flip it over) and *write* it on their white boards. Last, ask them to uncover the word or flip the card over, say the word, and *check* letter by letter.

Students can do the "look, say, spell, cover, write, check" routine three times for each word. To differentiate this activity, you can tell the students to start with a quick "buddy test" of their high-frequency words. Students can read their whole stack of high-frequency cards with a partner. If a student pauses too long or does not know a word, it can go in the "unknown" pile. Instead of only focusing on the five words of the week, each child can work on the activity with the words he needs to remember.

Children can also hunt for their high-frequency words in their reading and their writing. For this activity, channel students to work in pairs, hunting for high-frequency words in both their book baggies and their writing folders. As they come across high-frequency words, ask them to mark them, perhaps with highlighter tape. You might ask students to track their work by tallying how many times they find a particular word or how many words they find in all.

Chapter 12

Shared Reading

TO IMAGINE SHARED READING, think of the times when you've attended a concert of a favorite singer. The star performer picks up the mike and takes the lead in a hit song. The audience sings along, and whenever the performer pauses in the song, the crowd fills in the lyrics. The crowd's engagement is high, and their voices come together to almost overpower the lead singer. Then, the song reaches a tricky part and the performer takes over, singing louder to lead the crowd. After all, she knows every up and down of that song and can help the crowd sing with success, and she does that without talking about her interpretation of the song. She simply steps forward at key intervals, singing louder, takes the lead, then pauses for the crowd to fill in the space and sing alone.

No one in that room raises a hand to request permission to contribute a line; no one worries that he might have a word wrong. The mood is celebratory, participatory—a bit raucous, even—but that's what happens when everyone participates fully.

ESTABLISHING A CELEBRATORY SPIRIT FOR SHARED READING

If you watch teachers who are especially comfortable with shared reading, you'll see that they function very much like that singer. You'll get a sense of joyous participation in reading, and you'll grasp how shared reading can feel like a hootenanny.

The interesting thing about shared reading, though, is that although this is whole-group work at its finest, its roots are in the intimacy of a father reading with his toddler on his lap. That father of shared reading was Don Holdaway, the Australian literacy researcher who developed shared reading in an effort to re-create in the classroom the experience of what he referred to as lap-reading.

Since then, shared reading has become a staple in any balanced literacy primary classroom. Its honored position comes not just from the way shared reading brings a class together around a love of reading, but also from the instructional payoff. Shared reading provides a bridge linking direct instruction, active engagement, and independent reading, connecting the work of reading to students, with students, and by students.

First and foremost, you need an inclusive, celebratory spirit and a sense of intimacy. The goal is for all students to be comfortable participating in shared reading sessions, so that by the end of the week, a chorus of children's voices overtakes yours. To do this, avoid calling on students to read aloud sections of the text to the class, and instead, invite all students to read the text at once, saying, "Will you join me in reading this book? Let's read with one voice, saying the words together." Watch teachers who do this well, whether by visiting colleagues or by viewing videos, including those on the TCRWP website.

You may have practical questions: How long should these shared reading sessions take? Do I tap the pointer under each word or draw it across the page? Do I read fluently, or do I slow my reading to match that of my students?

Shared reading sessions move quickly. You'll likely find that your most productive shared reading sessions move students first through a warm-up text and then through the focus text, with a few pauses for conversation along the way, all in a span of ten to fifteen minutes. To engage students while keeping these sessions brief, you might weave in a few turn-and-talks, saying to students, "Whoa! That felt important! Turn and tell your partner what just happened." Then, instead of calling on individual students to share their thoughts, you might say, "I heard you saying that those darn squirrels found a way to get into the bird feeder, despite Old Man Fookwire's great plan," highlighting quickly what students shared. This keeps the focus on students' shared experience with the text, rather than on one child's comprehension or fluency, and allows you to maintain momentum while reading.

Whether or not you choose to point to words and how you do so will depend on students' reading levels and your goals for your students. For students reading at levels A through D—those who need support with one-to-one matching—you might point under each word as you read it, mirroring the work you hope your young readers do when reading independently. Then, as students move to levels E and F, you might move to sliding your finger under the line of words. By levels G through I, you'll likely remove that scaffold, putting your finger next to the end of the line so children have support tracking the line being read. Regardless, what researchers such as Tim Rasinski emphasize is critically important is that students are able to see the text and are encouraged to move their eyes across it as they read together.

A performer wouldn't slow down her singing to match the crowd, and in the same way, you'll want to avoid reading in a staggered way, slowing down to match the voices of your students. Instead, demonstrate fluency for students. Model how the book ought to sound, reading it as you hope students soon will, with words grouped together, silently urging kids to keep up with you. You'll find that the group develops momentum as you read along fluently, and before you know it, your meeting area will be filled with smiling, engaged readers.

During a shared reading session, closely watch your students to observe their strengths and needs. Watch for the places where they join you, leaping into the text confidently, and watch for the places where their voices trail off or one or two dominant voices take over. At these times, try to develop theories that will shape your later shared reading sessions. "This is a place where I know students will leap in," you might think, "so I can trail my voice off here and really let students take over." Since you're sharing the reading load with students, you can watch them closely, becoming more aware of what they can do and what they need to learn to access harder texts. These strengths and needs can later be expanded on in minilessons, conferences, and small-group work.

You can return to favorite texts day after day, time after time, until you and your class are at home with shared reading. Then you can extend your use of this powerful teaching method to a wider range of teaching points. Shared reading gives children in a classroom community the conviction, "Of course I can read!" It supports agency for all readers trying out what they know, drawing on their growing repertoire of strategies to tackle tricky words, build meaning, and reading with greater fluency and expression. With your coaching and modeling, students can learn more about reading while you learn more about their strengths and needs.

In this chapter, we'll first tackle the logistics of shared reading. We'll describe text selection considerations and outline a possible structure for shared reading sessions across a week that is replicable regardless of reading level, genre, or unit of study. Then, we'll suggest key ways you can gear your shared reading sessions to address the unique needs of your students to support comprehension, reading process, word study, and fluency.

TEXT SELECTION

Think about the texts that you and your class adore. Your children's love of those texts—perhaps the song "The Itsy Bitsy Spider" or a big book version of *Mrs. Wishy Washy*—will help you be at home with shared reading.

In general, it's a good idea to choose books that are slightly above the independent reading level of the bulk of your class. Imagine you have a class of first-graders. In September, the benchmark level for first grade is D/E. If most of your students are at this level, you'll need to teach and coach into skills and behaviors that will move them toward level F/G books and therefore use shared reading texts at these higher levels. If a larger percentage of your students are below or above benchmark level, you'll need to adjust the level of texts, as well as the skills and behaviors you highlight, to match students' specific reading needs.

You'll also want to select warm-up texts. These can be poems, songs, class charts, or interactive writing you've done together. We suggest you read one of these texts briefly, at the start of a shared reading session, as a way to build fluency and warm students up for the work ahead. Of course, these warm-up texts can also be added to students' book baggies.

You'll need some way to make the text you select accessible to students, so all eyes can gather on one shared copy. You might use a document camera to enlarge and project a text, gather students around a big book, or copy a selection of the text onto chart paper. If you choose a book of which you have multiple copies, be sure to give students access to these after the shared reading sessions, so they can read them independently.

We suggest that you give children copies of beloved shared reading texts to read on their own. Just imagine the excitement when children get to choose some of these texts to read during reading workshop.

PLANNING SHARED READING: POSSIBLE STRUCTURES ACROSS A WEEK

Each unit of study in this series includes a five-day plan for shared reading. These plans highlight one text and revolve around reading the shared text repeatedly, and of course, children will also be rereading the books in their baggies during reading workshop. As you take children through five days of work with one book, you can show them the ways readers return to a text again and again, each time getting more and more out of the text, showing readers that it's fun to know a book by heart.

One benefit of the five-day plan is that it serves as a template you can use with other texts. This plan shows how you can give your students a lot of practice with foundational skills across several texts so that they transfer these skills to the texts they read independently. Remember, you are not just

teaching a text; you are also working on sets of skills that students need to orchestrate and integrate in reading all texts. This plan will help you decide both what to teach and how to teach those skills through shared reading.

Here is one possible sequence to plan shared reading across a week.

Day One: Book Introduction, Comprehension, and Word Solving (MSV)

On the first day of shared reading, introduce the new book and several important vocabulary words or concepts. Be careful not to overdo the time spent introducing the book and the words, so you can spend most of your time reading. Invite children to chime in, even the first time you read the book. You'll be amazed how many leap right in! The first encounter with the text is a perfect time to practice using multiple sources of information (MSV) to tackle tricky words.

To prepare for your lesson, choose a few words in the text that you and the children will pay extra attention to. Cover these words with Post-its. Then, as you read with the kids, stop at each of these covered words and guide students as they use their word-solving strategies to figure the words out. In choosing which words to cover, keep in mind the word work students are doing at these levels. For example, if you are teaching digraphs (such as *ch*, *sh*, and *th*), you might partially cover words that begin that way. Allow students to see the digraph and to use those letters to help them guess the word you have covered. Then reveal the last part of the word so they can confirm or revise their guesses. After reading, think about any important comprehension points, possibly connected to the current unit of study.

Day Two: Cross-Checking

On the second day, we recommend you and your students reread the book, this time with a focus on cross-checking. As you read together, stop occasionally to say to students, "Wait, I'm not so sure about that. Is that word right? Let's check it!" When you do this, sometimes you'll read the word correctly and stop to check, "Does that make sense? How do we know?" or you might say, "What are three ways to check if that word is right?" Other times, you might purposefully make some errors while reading. You might say, "Wait a minute, I thought the word was *running*, and you think it's *raining*? Let's check it!" In this way, you can encourage kids to monitor their own reading and to become more self-reliant.

Day Three: Word Study

On the third day, use the same text, this time focusing on word study concepts, perhaps hunting for spelling principles you're working on with students. Again, choose activities relevant to the word work students need at these levels such as sight words, parts of words, short vowel patterns, plurals, rhyming, syllables, and so on. You might ask children to come to shared reading with personal word walls or white boards to reinforce the word work that comes up during this session of shared reading.

Day Four: Fluency

During the fourth time reading the text, you might focus on fluency. Remember, there are three parts to fluency: parsing, pacing, and using prosodic cues. First, work on parsing, or breaking up sentences and paragraphs into meaningful parts. This helps readers make their reading sound smooth and fluid. You can help them read all the way through phrases, sentences, and paragraphs without stopping to figure out words and without stumbling over pronunciation. Since this is their fourth time reading the text, children will most likely be able to read right through parts that were tricky for them earlier. Next, you can work on pacing. It's important to read not too quickly and not too slowly. When young readers read too slowly, meaning breaks down and understanding is lost. On the other hand, if they read too quickly, they often miss important ideas and information, also compromising understanding. Depending on the level of your readers, you might use your pointer to scoop up the words, nudging readers to follow at an appropriate pace. Finally, support your readers in using prosodic cues. Prosodic cues are all the meaning cues an author provides. You can channel students to study cues such as punctuation and font characteristics, italicized print, bold print, or enlarged print. Using all these bits of information in a text positions students to read with increased expression and drama.

Day Five: Orchestration/Comprehension

During the final time reading the text, rally children to put together everything they've practiced all week to read accurately and fluently. In addition, deepen their comprehension work, helping students to develop even bigger ideas about the text. For example, after reading the text, you might set students up to discuss it with the whole group or with a partner.

However, we also want to acknowledge that there are other ways to plan for shared reading. For instance, you may decide to use a *different* book each day of the week. This kind of shared reading work is particularly important if you want to show your kids how the reading process works in many different kinds of books. You may choose this plan when you want to get your readers involved in using a repertoire of strategies to make meaning from a text. Also, if you want to expose your children to a variety of text types, a book a day can be more powerful than a book a week.

Feel free to think outside the box when you're planning for shared reading. You might decide to take time to extend some texts, perhaps through interactive or shared writing, drama, or talking about the book. What is most important is that you support readers with comprehension, accuracy, and fluency while keeping the energy level high, whether you do this across five days using the same text, or on one day because you plan to move to a new text on the next day.

A SHARED READING SESSION

Just as reading workshops are highly structured and predictable, giving students a sense of how minilessons go and the confidence to take on new and challenging work, your shared reading sessions will probably follow a fairly predictable structure, beginning with a warm-up, followed by a choral reading of a chosen text, and ending with an activity to respond to or extend the text. We suggest you move through a session quickly, in a ten- to fifteen-minute chunk of time.

Warm Up

We recommend starting each shared reading session by quickly rereading a familiar text, such as a class chart, a poem, or even just a part of a favorite book. This warms students up for the work ahead and builds confidence and excitement. Also, because you'll be returning to a familiar text, this warm-up time reinforces fluency.

(Re)reading of the Text with a Focus

This portion of the shared reading session occupies the bulk of the lesson. Each day, you'll focus on a different aspect of reading. One day the focus might be fluency, another day, word solving or vocabulary. Always keep in mind that the primary purpose of reading is comprehension and the effective orchestration of strategies, so no matter what, put the focal skill into a meaningful context.

After Reading

On some days, you may want to lead students in a brief follow-up activity after reading. This might be a word work activity, such as a game with a star name (see Chapter 11) or work sorting magnetic letters on a white board. Or you can ask children to write a few words on individual white boards or find words on the word wall or look through their own writing for particular kinds of words. You may wish to do an inquiry study, in which you ask partners to tell each other what they noticed about the words they studied today. Other days, you might end with a quick turn-and-talk focusing on comprehension.

DEVELOPING YOUR FOCUS

Shared reading is most effective when the skills practiced are those that students especially need to strengthen. Closely analyzing your data can help you plan successful shared reading. Look over running records along with any other assessments, such as concepts about print or high-frequency word or letter-sound identification, as well as your conference notes, to look for patterns and trends. What kinds of comprehension, reading process, word study, vocabulary, and fluency work do your students most need?

Based on your students' needs, use the sections below to create your shared reading plans. If many students are struggling with fluency, for example, you might closely read the section on developing a focus on fluency, noting ways you can support fluency development across the week. Similarly, if you notice students need additional support with word study, you might scan that section for suggestions.

Developing a Focus on Comprehension

When focusing on comprehension during shared reading, emphasize key skills, such as using pictures, drama, predicting, and retelling to enhance understanding. One of the early ways to help children make meaning as they read is to channel them to glean as much as possible from the pictures. In the kindergarten unit *Super Powers: Reading with Print Strategies and Sight Word Power*, Amanda Hartman suggests you start by saying, "Super-readers, let's reread *Brown Bear, Brown Bear*. As we read, let's stop and study the pictures on the pages and try and say all the things that we see!"

It's important to help students actually study the pictures, looking around at the different parts of the animals. After you all read the first page you might say, "Let's look at this bear and say all the things we see!" Kids might notice four paws, two ears, and a black nose. Then you might add, "Let's zoom in closely here. Look at those paws. I see long sharp nails!" Of course, you'll want to balance an attention to detail with an attention to pace, shifting soon to say, "Let's read the page again and get ready for what's next." After the class rereads the page you might say, "So, what are we going to see next?" After children predict, you could say, "Let's see if you are right," and then turn the page to confirm the prediction and read the page together. In this way, you're helping children synthesize the text, accumulate more details, and understand the value of rereading.

Another way to deepen students' comprehension of texts and to support language development is to channel readers to act the text out as they read and reread it. During choice time, for example, you could provide materials for students to make simple props or puppets and then encourage them to use these to act out the story as they turn the pages of the book. Or you may be content with rallying children to use simple gestures and body language to perform scenes.

In the shared reading that accompanies the first-grade *Meeting Characters and Learning Lessons: A Study of Story Elements* unit, Liz Dunford Franco prompts students to share the details they learned about the characters and discuss how the characters' feelings changed across the story. She also shows how you can support students' ability to retell the big events of the story in order. Note that she channels partners to work together to retell the important parts. "Where did this story take us? What happened at the beginning, middle, and end? Turn and retell the story with your partner." You might model sketching a symbol (like a happy face or a scared face or the words *excited* or *afraid*) on a Post-it to track each character's feelings across the story.

Extending this work in the second-grade nonfiction unit *Becoming Experts: Reading Nonfiction*, Lindsay Wilkes and Celena Dangler Larkey prompt students to use the features of the text to revise and focus information predictions. It is important to support the thinking work readers engage in before reading, during reading, and after reading. After all, readers are *always* thinking. You can support this thinking work by saying, "Let's preview *all* the different parts that we will read to anticipate what information we might learn in *each* part!" You can use the table of contents page, pausing especially at the chapters you have selected to read. Continue the predicting work with the class by stopping at selected chapters and prompting partnerships to predict what they will learn about in each part, briefly flipping back to the table of contents and tapping a new chapter title before going to that chapter in the book.

After reading, you might go back and reread a chapter to help students accumulate information, holding on to more key details from the text. During this time, refer to your reading workshop anchor charts. This is another opportunity to reinforce the strategies children are practicing independently during reading workshop.

Developing a Focus on Integrating Multiple Sources of Information

Of course, shared reading is a prime opportunity to support children in orchestrating the reading process, drawing from a growing repertoire of strategies to read with greater automaticity and accuracy. For example, to support early readers' ability to integrate multiple sources of information, you can cover a few words and encourage children to use the picture and the pattern to help them read. In kindergarten, using *Brown Bear, Brown Bear, What Do You See?*, for instance, you could mask the noun (animal) on the page, so that students use the picture to consider what word it might be. Choose three animals your class knows well, such as duck, horse, and frog. Then prompt them, "What might this word be? Check the picture. Let's reread and see if that would make sense. It does! Now, what letter will we see at the beginning of the word if it is /d/uck?" Overexaggerate the sound /d/. "Let's check. It is a *d*! Let's keep reading." You also might cover the color word, such as *purple* or *white*, and say, "Let's look at the picture and think about this first word. I see a cat. I see a purple cat. Will it be cat or purple cat? Let's remember the pattern of the book. Purple? Do we see the letter that makes the /p/ sound at the beginning? We do! *Purple* starts with *p*! Let's read this page together!"

In the first-grade nonfiction unit *Learning About the World: Reading Nonfiction*, the shared reading text is Mary R. Dunn's *Owls*. Amanda Hartman covers up the word *gulp*. When the class gets to the covered word, she prompts kids to integrate sources of information by saying, "What words would make sense here? Let's think about what is happening and try to think about a couple of words that might fit. *Eat*, *slurp*, *chew*. These are all good guesses that sound right and make sense with what is happening. Now let's look at *all* the parts of the word. /g/ul/p/. Say it with me. Gulp. I guess they eat really quickly in one bite. Let's reread this page now." You might choose a few additional words to cover up and ask students to guess, such as *silently* on page 10 and *listen* on page 20. This is sometimes referred to as "guess the covered word" but is technically a close reading activity.

In the first-grade foundational unit, *Readers Have Big Jobs to Do: Fluency, Phonics, and Comprehension*, during a second reading of *Tumbleweed Stew*, by Susan Stevens Crummel, you might remind readers to continue using all they know to solve words and to check that they are reading with accuracy. Because it's a second reading, you might compliment children on all the word-solving work they did the previous day and let them know that their work isn't finished yet. Emphasize that even when readers *re*read books, they can struggle with tricky words. One of the most important jobs readers have is to make sure they check that words make sense, sound right, and look right. Make sure you always ask, "Does it make sense?" first, so that students start with meaning instead of just visual information.

Choose a few words ahead of time that you'll coach children to check. There are a few ways you can set this up. You might use highlighter tape or flexible sticks (such as Wikki Stix®) around or under the words to signal that they need to be checked. Or you could mask each word with a label or Post-it note on which you've written either the correct word or a partially correct attempt. When you reach each word in the text, prompt students to check if it makes sense and sounds right before revealing the covered word to check that it also looks right. Occasionally, you may insert the correct word to emphasize that when readers check words, they sometimes find that they were already right.

Another way to set children up to check is to let your voice trail off at key points in the text. If you've arrived at a tricky part, you're likely to hear the group begin to mumble or try out several words. This is a perfect spot to stop and say, "Readers, it sounds like we have some different ideas about what this word could be. We'd better check it!"

Or you might simply pause with the students as you read, modeling your own uncertainty. For example, when Buzzard arrives you might read, "Buzzard floated," and then exclaim, "Wait a minute readers, *buzzard floated*? Does that make sense? We'd better check it!" Then guide students to triple-check that yes, it does make sense, sound right, and look right!

As always, be aware of your pacing, making sure you don't stop to check so many words that the story is lost. You want to model reading a text just above the level of the majority of your students, one in which children have work to do but not so much that they are constantly stopping and losing meaning.

Developing a Focus on Word Study

A shared reading focus on word study supports early concepts about print and phonological and phonemic awareness and helps students transfer the principles they are learning and use them in context. To support students' growing understanding of print concepts, for example, you might pause at the start of a new page and think aloud, "Hmm, . . . How many words are on this page? Let's count them together. Now, Brandon, come up and point under each word as we all read this page together. Make it match!"

You can also use shared reading to develop students' phonological awareness. In kindergarten, for example, you might choose a specific letter sound, using the first letter of a child's name. In the kindergarten *We Are Readers* unit, Natalie Louis asks students to clap if they hear a word that starts with that sound. You might say, "As I read this next page, listen closely for words that start with /w/ like *William*. If you hear a word that starts the same way, clap once!" After reading a shared text, you might play a quick rhyming game with young students, choosing different words from the text and inviting students to name both real and nonsense rhyming words.

Word meaning and vocabulary are crucial areas of word study, and daily shared reading sessions are a perfect opportunity to support these concepts. In the kindergarten unit *Becoming Avid Readers*, Marjorie Martinelli and Christine Holley show that when reading *Gossie*, by Olivier Dunrea, you can point out that little words can hold big meanings. They suggest beginning the third reading of this book by asking the question, "Do you think Gossie is a boy or a girl gosling? Let's read today trying to figure that out." When you read on page 6, "She wears them when she eats," they suggest you stop and say, "Wait a minute. It says, '*She* wears them when *she* eats. That word *she* might be the clue we are looking for! What do you think?" You can expect that several children will be jumping up and down declaring that a *she* is a girl, so Gossie must be a girl gosling.

You can commend children's highly skilled detective work before posing another question about another word. You might say, "You know what? You did a really good job of figuring out that the word *she* referred to Gossie. Now as I reread this sentence again, I am wondering what the word *them* refers to. 'She wears *them* when she eats.' What could *them* be referring to?" If needed, follow up with prompts like "Hmm, . . . it says she wears *them*. What is Gossie wearing?" Once you hear "Boots!" show how you can check this by substituting the word *boots* for *them*. "She wears *boots* when she eats. She wears *boots* when she sleeps," and ask if that makes sense and sounds right.

As students move into these higher-level texts, the ability to fluently and flexibly break apart words is critical. Be sure to provide plenty of opportunities for them to practice this work. In the first-grade unit *Readers Have Big Jobs to Do: Fluency, Phonics, and Comprehension*, Havilah Jesperson suggests that prior to reading the text, you might choose several words from it to break apart in multiple ways, beginning with easier words. Say, "Readers, let's see if we can think of a few ways we might break this word into parts." Then you could use magnetic letters to demonstrate, sliding the letters apart to emphasize the different options. As you read further into the text, you could set partners up to do this work with one or two words that they write on their white boards. You might say, "Readers, now you and your partner can try this work. Choose a word on this page that you'd like to work with, and write it on your white board. Then think, 'How can we break this word into parts?'"

Children who are reading level J–M books might need additional practice using prefixes and suffixes to solve words. In the second-grade unit *Bigger Books Mean Amping Up Reading Power*, Brianna Parlitsis and Lauren Kolbeck support children with this after reading a selection from *Happy Like Soccer*. If you decide to focus on this work, you might let students know that, in this book, you have noticed some words with prefixes and suffixes. Students could then try adding a prefix or suffix to a word on their white boards, changing its meaning. You might say, "Write the word *read* on your board. Now, change the word *read* to mean *read again*. Do this by adding just a few letters to the beginning or the end of the word." Coach students as they turn *read* into *reread*. "Wow, you're really getting the hang of this. Many of you knew to add the prefix *re-* to the front of the word, and now you have made the word *reread*."

Practice a few examples on the white board, and then transfer the work to *Happy Like Soccer*. Reread sentences that have prefixes and suffixes, and let students know that when they come to these words, they can use the prefix and/or suffix to help them decode and think about meaning.

You can also use shared reading to support students in understanding what words mean. As children move into more complex texts, your word-solving work will likely move toward a greater focus on vocabulary. In *Series Book Clubs*, Amanda Hartman coaches students to focus on the meanings of words that they know in different ways. In "My Very Strange Teeth," from *The Stories Julian Tells*, Amanda starts to read the text together with students. In advance, she covers the word *pliers*, knowing it may be new to the children, or it may be a word they need to figure out from context. She then prompts students to describe a pair of pliers to their partners, saying what they look like, what they do, and giving examples. If you do this with your class and students do not know the word, have them think about what kind of word it is, what it is similar to, and what it does. Then reveal the word and continue reading. You may stop and explain in *your* own words what it means, using as many words as you can to describe it. Repeat this with other possibly unknown vocabulary words.

You may want to do this same work to help students monitor and build meaning when reading lines containing literary language. In the second-grade unit *Bigger Books Mean Amping Up Reading Power*, Lauren Kolbeck reminds students of the strategies they know for paying attention to special language. As she leads the shared reading, she asks them to put a thumb up if they notice a place where the author uses special language to communicate something to readers. She demonstrates that readers pause and think, "What special meaning might the author want me to get from this?" For example, when children heard the passage "my shoes have flames" in *Happy Like Soccer*, by Maribeth Boelts, most of them felt sure that Sierra's shoes didn't actually have flames. They decided that, instead, Maribeth Boelts is trying to show that Sierra is running very fast.

Some students may notice not only that Maribeth Boelts uses comparisons in *Happy Like Soccer*, but some of her words—her descriptions—create special images. As you read, students may put their thumb up at the part where it says, "low around the edges." Point out that this phrase is not typically used to describe a feeling. Suggest that students reread that part, bearing in mind what is happening in the story. Prompt them to think about how Sierra must feel, knowing that she loves her auntie, who couldn't come to the soccer game because she had to work. Coach students to use clues in the phrase, such as the word *low*, to see that this phrase shows that Sierra is feeling sad.

Developing a Focus on Fluency

Shared reading is a great time to work with students on phrasing and other core aspects of fluency. You can, for example, move kids beyond reading one word at a time to reading half a line at a time. You can frame out half a line with your hands and have kids say all the words. Then frame the other half and have them say those words. Then have them read the entire line with phrasing. Some teachers do this by scooping half a line at a time. You might also work with students on using punctuation to help with phrasing.

A shared reading warm-up provides ample opportunity to build students' reading fluency. Returning to a favorite familiar text again and again means that children will read with growing ease and confidence. To warm up for shared reading, enlarge a nursery rhyme or poem that is likely familiar to your readers and sing it together. In the kindergarten unit *Bigger Books, Bigger Reading Muscles*, we use "Hickory Dickory Dock." Keep the tone welcoming and upbeat. Say something like "Readers, let's warm up today with a song I think you may know already! It is very catchy, so if it is new for you, you'll get to know it by the second or third round! I'll point under the words. Join me in singing as soon as you are ready!" Remember that after reading the warm-up text across the week, you can give children copies of this text to read during independent reading.

In the shared reading section for *Bigger Books, Bigger Reading Muscles*, the authors suggest helping children pay attention to punctuation and the way it affects readers' voices, using the book *My Bug Box*, by Pat Blanchard and Joanne Suhr. They prompt the class to make an inference about the character to bolster prosody. If you use this book with your class, on its last page, you might point out that the character is asking a question. "Readers, look! This sentence ends with a question mark. Hmm, . . . let's look back. I think all of the other sentences end with periods. Yes, they do. So the authors want us to read this last page differently. On this page, we have to make our voices sound like we are asking a question. But before we reread these words, let's look closely at the picture. How do you think she is feeling? How do you know? Turn and tell your partner."

In the first-grade unit *Learning About the World: Reading Nonfiction*, Amanda Hartman suggests reading and rereading songs with related themes, focusing on fluency and expression. Singing songs is a wonderful way to build fluency and to develop a greater repertoire of texts. You might choose a song to read and reread as your warm-up. You might read it along with a recording or sing it without accompaniment.

Read and reread the song, working with students on first understanding the phrasing, how words in the song are grouped together. After you have read the song once, make sure you take the opportunity to quickly retell what it is about. Then proceed with a few consecutive rereadings. You might do this with students, thinking together about where your voices could place extra emphasis. Finally, reread it once more, thinking about the expression of your voices, gestures that would be fun to accompany the singing, and ways to show expressions on your faces.

In the unit *Second-Grade Reading Growth Spurt*, Shanna Schwartz suggests using *Mercy Watson to the Rescue* by Kate DiCamillo to help students read with expression by paying attention to font characteristics and what is happening in the text. Just as students have had a chance to notice the punctuation, they should have the opportunity to notice and use font characteristics bolds, italics, all caps, enlarged print—to help them read fluently.

When using this book, remind readers that the author puts all of these clues in the text to help them figure out how the book wants to be read. You might add, "But you also need to use what's happening to help you know how to read the words!" Then have children think about how to read a sentence or two, letting the meaning of the words and their font characteristics guide their intonation. You can lead children in reading the passage once and then discussing how it wants to be read. You might ask them to think about which words in the passage should be stressed. Children might decide to slowly say the word *lovely* to give the sentence a dreamy effect, or they might decide that *hopped* should be said quickly and with a high lilt to mimic the ease with which Mercy jumps from the bed.

Shared reading is a powerful tool in primary classrooms. You may find it helps to draw on this method regularly, carving out time each day for shared reading. We think you'll find it particularly helpful, though, when students are having trouble doing the work you're teaching in your minilessons, or it seems your reading workshop is not going smoothly. When that is the case, draw on the shared reading structures detailed in this chapter to support your readers, doing the tricky work alongside them. You'll probably find they're more likely to approximate the work during shared reading, when you're almost carrying them along on your back to offer additional support. Once you've targeted what's difficult for students in shared reading, you might return to the concept in your minilessons and in independent reading, confident that students will now be able to do the work at a higher level.

Chapter 13

Reading Aloud

READING ALOUD is the best way we have to immerse children in the glories of reading, showing them both how and why one reads. "Great literature, if we read it well," Donald Hall has said, "opens us to the world and makes us more sensitive to it, as if we acquired eyes that could see through things and ears that could hear smaller sounds." Together with our children, we gulp down stories—stories that allow us to visit a construction site, work on a farm, and solve mysteries. We construct knowledge about extreme weather, and we assemble a mental model of how to make a pizza. Together with our children, we experience what it means to lose—and to find—ourselves in a story, in history. Word by word, chapter by chapter, we are led into another time and another place, or another field of study.

"Read to them," Cynthia Rylant says. "Take their breath away. Read with the same feeling in your throat as when you first see the ocean after driving hours and hours to get there. Close the final page of the book with the same reverence you feel when you kiss your sleeping child at night. Be quiet. Don't talk the experience to death. Shut up and let those kids think and feel. Teach your children to be moved."

We read not only because it is good for children as readers, but also because it is good for all of us as people. I think, for example, of a teacher in Queens, New York, whose classroom had for years been one of those rooms where everything seemed to be done perfectly well, but there just was no chemistry. The teacher had a lovely author's chair at the front of her meeting area, lovely charts around her room, a daily reading workshop and writing workshop, but it often seemed like her students were going through the motions when they were reading and writing.

Then one day, when the Teachers College Reading and Writing Project staff developer arrived in this teacher's room, she noticed that everything seemed utterly different. The room was charged with energy and intensity. During writing workshop, kids were pouring their hearts out onto the paper, and during reading, the room felt full of care and investment. "What happened?" my colleague asked.

The teacher nodded, knowingly. "Can you believe it?" she said, scanning the room.

"What'd you do?" my colleague asked, big-eyed with amazement.

"We read together," the teacher said. "That's all. We read stories that brought tears to our eyes, like *The Velveteen Rabbit, Love You Forever,* and *Fly Away Home.*" Then she said, "I think I'd been pretending that stories always have happy endings. Reading those books, it tapped into the pain in children's lives and in mine. I started telling the children about how my parents are moving and it's killing me. I told them my stories, and they started telling me their stories, too, and writing them."

A little boy had written about seeing his father go into diabetic shock, and a little girl had written about seeing her father released from jail and how she hugged him and he hugged her and "it is like the greatest love of all."

How powerful it is to read aloud, right smack in the midst of the hopes and heartaches of a classroom, amid friendships that form and dissolve, invitations that come and do not come, clothes that are in or out of fashion, and parents who attend or do not attend the school play. Here, children work out their life and death issues. Doing so with books at their side is a way to help them make sense of it all. Ralph Peterson, author of *Life in a Crowded Place* (1992) suggests that we respond to the challenges of elbow-to-elbow classroom living by using ceremony, ritual, and celebration to create a sense of community in the classroom, and he further suggests that one way to create that sense of community is to read aloud poems and stories as a way to cross the threshold, to mark the classroom as a world apart.

And so we read aloud. We read aloud several times a day; we read to greet the day, to bring a science inquiry to life, to learn about leaves or gravity, and to fall through the rabbit hole of story.

CHOOSING TEXTS TO READ ALOUD

So how does one choose texts to read aloud? My advice is this: choose carefully. Spend your summer reading one book, another, and another, and mulling over your decisions. Think about texts that will open up new topics for your class, turning your students into scientists, historians, or anthropologists. Think about the texts that will bring your class together—to laugh together, to be outraged together, to cry together. Consider books that are more complex

than your students can read on their own, books that can move children toward more complex understanding of characters or settings or issues. Books such as *George and Martha* can promote grand conversations and make students think and think and think.

As you mull over your choice of books, consider their length. You might want to read aloud powerful, complicated books such as *Ramona the Pest, Fantastic Mr. Fox,* or any of Dick King-Smith's books. If you make reading aloud a mainstay in your classroom, by all means turn to books such as these. But if you tend to have a bit of trouble actually finding twenty to thirty minutes a day for reading aloud, then opt for shorter books such as *Pinky and Rex, Chrysanthemum,* or *Koala Lou,* because you won't want your read-aloud to drag on over too many days.

Reading aloud can invite children into heady intellectual work, and more complex books are especially supportive of that work, so don't limit yourself to reading aloud only books that are similar to those your children can read.

For beginning readers, it is important to read texts that invite new concepts, vocabulary, and big ideas to surface. Again, many of these texts will be well above your students' reading levels. For example, if most of your first-graders are reading levels D and E at the beginning of the year, you may read aloud not only texts that are a couple of levels above this, but some that are well above. First-graders can listen to and love *Charlotte's Web.* Reading a wide range of literature also helps to develop thinking readers.

When selecting nonfiction to read aloud, choose with equal care. Often, it's helpful to assemble a text set of related nonfiction read-aloud books so that your read-aloud work can lead and mirror the work you want children to do in their own texts. When you read nonfiction aloud, remember to attend to your tone of voice and body language, just as you do when you read fiction. Watch some great nonfiction videos, such as the Planet Earth series, and listen to the narrator's tone of voice, which imbues great drama into even topics such as flight patterns of geese. Just as you use your voice to help children follow a story, you can use your voice to help them attend to meaning in nonfiction. You can also exaggerate your own response to the content of what you are reading, giving a kind of "Wow, can you believe that?" expression, or a "Hmm, . . . what does *that* mean?" look, to show kids what engaged readers look and sound like. Children need to see how engaging nonfiction can be, and reading aloud offers a chance to bring a sense of burning curiosity and excitement to those texts.

When considering texts, try to choose ones that are well written as well as informative, both so kids will fall in love with nonfiction, and also so if you decide to teach craft techniques, the texts are rich enough to warrant that lens.

USING THE READ-ALOUD TO TEACH THE SKILLS OF PROFICIENT READING

In the classrooms we know best, although texts are read aloud throughout the day for multiple purposes, there is one time, several days a week, that children refer to as read-aloud time, and it's an instructional, interactive read-aloud. This is often at an entirely different time than the reading workshop—perhaps after lunch, or at the end of the day—and it generally lasts at least twenty minutes.

The books that weave their way in and out of a unit of study are sometimes read aloud during this time, with the teacher pacing that read-aloud so as not to read past the portion of the book needed for an upcoming minilesson. Other times, other texts are read aloud. Often in a minilesson, the teacher returns to portions of a text she has read aloud previously—perhaps even months earlier.

Choose the Skills to Teach

To decide what skill you want to highlight in a read-aloud, it helps to read the text to yourself, spying on the intellectual work you do as you read. After (or before) spying on yourself to see the work that you tend to do as you read the passage, you need to decide on the purpose of the read-aloud. While reading those five or six pages, you will have envisioned, predicted, monitored for sense, made personal responses, asked questions, inferred, interpreted, developed theories about characters, and so on. This work may have been especially complex and rich, but you can probably review the work and discern some dominant skills in action. Then you can think about whether that is the work your students need to learn to do, and if so, you'll need to decide on a sequence of thinking that you'll highlight to bring them along. So it is important to decide which sequence of skills the read-aloud will demonstrate and channel readers to use themselves, first with more and then with less scaffolding.

Riding a bicycle requires the seamless integration of many different actions. A biker pedals, steers, balances, distributes his weight on a slope, monitors speed and momentum, and occasionally brakes. Yet while teaching someone to ride a bike, we support a few of these actions ourselves so that the learner need only focus on a handful of skills. With training wheels, we take balance and weight distribution *off* the instructional radar completely so learners can focus on pedaling and steering—and ringing the bell.

Teaching reading, in many ways, is similar to teaching swimming or dance or tennis or painting. When any of these activities are done proficiently, the effect is that of effortless synchronization. But to the practicing novice, it is easiest to focus on a small cluster of related skills, learning to achieve fluidity or fluency with those skills before adding others.

When you do teach three or four reading skills at a time, you might pass the read-aloud text through the sieve of just these skills. That is, reading a text as rich as *Charlotte's Web* or even *Pinky and Rex* might lure you into focusing on envisioning, predicting, critical thinking, and empathizing—often all on the same page. If, however, your instructional aim at a given time is to support readers in envisioning, retelling, and growing ideas about characters, then you can prepare for teaching by spying on yourself as you read the text, this time focusing on those skills.

READING ALOUD ACROSS THE CURRICULUM

What a powerful tool the read-aloud can be for teaching science, social studies, and history! Children learn that they can climb into the skin of the character or subject, whether the skin of a caterpillar as it eats its way out of its cocoon to become a butterfly, experiencing the thrill of metamorphosis, or the skin of George Washington, gathering his weary troops on a wintry Christmas morning, trying to inspire the men to stay with him. You can expect that the child who can stand with other soldiers on that snowy battlefield, who can climb aboard a red blood cell to ride the roller coaster of arteries and veins, will be an avid reader.

You can bring this magic to expository nonfiction as well as to narrative nonfiction. Reading aloud is one of the most effective ways to demonstrate that expository and narrative texts sound and feel different and are structured differently. In fact, you can read expository texts aloud in ways that highlight specific text structures. You might read aloud a part, then stop to think aloud about how that part was organized. "Do you see how on this page the author is teaching us about butterflies by comparing them to moths?" you might say.

Then again, if your instructional focus is on synthesizing and retelling, you might say, as you read aloud, "Let's listen to this next part and see if it builds on what we just learned or if it's about a whole new topic."

MAKING READ-ALOUDS MORE INTERACTIVE

Reading aloud in a way that is spellbinding is an acquired skill, one that requires practice and planning. Those who are well versed rise to the occasion when encountering the thump-bump scary parts, the balloon-floating happy parts, and the slow, sad, knot-in-the-throat parts. These teachers use their hands, their eyes, their posture, their voices, and their hearts. But no matter how thrilling your dramatic interpretation of a read-aloud text may be, to optimize instructional potential, it is important to provide children with the chance and space to respond to the text.

Imagine for a minute that you are learning to drive. There's something to be said for getting into a moving car with a proficient driver, hearing a steady commentary on why he's choosing to brake, why he's accelerating *just so* during an overtake, or what he'd do at a busy roundabout. The next step, however, is for you to actually take your *own* spot behind that wheel, to have that proficient driver egging you on with advice and encouragement when you enter the traffic flow on your first busy roundabout. A read-aloud accompanied by your out-loud thinking serves as a great demonstration, but instruction requires the learner's active involvement.

To pass the baton to children, you need to shift from pausing and thinking aloud to saying, "Stop and think," and then leaving a pool of silence, or saying, "What are you thinking? Turn and talk," and sending children into partnership conversations. Sometimes, instead of saying "Turn and talk," to a group of more proficient readers, you might say "Stop and jot," or "Stop and sketch." Of course, there are many variations on these prompts. Instead of saying "Stop and think," you can say, for example, "Oh my gosh, what's going to happen next? Can you predict? Make a movie in your mind of what will happen next." Then, after a minute of silence, "Let's read and find out." That is, any prompt can be made more specific. "Turn and talk" could be "Turn and talk. What's going to happen next?" or "Stop and retell. What's happened so far?" Still, the two main invitations to give are to think and to talk.

Each of these prompts invites children to develop and articulate their own independent responses to the text, and each does this in a different way. Silent thinking is the most introspective prompt, perfectly suited for especially moving or poignant parts. Turning and talking incorporates a social element, allowing peers to model, imitate, or reinforce each other's ways of responding to text. Asking students to turn and talk also allows you to listen in on their conversations and to assess their understanding and skill work. Stopping and sketching or jotting allows children a moment to sketch a quick image or write a few words, capturing the pictures or thoughts that bubble to the surface of their minds before being pulled back into the flow of the continuing read-aloud. When you plan, think about not just the specific skills that you'll teach during a read-aloud, and not just the points

at which you'll nudge children into responding, but also about the various ways you'll engage them in responding—through silent thought, through talk, or even occasionally, through pencil and paper. You can also combine these prompts in one interaction, asking students first to stop and think briefly to collect their own thoughts, and then to turn and talk about those thoughts with a partner.

Of course, there will be days when you pause more or less or not at all. Indeed, there will be days—and books—that remind you of Cynthia Rylant's advice to end with quiet reverence, to "be quiet" and not "talk the experience to death." There will be other days—and books—that will invite, even beg, questions, discussions, or hot debate. You and your students will decide which of those kinds of days and books are best for your classroom community. A wonderful thing about a read-aloud is that it can be tailored to fit available time and relevant instructional needs and goals. When done often and done well, it can be the binding cement that holds your community of readers together.

SUPPORTING A WHOLE-CLASS CONVERSATION

When you finish reading for the day (or sometimes in the midst of a day's reading), you may want to support children in talking together as a class about the text. You can use these whole-class conversations as opportunities to teach children how to develop ideas about texts, to hold themselves accountable to what the text actually says, to mine passages of the text for interpretations that may not at first be apparent, to think across texts, and to use their higher-level comprehension skills to comprehend with depth, harvesting all the insights and feelings, understandings, and knowledge that the texts can yield. These conversations are enormously important.

Early in the year, you might pause half a dozen times to think aloud in the midst of a story or a nonfiction book. Perhaps once or twice, you might pause to support children in thinking to themselves about something by talking with a partner. "Hmm, . . . I'm really wondering why he did that, are you? Turn and tell your partner what you're thinking."

When you come to the end of a chapter, section, or whole text, you'll need to decide whether to channel the conversation in a particular direction or whether to let the children develop the starting idea. Let's imagine that you choose the latter alternative. You might close the final page of the chapter and

say, "Oh my gosh, my mind is on fire. Is yours? So many thoughts right now. Whoa! Turn and tell your partner what *you're* thinking. Go!"

The room will likely erupt into conversation, and as the children talk, you might crouch among them, listening in. You may overhear a child who is full of an idea that you believe will lead to a generative whole-class conversation. Or, you might enter into a peer conversation and get a couple of kids going on a question or an idea that you're excited about. Make note of these, but let the children keep talking.

At first, students might struggle to generate discussion-worthy ideas. A comment such as, "My Uncle Dave has a hat like the one the main character wears," isn't one that the class as a whole could think about for a long while. And if a book doesn't really provide much information about a minor character, discussing him may not yield much. On the other hand, a question about a main character's motives or a comment about how one event led to another might invoke sustained, thought-provoking conversation. At some point, if children have trouble getting started pursuing generative lines of thought, you might step in to teach them that there are some universal questions about a text that are usually worth discussing.

Questions Readers Ask of Fiction

- What were the important things I learned about the character?

- Why has the character acted that way?

- What is the character thinking, inside (and how do I know)?

- How has the character changed?

- What do you think about the problem(s) the character ran into? Do you agree or disagree with how she responded to this problem?

- What lessons did the characters learn, and what is important about this?

You might model for students how thinking about one of these questions can lead to a line of powerful thinking. Then, signal for them to return to their conversations, now armed with a new way to grow ideas.

After children talk for a few minutes, call for their attention and start the whole-class conversation with an invitation that can become a familiar part of the fabric of the classroom. You might say, "Who can get us started in a conversation? Who's got an idea or a question to share?" Or, you might decide to ask a particular student to share a generative idea that you overheard, thus channeling the conversation to begin with an idea you feel will lead to fruitful talk.

In any case, once you have nodded to a child to get the conversation started, make sure that members of the class look at that child, giving him their attention. "All eyes on Tyrell," you might say, and signal for Tyrell to wait until he has his classmates' attention. It's also a good idea to coach Tyrell to say his idea to them—not to you, not to his collar, and not to a hand held over his mouth.

The hope is that when he puts his idea out there, others will ponder it, and it will spark thoughts in them. It will help children to think in response to the idea if you do so as well. You can model the way you listen deeply, taking in the idea that someone else has put onto the table. "Hmm, . . ." you might say as you reflect on the idea, repeating it aloud to yourself while you think about a response.

If you think the children don't have much to say in response to the idea yet, you can give them a few minutes to develop their thinking. You might ask them to turn and talk to a partner to give them space to mull over ideas without the pressure of sharing them with the whole group.

If you want to support children as they talk together, you might voice over some ideas you're hearing. Or you might whisper tips to some partnerships: "Ask your partner for an example." Or "I was wondering why the character did that. I think it seems rude. What do you think?" In these ways, you can generate more thinking that can then be shared in the whole-group conversation.

After a bit, you might say, "Who can talk back to the idea that Tyrell shared?" and reiterate the idea. The next speaker may address her comments to you, in which case you can signal that she needs to speak to the group and to the original speaker. Then a second, related idea will be on the floor. You may raise your eyebrows and scan the group, asking without words for someone to add on. When one child catches her breath like she can hardly contain the idea that has come to her, try to refrain from calling on her with words, using a gesture instead. The hope is that before long, one child will speak, then another and another, without raising their hands and without you needing to facilitate the entire conversation.

This portion of the conversation, again, merits instruction. There are lots of ways to help students interact with each other directly.

Ways to Help Children Talk Back to Each Other's Ideas in a Book Talk

- You could repeat the idea on the floor and then say, "One way to respond to an idea is to say to yourself, 'I agree (or I disagree) because,' and then say, 'For example . . .' Then, retell part of the story that goes with—or doesn't go with—the idea." Then you could say, "So right now, with a partner, before we talk in the large group, share what you think. 'I agree/disagree because . . .' Then retell a part of the story that goes with your idea."

- You might say, "Readers, one way to grow an idea is to repeat what you heard in your own words and then try and add to it. You can add by giving an example or saying how it is important. You could say, 'That is important because . . .' Or 'One example of that in the book is . . .'"

- You might say, "Another way to grow an idea is to ask questions. After someone says something, make sure that you understand what they

are saying. You can ask your friend to say more or to explain what she means. You could say, 'What do you mean?' or 'Can you give an example?' or 'Why is that important to the book?'"

- You might say, "Get with a partner. I'm going to help you say more about this idea. Partner 1, repeat the idea, and then, after a minute, I'm going to shout out a prompt, like 'This important because . . .' Whatever I say, Partner 2 should repeat the prompt and then use it to keep talking and thinking about the idea." Then, give Partner 1 a few minutes to talk before calling out a prompt such as "That means . . ." Signal for Partner 2 to repeat the prompt and then carry on talking. You might continue switching partners, using different stems, such as, "This is important because . . ." or "What I wonder is . . ."

- You can retell the conversation that children just had and show them how they jumped from topic to topic. Then you can suggest that the class rewind the conversation and try it again, this time using some of the prompts and questions you've shared to develop an idea before jumping to a new idea.

As the conversation unfolds, other ways to support students will likely emerge, and all of these conversational moves can later be taught explicitly. You might, for example, teach students to stop after a bit to retell the conversation, just as they would retell a book.

There are other conversational moves you can teach children to make on their own.

- If someone shares an idea with the group, you can model an appropriate response, for example, "Why do you think that?" or "Can you show us what part of the text made you think this?"

- If an idea has been stated without being grounded in a text, you might whisper or gesture to one child, hinting to him that it would be great to ask his classmate, "How does that go with what is in the book?" When the child takes your suggestion, give a thumbs up.

- If a child takes the conversation to left field, saying something totally unrelated, you can make it clear to the class that it is okay to say, "I'm not sure how that goes with this idea." If, in fact, it doesn't go with the current line of thinking, it is perfectly acceptable to say, "Can we talk about that later, 'cause right now we're talking about . . ."

All of these moves are intended to grow not only students' conversations, but also their thinking. Teaching students to *talk* well about a book teaches them to *think* well about a book. What could matter more?

Chapter 14

Differentiation
Helping All Learners Access the Curriculum

THE STRUCTURE of the reading workshop and its sister, the writing workshop, are both deliberately kept simple and predictable, because the work of helping individual readers and writers requires teachers to be able to do the complex work of listening, adapting, and teaching responsively. The simplicity and clarity of workshop structures have allowed both reading and writing workshops to be built around what is almost a reverence for listening and for responsive teaching. Open any page of the texts written by Don Graves and Marie Clay, two of the most influential people upon whose shoulders reading and writing workshops have been built, and you will hear them rhapsodizing about the need for teachers to take cues from learners. Visit any school that leads effective reading and writing workshops, and you will come away describing those classrooms as responsive and intimate.

The aim of this chapter is to address the challenges and promises of responsive teaching. Clearly, this is one of those topics that deserves a book unto itself, and this may in fact be a topic I take up soon. Surely, there are few topics that matter more. This chapter touches upon ways of helping all kids access the curriculum—and also on approaches that I don't think make sense. I do this on the assumption that saying *yes* involves saying *no*. Warren Buffett, one of the world's top investors, recently said, "People ask me for the secret of my success. It's my ability to say *no*. Day in and day out, I look at investment proposals and I say, 'No, no, no, no.' Then one comes along that looks exactly right and I say, 'Yes.' One *yes* can get you very far." You and I are, in a sense, investors. We look over proposals for what will help our students, and we, like Warren Buffett, need to say "No, no, no, no." Then when one comes along that looks exactly right, we can say *yes*.

READING WORKSHOP AND RTI

Meeting the needs of the diverse learners who enter our classrooms each day is a shared concern for school districts across the country. As outlined in the Individuals with Disabilities Education Improvement Act (IDEIA), reauthorized in 2004, schools must meaningfully and proactively address the needs of all students, including struggling readers, within the regular education classroom, thus reducing the need for special education services. IDEIA mandates that before school districts can identify a child as having a specific learning disability, they must first determine if a child responds to "scientific, research-based intervention" (IDEIA 2004).

Many districts have turned to response to intervention (RTI) as a way to best meet students' needs. RTI requires teachers, schools, and districts to administer research-based universal screening assessments at the start of the school year to all students and then to design classroom-based and out-of-classroom interventions based on that data. Those interventions are to be implemented with fidelity, so they are closely aligned to the curriculum taught in the classroom.

Running records are an approved universal screening tool for RTI, and these assessments provide useful data about which students are not making expected progress (on reading rate, accuracy, and comprehension), data that teachers can use to provide appropriate data-based instruction to meet students' needs within the classroom setting. For additional information about administering running records and analyzing assessment data, see Chapter 6 on assessment in this book. It's important to create a protocol within your school that details how staff will administer running records to ensure reliability of the data.

RTI relies heavily on high-quality instruction within the general education classroom, referred to as Tier I instruction, with the goal of meeting 80–90% of student needs within this setting. This is done through the use of scientific, research-based approaches that include explicit and systematic instruction in phonics and phonemic awareness, vocabulary, fluency, and reading comprehension. These are precisely the principles on which the reading workshop is based. Schools and districts that adopt reading workshop and RTI find that they are well-equipped to meet the needs of their students.

Within an RTI model, children spend the bulk of their time in Tier I instruction, which means that high-quality classroom instruction in reading is critical. The very best pull-out reading intervention, administered in a 30-minute chunk of time, cannot make up for the time children spend in the classroom. Because of this, school districts are wise to invest a significant amount of time and energy into strengthening classroom teaching and learning.

Reading workshop is designed to support all learners, whether or not they are reading on grade level, through differentiated, small-group work and one-on-one conferences as well as through minilessons which are broadly supportive and sometimes include differentiated supports. Reading workshop classrooms are proactive, rather than reactive, with teachers modifying instruction based on the specific needs of their learners. Suggested modifications that can be made to units of study based on student data are detailed across this chapter. Teachers can plan and pull together flexible small groups based on a host of data collected

First Grade Whole Class Data

Students	Level	Monitoring	Searching for			Self-Correcting	Word Test	Spelling Features	Fluency	Comprehension		
			Meaning	Structure	Visual					Summarizing	Character	Synthesizing
1. Jason	F	E	E	C	C	E	86/100	Blends	2		*	
2. Glenda	D	E	E		C		54/100	Blends and Short Vowels	1		*	*
3. Rafi	C		E	E			47/100	Final Consonants	2			
4. Matt	D		E	E	E		99/100	Final Consonants	2	*	*	
5. Jesse	F						139/200	Short Vowels	3			
6. Rewayda	C	E			C		115/200	Short Vowels	1		*	
7. Jazmin	B	E	E	E		E	119/200	Final Consonants	1	*	*	
8. Lucas	B	E		E		E	41/100	Initial Consonants	1		*	
9. Emmy Ruth	E		E	E	E		115/200	Short Vowels	2			
10. Kareem	D	C	E	E	C		149/200	Short Vowels	2	*	*	
11. Christian	G	E	C	C	C		125/200	Long Vowel Patterns	2	*		
12. Yoselin	E	E	C	C	C	E	181/200	Short Vowels	2		*	
Students	Instructiona	Monitoring	Searching For			Self-	Word	Spelling	Fluenc	Comprehension		

KEY: C=CONSISTENT/INDPENDENT E=EVIDENCE/SOMETIMES BLANK=NOT YET APPROXIMATING *=EVIDENT IN THEIR RETELLING
Created by Mary Ann Colbert and Enid Martinez 2010

First Grade Whole Class Data

Students	I Level		Meaning	Structure	Visual	Correcting	Test	Inventory	y	Summarizing	Character	Synthesis
13. Sanai	D	E	E	E	E	E	110/200	Short Vowels	2	*	*	*
14. Kevin	B	C	E	E	C	E	52/100	Initial Sounds	1	*	*	
15. Mya	D		E	E	E		75/100	Short Vowels	3	*	*	
16. Oumar	H	E	C	E	C	E	121/200	Consonant Blends	3	*		
17. Jaime	F	C	E	E	E	E	146/200	Final consonants	2		*	*
18. James	D	E	E	E	E	E	93/100	Short Vowels	3	*	*	*
19. Hailey	G	C	C	C	C	C	119/200	Blends and Short Vowels	2	*	*	
20. Joseph	F	C			C	E	149/200	Short Vowels	3			*
21. Justin	D	E	E		C	E	182/200	Short Vowels	2		*	*
22. Zoe	G	E	E	E	C	E	195/200	Digraphs and Short Vowels	1	*	*	*
23. Enrique	C	E	E		C	E	9/100	Initial Consonants	2		*	*
24. Jesse C.	E	C	C	C	C	C	82/100	Final Consonants	3			*

KEY: C=CONSISTENT/INDPENDENT E=EVIDENCE/SOMETIMES BLANK=NOT YET APPROXIMATING *=EVIDENT IN THEIR RETELLING
Created by Mary Ann Colbert and Enid Martinez 2010

FIG. 14–1 Whole-class data sheets

from progress monitoring tools, including letter-sound identification inventories, high-frequency word lists, spelling inventories, and running records.

A great example of classroom-based interventions came from a first-grade classroom I recently visited. The class was engaged in a reading unit on non-fiction reading skills. The teacher gave a minilesson on studying the page more carefully to learn more information, and then she sent students off to read independently in their just-right books. From her analysis of students' running records, the teacher identified a small group of readers who needed additional support with fluency, so she designed a series of small groups to support students with their intonation. After providing a quick demonstration to highlight how she used her voice to pop out the structure of the text, she coached the readers while they tried the same work in different accessible texts. Then she conferred one-on-one with a student whose spelling inventory and running records suggested she needed more support with short vowel sounds. Next, the teacher conferred with another child who needed to work on checking to see that what he read made sense. While delivering these small groups and conferences, the teacher kept careful records that she could study later to design her ongoing work with these students.

While classroom-based interventions are underway, teachers are expected to regularly monitor student progress toward goals and benchmarks and make adjustments to instruction, providing necessary levels of support until all students are able to achieve success. At times, progress monitoring of student achievement may reveal that students are not making sufficient progress toward benchmarks, and students may be referred to Tier II support. At Tier II, support becomes increasingly intensive, with teachers gathering smaller groups of students several times a week for extended periods of time. This support is provided in addition to, not in place of, Tier I reading instruction, and students cannot be removed from reading, writing, or math instruction for this intervention.

Of course, it's possible that a small number of students will not make adequate progress with the Tier I and II supports provided and will need Tier III support. This support occurs outside of the classroom in addition to the Tier I interventions provided in the general education classroom. This level of support is typically reserved for 1–5% of students. For these interventions, teachers and specialists often choose to draw on supplemental programs designed to target students' specific needs.

It may be useful to keep your school's response to intervention framework in mind as you read through the remainder of this chapter, considering ways your school's RTI program already meets the needs of your diverse learners. As you read on, be on the lookout for additional ideas to which you can say *yes*, ideas that data show your students need.

ADJUST TEACHING BASED ON YOUR DATA

The start of the school year is a critical time for assessment. In Chapter 6, the assessment chapter of this book, there are detailed suggestions for how you can assess readers to determine their precise needs before making adjustments to your instruction. Your students' previous year's teachers may have passed along data about the reading levels of your students, and your own running records will confirm or update that information.

As you get to know your students, you'll construct a portrait of each reader in your class. This will be based on your running records and performance assessments, and it will also draw on your studies of behaviors during reading workshop. For example, it will be important for you to sometimes scan the room to see whose eyes are focused on text and whose are roaming the room. It will be important for you to analyze students' Post-it notes and talk. You can draw on this data as you design your instruction.

If you have analyzed your initial assessments prior to launching your reading instruction—that is, if the sequence of units you will teach is still an open question—and if your students' skills are extremely low or extremely high, I recommend that you and your colleagues turn to the the *If . . . Then . . . Curriculum* book. The introduction, in particular, will suggest ways you might alter the sequence of units to meet the needs of your students. For example, a second-grade teacher might decide to support students' foundational inferring skills in lower-level texts before embarking on the unit of study *Series Book Clubs*. The teacher might decide to first teach on the unit "Readers Get to Know Characters by Performing Their Books" from the *If . . . Then . . . Curriculum* book.

One caveat: if you and your students are new to reading workshop, we recommend you start with the first Unit of Study book for your grade level. If you decide to teach your first unit of study by relying only on the summary of a unit (such as that which is provided in the *If . . . Then . . . Curriculum* book), you will be foregoing the tremendously supportive scaffolding of a Unit of Study book—the day-to-day guidance that details how your instruction might unfold and the coaching, support, and materials to teach that unit well. My advice, then, is for you to self-assess, and if this teaching is new to you,

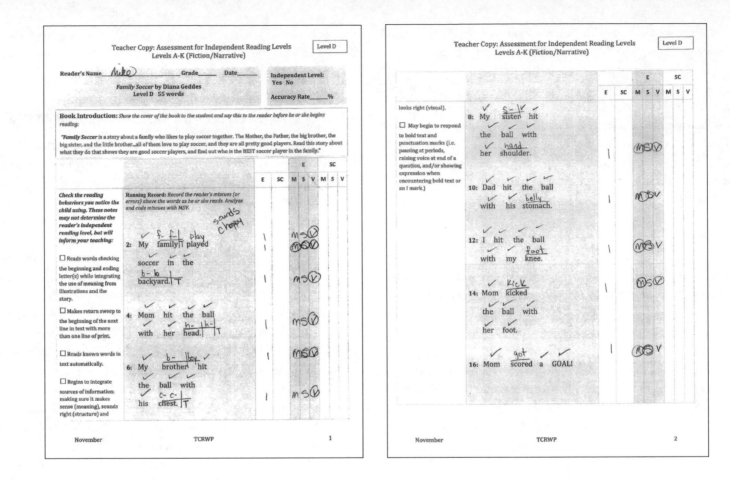

no matter what your students' skill levels might be, stay with the first Unit of Study book, adjusting it somewhat based on your assessment of your students.

Know that the series as a whole provides you with many resources to help you add sessions designed especially for your students, should your assessments reveal additional needs. For example, if you are teaching second-grade foundational reading skills, you might find that some children are having trouble using the first couple of sounds to help them read or still don't know the short vowel pattern work. To address these needs, look through the kindergarten or first-grade foundational skills units focused on beginning reading strategies or through the *If . . . Then . . . Curriculum* book for an alternative unit, and you'll find lots of lower-level tools, mentor texts, teaching points, and minilessons. You can also invent minilessons yourself that address the

skills students need to learn. To develop those minilessons, conferences, and small groups you can draw on your students' reading levels, the strategies and skills needed at those developmental stages in reading, as well as other data from your assessment of students.

Although it is entirely reasonable to plan a detour in your unit of study, I advise against stretching out a unit longer than six weeks, because after this amount of time, most youngsters are best served by wrapping up a chunk of work and getting a fresh start on some new work. If you do bring some supportive instruction into a unit, you might need to lop off the last bend. Always, the most sophisticated work in a unit is what comes in the final stretch. Rest assured that there will be opportunities to cycle back to skills with which your readers need particular support in future units of study.

DIFFERENTIATING MINILESSONS

There are a number of very accessible ways you can make any minilesson more differentiated. Below, I outline a few of these in greater depth.

Assigning Roles within Partnerships

Think for a moment about the typical partnership work that occurs in the midst of minilessons. My colleagues and I have often noticed that if partnerships are left on their own, often the same student—usually the more proficient or dominant student—will take the lead. So if you say, "Turn and tell your partner how you think this part of the text connects to what we read before. How does it fit?" and you give just a minute or two for students to talk about this, the dominant partner is apt to talk first, while the less dominant partner listens, nods, and follows along. There often isn't time for both youngsters to talk, so typically the stronger student does the work, and the less proficient one becomes the sounding board.

Because this is predictable, you can add a layer of support to your minilessons by assigning roles to students within their partnerships. I recommend identifying one student as Partner 1 and the other Partner 2. You can make a point of asking for one or the other to talk first, alternating this over the course of days.

If you assign which member of each partnership will be Partner 1 and which will be Partner 2, and you consistently make the more proficient one Partner 2, you can make deliberate decisions about whether you want the more or less proficient reader to do the talking at any one time. For example, if you ask partners to share what they know about a character, the first person to be able to offer a thought is probably in the easier position, able to choose the low-hanging fruit. Sometimes, of course, if the more proficient partner goes first, this can provide the less proficient partner with a helpful demonstration.

Embedding Assessments and Coaching Responsively

Another way to differentiate minilessons is to embed quick assessments in them and coach responsively based on your observations. In the midst of a minilesson, you'll often channel students to turn and talk to practice what you have just taught. While they do so, you can listen carefully to ascertain whether or not they are grasping what you are trying to teach. If your students

are able, you might ask them to draw or write on white boards or on a Post-it instead of talking to a partner, and then to hold the white boards high afterward so you can quickly keep tabs on their work.

Be prepared to coach students in response to what you observe them saying or writing. You might say something like "Many of you are talking about who the character is and what she looks like. Let's try not to name just what she looks like, but what she actually does and feels across this story. " You may also choose to share the responses of one or two students to serve as a model for others.

Just a word of caution: the trick is to do this without extending the minilesson beyond ten to twelve minutes in length. You may need to crop part of the minilesson as you'd planned it to stay within that time frame, and you certainly will need to leave many issues left to be tackled in small groups.

Providing Visual Texts as a Scaffold

Another way to adapt your minilessons so they support all students is to offer visual examples as scaffolding across the parts of the lesson. If you think the work might be particularly difficult, or if a strategy taught includes several steps, you might post a chart listing those steps. During the teaching portion of the minilesson, touch each step on the chart as you demonstrate that step, helping students connect your demonstration with the step of the strategy. Then, during the active engagement, you might say something like "Remember, I have a chart up here with steps you can follow to do this work. Use it if you need it." Adding illustrations to your charts whenever possible will offer additional support. Illustrations often function to make an abstract concept more concrete and accessible for learners. Study the suggested anchor charts in the online resources for examples of how illustrations can capture complex activities and concepts. Whenever possible, keep your illustrations consistent across charts, so that, for example, whenever you ask students to stop and think, you use the same thought bubble.

Your charts can also provide broader access with examples for students working below and above the text level used in the minilesson. You might even provide a small group of students with a copy of the day's chart and ask that they hold it as you demonstrate, touching each of the steps as you model how a proficient reader does the work. Then, as students work with their partners, the chart could function in a similar way, guiding them through each step in the active engagement.

Be the Boss of Your Reading!

1. STOP at the first sign of trouble.

STOP

2. TRY SOMETHING!

tools

3. Try something ELSE to get the job done!

4. Check it. Do a triple-check!

Using videos or digital texts in reading instruction can increase engagement and can be particularly helpful in ensuring that high-level thinking work is accessible to all children. Two kinds of videos particularly spring to mind as useful for classroom teachers: short narratives (which tell a story), and short documentaries or other informational videos (which teach). For example, if you were teaching your readers to think about lessons characters learn at the end of their books, you might gather children around a familiar television show and invite them to rewatch the ending to think about lessons learned. Then, when you introduce students to similar work with print texts, children will already be familiar with the thinking work involved.

A word of caution: you can't rely on having fast or open Internet service while you're teaching. You don't want to depend on an online video for your minilesson, only to find that the server is down that day and the video is unavailable. To avoid that, download the videos you want to use ahead of time (using one of several available online tools) and place them in a folder on your

desktop and/or a flash drive. You can find a wide variety of short videos in the online archives of museums and other educational websites such as PBS, National Geographic, Discovery, or The History Channel. If you can download them, do so, because they may disappear later!

Guiding Students toward Appropriate Texts

You can also decide to differentiate your minilessons by channeling groups of students toward texts that your assessments reveal to be especially appropriate for them. This type of differentiation occurs naturally anytime you ask students to pull out one of their own books to use during the active engagement, because students will then be working with texts at their independent reading levels. You can also provide different practice texts to different groups of students based on their needs. Or you could choose to ask all students to read the same text, and suggest they work with each other to read the text.

Seating Students Strategically

Seating students strategically can also help boost success during minilessons. Many teachers assign students to spots on the rug, next to their reading partners, and make careful choices about which students to seat in the most easily accessible spots on the rug. If you have a paraprofessional or another colleague in the room during your minilesson, you might suggest that he sit near particular students.

Supporting Students Who Need Additional Help Getting Started

You may be concerned that, despite your best efforts to differentiate during a minilesson, some students still cannot access the content. If so, you can end the minilesson by asking students to get started on their independent work, suggesting those who want help getting started remain with you. Sometimes you'll also want to scan the room, looking for students who aren't able to get started. The students who need further scaffolding will become apparent to you, and you can ask them to join you for some follow-up instruction. This approach is especially useful if the strategy you are teaching is particularly new or essential.

USING CONFERENCES AND SMALL GROUPS TO TEACH RESPONSIVELY

By their nature, conferences and small-group lessons are differentiated instruction. When you confer and lead small groups, you are authoring and delivering instruction that stems directly from your observations of your students' needs. It can help to envision your small groups and conferences not as stand-alone conversations with a child, but as sessions that make up a larger course of study on a topic. For example, if you identify that a major need for one reader is word solving, you might plan several conferences on this topic, accelerating the student in this particular area.

It is important to set clear short- and long-term goals with students. Frequently, students performing below grade level feel overwhelmed by the amount of growth they need to make. By setting short-term goals that you share with students, you allow them to work toward something attainable and to see their progress. Always, your small-group work and your conferring will show children how to do something they can do first with scaffolds and supports, and then, soon afterward, with independence. Rest assured that even if your conferences for a chunk of time all support a simple focus, helping students to become more proficient with that work, your students will still have opportunities to practice a broader repertoire of skills during minilessons and read-alouds and their own reading time.

You might choose to use small-group work as a way to orient readers who need support to upcoming work you anticipate will be difficult. Let's say you are planning to teach a lesson on becoming an expert about the characters in a book. In a small group the day before the lesson, you might preview some of this work by using a video or a comic strip. In this way, you provide multiple means of representation for the content you will teach while you also help students practice the work first on a more accessible text. The next day, during a minilesson on characters using the class read-aloud as a demonstration text, these students should be better able to access that content.

Support Readers with a Variety of Methods

In addition to your minilessons, conferences, and small groups, you may provide differentiated instruction in a number of other ways. These methods can be used flexibly as part of small-group work and conferences for specific readers, and some can be brought into share sessions, mid-workshop teaching, and connections.

Shared reading, which is detailed in Chapter 12, is a particularly effective method for helping students who need extra support with particular skills and is often underutilized as a form of small-group instruction. Gathering students around a shared text and reading the text together is especially useful for teaching word-solving strategies and for helping students orchestrate sources of information, as well as for supporting fluency. In primary classrooms, teachers may do shared reading with the whole class every day, but you might also decide to use this structure to support small groups.

Guided reading sessions are very useful to support students in accessing texts a notch above those they would be able to read independently, and you can read more in-depth information about these sessions in Chapter 9 of this book. When planning a guided reading session, design brief text introductions that focus on the tricky aspects of the text, keeping these to just a minute or two in length so you move students quickly toward reading the text. Students sit alongside each other reading the text silently until you come close and ask for them to read a bit aloud. Coach the first reader quickly, with lean prompts, and then move on to offer brief support to the next reader. You can tailor these groups to meet individual student's needs by layering in scaffolds, such as coaching students to carry bookmarks with questions to remind them to self-monitor as they read. These extra supports can help students progress to more challenging texts.

Reader's Theater, which connects oral reading to genre and drama, allows students to work on fluency while being part of the story. This allows students to work on fluency and character theories simultaneously. Students who have difficulty inferring character traits when reading can benefit from Reader's Theater as well. There are Reader's Theater sets from Benchmark Education that are leveled. Within one text, the character lines are leveled as well. For instance, one text might have character lines that range from level F to M. They are available in Spanish as well.

Partner reading is another structure that can help when differentiating instruction. In the early grades, students transition from independent reading to partner reading midway through the workshop. The transition to partner time gives those readers a second wind, allowing for more time dedicated to eyes on print, this time reading with the company of a peer. Partner time can also give students time to practice fluency or can serve as an alternative to jotting, where students read side by side and turn and talk when they have ideas.

Over time, you can move students toward progressively longer and longer periods of uninterrupted reading time so that eventually the bulk of their time is spent on independent reading. Likewise, you may have first-graders who are more advanced readers and could benefit from a structure that is more similar to that of the second- and third-graders. Think about partnerships, text complexity, and your students' skills work and decide on a structure that is most supportive and engaging for them.

You may find that some of your students, particularly those who have difficulty with fluency or word work, may benefit from having a book buddy in a class a grade or two below theirs. This arrangement can provide powerful support to the younger buddies, and it also can reinforce important foundational skills for the older buddy and dignify the time he or she spends reading very simple texts. It's lesson planning! Above all, keep in mind that students who are having difficulty reading need even *more* time to read, not less. Buddy reading time can be valuable for these readers if it offers them authentic, powerful reasons to practice their reading, but this needs to happen in addition to reading workshop time.

Use Materials to Differentiate

You may wonder how it is possible to support all your students, working at their just-right levels, while still teaching a compelling unit. The easiest way to do this is to differentiate expectations by differentiating the materials you provide to students.

Your first running records may have revealed that your students are reading at a wide range of levels. Be sure your classroom library features books at the reading levels of all students in your class. Your library showcases your beliefs about literacy and lets students know what books are valued in your classroom. So if you are teaching a second-grader who is reading at an end-of-kindergarten reading level, you need to have books in your classroom library at levels D/E, perhaps borrowed from a kindergarten teacher who isn't currently using them, so the reader can fill her baggie with books from those bins. Finding books at levels D/E that a second-grader finds engaging can take some effort.

The time that you spend finding engaging materials for this child will be well worth it, because this can help you support a love of reading. You might rotate lower-level high-interest book bins with other teachers in your grade,

trading book bins every few weeks to give students access to a broader variety of books at their reading levels.

Certainly, book baggies for students who are reading below grade level must be filled to the brim with books they can read well. You might also include shared reading and shared writing texts with which students are familiar. Some teachers find it helpful to type up (and correct) student's writing and put it in their book baggies to read during reading workshop. Many students write a level or two above their reading level. They can use their knowledge about their own stories to read more complex sentences.

SOME GENERAL PRINCIPLES TO KEEP IN MIND ABOUT SUPPORTING ALL LEARNERS

When supporting struggling students, the same strategies and accommodations will not work the same way for everyone. For example, picture Gene, a student who has great difficulty organizing his thoughts and articulating what he's thinking. He has no shortage of ideas, but he finds it challenging to express those ideas. Now picture Stephanie, a student in the same classroom who is considered to be on the autism spectrum. Inferring emotions is challenging for her, which makes it especially difficult for her to infer characters' motivations. She also finds it difficult to be flexible in her thinking and to revise her ideas. She loves nonfiction and is always carrying around the latest issue of *Ranger Rick* magazine. Just looking at these two students, it's clear that they need totally different types of support to help them access the curriculum.

As different as every learner is, however, there are some important principles to keep in mind. These apply to working with any learner, but they are especially important when working with students who need the most support.

Access to curriculum is the overall goal.

The objective is always to support all learners in accessing the curriculum. That means that when planning, you should ask questions such as "What might be difficult for certain students about this lesson (or series of lessons)?" and "What will it look like when students do this work?" It also helps to ask, "What content from this unit is essential—and what content is nice, but not crucial?" Thinking about these goals can help you prioritize the accommodations you'll need to make for your learners.

There are some who suggest that children should not attend minilessons if they are reading at what is considered far below grade level. They suggest to teachers that a few students for whom the whole-class minilesson does not seem exactly suited should instead work on word work activities or something of that nature while the rest of the class gathers for the minilesson. The idea that a few students would be segmented from the rest, and perhaps, thus be made to feel that they are not capable enough to attend the whole-class lesson troubles me. I view the minilesson not just as the teaching for that day, but also as a community-building experience. Just as I believe you might read an Emily Dickinson poem aloud to students who are not yet sophisticated enough to grasp its full meaning, but who will benefit from hearing the poem, there are important reasons to give students access to ways of talking in the intellectual community of the class. Minilessons can help to develop the language and the ways of being that characterize the intellectual community in your classroom.

Prioritize your accommodations to offer what is most important for each student, and teach toward independence.

It is true that there are endless things you could do to support learners. You could cover the feet of your chairs in cut-out tennis balls to minimize any undue background noise. You could set up listening centers. You could create bookmarks of every sort for every lesson. You could make graphic organizers. You could illustrate every chart. You could enlarge any text or make individual pocket-size copies of it. The hard truth is that there are a thousand things you could do for any student, but not a thousand hours in the day.

Prioritizing the supports for your learners is important. This means that some days you will offer more support to some groups or individuals than others. I want to caution you against believing that you need to spend endless hours developing materials so each child is always being given a new scaffold. In some cases, a particular graphic organizer may be useful, but too many can be overwhelming. Certainly, if you do introduce a scaffold, introduce it as a temporary scaffold, saying, "I'm giving you this chart now to help you organize your thinking about how these parts fit with the rest of the text. In two weeks, you'll need to do this organizing and thinking on your own, without the support of this tool." Make it clear to students from the onset that the ultimate goal is for them to work independently.

Stay focused on students' individual goals and how you are helping them make progress toward those goals.

When you are deciding what to prioritize, setting goals for a student (which could be goals from the student's IEP) can help you to know what accommodations to make. For example, if a primary goal for a student is to express herself and participate in class conversations more, then before reading workshop starts, I might talk to the student a bit about the content of the day's lesson, even perhaps helping her to think about what she might say during the lesson. If that student worked with an adult volunteer during breakfast time twice a week, I might ask that volunteer to read parts of that day's read-aloud text and to converse with the reader about the passage, setting her up to feel more confident in class. In this example, my goal for the student would not be so much to master the content of the lesson as it would be for her to express herself and participate. Having clear goals for students will ensure that you are helping them to make progress as effectively as possible.

Collaborate and communicate with other invested adults.

Too often, the invested adults in a student's life don't always talk together about the instruction they are providing for that student. That is, the reading intervention specialist has one goal and pathway for instruction she is following, the classroom teacher has another, the speech therapist a third. The result is that the student ends up feeling scattered. Be sure that all service providers talk together about their goals for the student and how to help the student meet those goals. This matters tremendously. Service providers are invaluable to both the student and the classroom teacher. Making sure that the classroom teacher, service providers, and parents/guardians are all on the same page is crucial for ensuring that a child has a cohesive, effective education.

Know what resources are available to you for support.

It is a Herculean task to support all learners—a task that changes from year to year, class to class, and child to child. My respect for you is enormous. It is my hope that you will find the resources provided in these Units of Study helpful to you as you work to support all of your students in accessing the curriculum. The *If . . . Then . . . Curriculum* book can help you adjust your teaching based on your data and also offer you support in your conferring and small-group work. The assessments outlined in Chapter 6 can help you to assess your students' needs and plan instruction accordingly. The Units of Study themselves are filled with examples of small-group instruction and conferring to offer support and enrichment, as well as coaching notes for how to adjust the teaching of certain lessons, if needed.

In addition to the Units of Study, there are other helpful resources and materials I would suggest to you. Two books that I recommend are Richard Allington's *What Really Matters for Struggling Readers: Designing Research-Based Programs*, and *Understanding by Design*, by Grant Wiggins and Jay McTighe. And, of course, remember that you and your colleagues are each others' greatest resources. When instruction is aligned across grades, whole-school conversations around reading instruction are possible. Your colleagues are treasure troves of information, and I highly encourage schools to make time, not only for grade level teams to meet and plan, but also for cross-grade teams to meet and share tips, ideas, insights, and resources.

A SPECIAL SECTION ON SUPPORTING ELLs

Because the Teachers College Reading and Writing Project is deeply involved with schools where classrooms brim with ELLs, we spend a lot of time thinking about ways the reading workshop can be adjusted so that it is especially supportive for these students. In many of our schools, teachers, coaches, and administrators have been working for decades on teaching reading and teaching language simultaneously throughout the workshop.

Balancing both—teaching reading and teaching language—is challenging but greatly rewarding for students and teachers.

Provide Consistent Teaching Structures

The fact that workshop classrooms are organized in clear, predictable, and consistent ways is very helpful for English language learners as the predictability allows children to quickly become comfortable participating in the work of each day. Very early in the school year, ELL children come to understand that reading workshops start with the teacher giving a minilesson and that during the minilesson they learn strategies that they are then expected to apply to their independent work. Children know that after the minilesson they will be expected to read independently and that the teacher will circulate around the room, conferring with individuals and with small groups. Children

also know that they will be expected at some point to share their work with a partner. When the reading time is over, children know that they need to put their materials away and gather with a partner (or in the meeting area) for a share session. When teachers follow these routines day after day, students can focus their energies on trying to figure out how to do their work, rather than on worrying over what they will be expected to do. The predictability of the workshop provides tremendous reassurance to a child who is just learning English, and this is amplified if workshop structures repeat themselves across other subjects.

Use Consistent Teaching Language

In addition, reading workshops are characterized by consistent instructional language. The consistency of this language scaffolds each child's classroom experience, making it easier for a child who is just learning English to grasp the unique content that is being taught that day. For example, it helps that most minilessons start in a predictable manner, with teachers saying, "Readers," and then reviewing the content of previous minilessons, perhaps referencing a bulleted entry on a class chart. It helps children that every day the teacher encapsulates the day's minilesson in a sentence or two (the teaching point), which is repeated often, using the same language each time it is referenced. It helps that the teaching point usually becomes a bullet on a chart. This consistent language signals students to know what to pay particular attention to.

Offer Plentiful Opportunities for Reading Practice

Of course, the predictability of the workshop also means that teachers need not invent a new way each day to support their ELLs. Because the same classroom structures are in place day after day, solutions that help on Tuesday will also help on Wednesday, Thursday, and Friday. In a workshop classroom, partners can refer to a sheet of conversational prompts during the partner share time that will end each day's workshop predictably.

The predictable structures also mean children can count on having time to practice. Whether your ELL is a beginning speaker of English or an advanced one, she will have the opportunity to work on her reading and language skills each day. Repetition and practice are two important scaffolds that ELLs need to develop their literacy skills. They need to expand both their receptive language skills—their listening and reading—and their expressive language skills—their speaking and writing. The reading workshop is one place where all of these skills can be cultivated.

Provide Access to a Broad Variety of Texts

All students benefit from seeing books in the classroom library that match their own experiences and culture. That is, it is extremely important, that your ELLs have books in your library that they can relate to. This includes having books in other languages when possible. It is easier to find popular titles and series in different languages than you would think. Mo Willems' *Pigeon* and *Knuffle Bunny* series are available in Spanish, as are several Dr. Seuss books and The Magic Tree House series, just to name a few.

Carefully considering book selection also applies to read-aloud texts. If you have a few students whose home language is Spanish, think how much they would appreciate it if your read-aloud text is written in both English and Spanish. Think how much those students would appreciate a read-aloud text about a main character for whom English was not her first language. Teachers love titles such as *How My Parents Learned to Eat*, by Ina R. Friedman, *I Hate English*, by Ellen Levine, *Everybody Cooks Rice*, by Nora Dooley, and *Home at Last*, by Susan Middleton Elya. A few titles that include lines in Spanish are *Abuela*, by Arthur Dorros, *I Love Saturdays y domingos*, by Alma Flor Ada, *Too Many Tamales*, by Gary Soto and Ed Martinez, *Hairs/Pelitos*, by Sandra Cisneros, and *Subway Sparrow*, by Leyla Torres (which has Polish lines, too).

Use Assessment to Provide Extra Support for ELLs in All Stages of Learning English

Of course, there is no such thing as a typical ELL. Like all learners, ELLs differ one from the next in many ways. Two significant factors contributing to their unique needs are the child's level of competence in his first language and his English proficiency.

Knowing where each student is in his English acquisition can help you plan minilessons, confer with students, and set up supportive partnerships more strategically. Assessing your students' language proficiency, just as you assess their reading skills, allows you to identify goals and expectations to help them work toward in reading workshop. Ninety percent of the language we have is acquired over time. So knowing what areas of language your ELLs know—for example, conversational English versus academic English—will help you coach those students during reading time. For language they don't know yet, you can create partnerships where they will hear that sort of language in context, and you can use that language with kids during conferring and small-group sessions. Identifying language that kids use but confuse can help you identify goals that you can work on with kids, encouraging them to use those words with more effectiveness in their talk (and in their writing about reading).

Most school districts have a formal language assessment, but you can collect language samples from your ELLs every day during reading workshop. Every time a student talks during the minilesson, during partnership time, and during small-group work and conferring, you can consider her language skills and needs. Some days you will also have examples of the student's writing about reading to consider. The more you listen to the language she uses throughout the day in different contexts, the more you will be able to identify where she needs to move next linguistically and support her in reaching that goal.

Each component of a reading workshop can be altered to provide ELLs with the language support they need. Most language learners go through predictable stages of language acquisition as they move to full fluency in English. When you plan the reading workshop, you need to think about how you are going to meet your students' needs as they develop English language skills and how you are going to adjust your expectations while children are moving toward full fluency.

Methods such as shared reading and interactive writing can provide immersion and practice in grammar and language, in addition to fluency work, word work, and comprehension. You will always want to consider vocabulary—both content vocabulary (which words are specific to the content of the lesson that students need to know?) and academic vocabulary (which words that run across many disciplines can be taught in this lesson?). All students who are learning English benefit from targeted instruction about a few vocabulary words with extended time to study those words across a period of time—say, a week. They benefit from seeing the words illustrated, generating (or being provided with) examples and nonexamples, and using the words in conversation and in writing.

Let's think now about specific ways each component of the reading workshop can be altered just a bit so that the workshop as a whole is especially supportive for ELLs at different stages of English language acquisition.

Support students in the preproduction and early production stages of learning English.

When students are in the first few stages of language acquisition (in the silent period, called the preproduction stage, or in the early production stages), they are generally working on learning such things as common nouns, prepositions, pronouns, and present tense verbs. To support these students, make your teaching and the words you use as clear as possible. It's important to help students build language by exposing them to language they can understand. Let's consider some ways you can make your teaching and talk more comprehensible to these learners.

Use visual examples in your teaching.

You might, for example, display an illustration of one of the characters you're discussing or an image from a book that captures some information about the character. Or you might sketch an abstract concept to make the meaning clearer to students. Sometimes I see teachers using their whole bodies when teaching a lesson, becoming highly animated. Animated teaching can grab students' attention, and it makes the teaching and language more comprehensible. These teachers use gestures, facial expressions, and intonation to bring their words to life. Recruit students to join you in these dramatizations, acting out new vocabulary words or becoming characters and role-playing their feelings.

Modify your minilessons to be as concise as possible.

If you are working with a large ELL population, you may want to trim the minilessons in this series. Make a special point of using examples that children can relate to. It's also helpful to repeat the teaching point more often with children who are learning English. Similarly, when asking children to turn and talk, it can help to set them up with cue cards. In a lesson on considering author's choices, for example, you might give them cards that say "The author wrote/drew . . ." or "This makes me think . . ." and so forth.

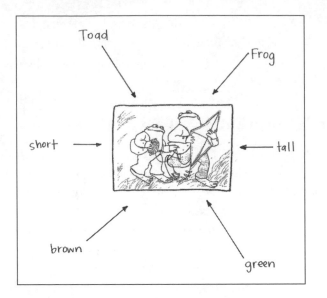

Weave a double active engagement into some of your minilessons.

You may find that, if you've demonstrated something slightly more complex and want children to learn from your example, they profit from first repeating your model before applying the strategy to another section of text or their own books. This may lead you to set up a double active engagement within many minilessons.

Provide readers with topic-based text sets.

Many teachers find it useful to provide students with text sets of leveled books about a topic. Within a baggie of books on the topic of food, for example, readers might encounter the words *lunch*, *eats*, and *hungry* several times. Repeated exposure to words supports students in the early stages of learning English by building vocabulary. When introducing a new baggie of books to a reader, you might preteach a few words using labeled pictures to help readers access the texts. To prepare these baggies, look for similarities among books in the bin at the appropriate level. You might create simple text sets on food, families, animals, homes, sports, cities, or other relevant topics.

Provide opportunities for listening and learning the social language of the reading workshop.

Children who are in the preproduction or early production stages of learning English will have few oral English skills, but they will be listening carefully, trying to interpret what is going on around them. It is okay for them to be quiet at this stage, and it is important to understand that they are taking in a lot of information. Opportunities for listening, really listening, are essential to language learning.

The English words, phrases, and sentences that make sense to these learners first will probably be the predictable sentences related to concrete classroom activities, such as "Get your books," or "Start reading," or "You can go to your seat now," or "Let's gather in the meeting area." It can help to accompany these directions with illustrative gestures, such as holding up a book baggie or tapping a chair. The expectation that these children will participate in the regular comings and goings of the class spotlights the value of learning the social language that is most within their grasp.

Establish partnerships and triads that support ELLs' burgeoning language development.

Language is learned through interactions with others. The reading workshop is an especially rich context for language development because children are not only reading and listening, but they are also talking, and much of that talk happens in the small, supportive structure of partnerships. Eventually, these partnerships will give children important opportunities to discuss their ideas about texts, but when children are in the preproduction stage of learning English, a partnership with one other child could make the child at the early production stage feel trapped, like a deer in the headlights, with nowhere to hide. Still, it is crucial that new arrivals are expected to join into the class activities as best they can right from the start. There is never a time when new arrivals should sit on the edge of the community, watching. Instead, the rug spot for the new arrival needs to be right in the center of the meeting area. From the start, when children turn and talk during the active engagement section of a minilesson, these children must know that they belong to a conversational group.

Children in the early stages of learning English benefit from being in triads rather than partnerships. Ideally, one child in that triad will share the new arrival's native language but be more proficient in English, and the other child will be a native speaker of English and a language model. Make use of every opportunity possible to pair students learning English with the strongest English language models in your class. Granted, children who are in the preproduction stage of learning English will mostly listen. You can teach their more English-proficient partners how to use lots of gestures and ask questions that can be answered with a yes or a no, a nod, or a head shake. Additionally, you could invite upper-grade students to serve as strong language models for your lower-grade language learners, inviting them in regularly for conversations or buddy reading.

Coach your students on how to work together in various configurations in the classroom. Many students benefit from meeting often with a peer to read pages of their books together or talk about them. These conversations not only give them valuable feedback, but they also create opportunities for comprehensible language input from a peer. This is a good use of partner time in both upper-grade and lower-grade classrooms.

Provide your ELLs opportunities to read in both their home language and in English.

When a child in the first stages of acquiring English arrives in a classroom, the first goal is to make sure that child is immediately active and interactive. If this child is literate in his home language, then by all means it is important for him to read and to write in that language. If there are people in the classroom or the school who can speak the child's home language, you can rely on these buddies to convey to the child the kind of text the class is reading and some of its main features. For example, a buddy might convey, "We are reading stories and thinking about the people who are in them. We are trying to say ideas we have about the people in the stories."

Whether or not the new arrival is literate in his home language, you will want him to also have opportunities to begin doing some reading in English. You may find that it helps for these children to have time slots for home-language reading and for English reading, with the child perhaps starting the reading workshop with fifteen minutes to read in his home language. During this time, the child can read with volume that is comparable to other children and build his identity as a child who reads a lot. Then, the child can transition to reading books in English.

You might start by asking the child who is in the early stages of learning English to read texts that are very short and have recognizable patterns when reading in English. These texts are generally filled with pictures that support readers in making sense of what the text says, often before they can even read all the words. This, of course, is reminiscent of what we ask kindergarten and first-grade children to do. There is nothing elementary about learning a second language, and yet taking children new to English through the progression of work that younger children in a reading workshop experience has all sorts of advantages. After a child has read at one level for a bit, you can informally or formally assess her and then move her to the next level with a transitional book baggie that contains her previous level and current level. If possible, providing students with theme-based books can be very supportive. These children need the same kinds of teaching methods that are so powerful with primary readers. You may find it helpful to do interactive writing in small groups with ELLs specifically creating writing that matches the language goals for a group of students. This interactive writing can take the form of books, which can then be added to a child's book baggie, and the student can read these books in addition to others. This way, stories or informational texts can be tailored to the student's interests or home culture.

Plan instruction with your ELL instructor to maximize learning in the reading workshop.

If you have children who are in the early stages of English acquisition, it is especially important to provide them with extra help understanding the content of a minilesson. If there is a teacher of English as a second language (ELL) who can provide support, this can also be extremely beneficial. Some ELL teachers "push in" to classrooms, and some "pull out" children for work in the ELL room. While not always possible, we recommend that ELLs remain in the classroom to maximize interaction and instructional opportunities. In either case, working in tandem with an ELL teacher will benefit your ELLs.

If classroom teachers and ELL teachers have opportunities to plan together, the ELL teacher can support the children during reading workshop by preteaching the concepts and developing the vocabulary necessary to understand what will be taught in the minilesson. For example, if the minilesson teaches children how to identify important ideas in a nonfiction book, the ELL teacher might use gestures to convey that the book's title provides the main topic, and the table of contents and bold headers identify subtopics, which point to some of the big ideas addressed in the book.

Support students in the later stages of learning English.

It is important to celebrate the work that children at this stage of early emergent English are producing, focusing on the content of their speaking and writing about reading, not only on the correctness of the syntax. These children are taking risks, and your job is to help them to feel successful while also accelerating their forward progress. There are many ways you can tailor your teaching to provide particular support to students at these stages of English language acquisition.

Move students in this stage from triads to partnerships or pair them with an early emergent ELL.

As children become more fluent in English, they will be better able to understand written and spoken English when there are context clues, such as pictures, actions, sounds, and so on. Partnership work can provide helpful context when reading and talking about texts. As students develop their proficiency, you might move them from triads to partnerships, or you might nudge them to become one of the more vocal members of a triad, with a new preproduction ELL joining in as much as possible. These learners may not always use correct syntax, but they can and should participate fully in partnership work. Remember that all language learners need the best language models possible, so keep this in mind as you determine your partnerships and triads.

Extend the language ELLs are producing.

As children become more proficient in English, their answers to questions will become more extended, even though their hold on English grammar and vocabulary may still be approximate. Again, partners (and teachers) can be coached to realize that this is not a time for correcting grammar. Instead, it is a time for expanding on what the child says. If the child points to a picture in her book and says, "Shark," then you can expand on that. "That's a shark?" Pause for a nod. As you point to the picture, you might say, "Do sharks have sharp teeth?" Wait for another nod. "Yes, you're right. What else do you notice about them?" Gesture to illustrate that the question pertains to sharks' bodies. If the child isn't sure how to answer, you can eventually supply options as you point to the relevant pictures. "They have tails, right? And fins. What else?"

Support students in acquiring academic English.

Children who are in later stages of language acquisition also need special support during reading workshop. When children reach intermediate fluency, they demonstrate increased accuracy and are able to express their thoughts and feelings in English. They often sound as if their English is stronger than it is. Although these children may have developed conversational skills, they may not have academic English language skills. These children have a strong command of social English and can use English to chat with each other, to learn what the teacher expects them to do, and to talk about the events of the day. They may sound fluent in social conversation, where complex structures can be avoided, but it is often difficult to follow them when they describe events from another time and place.

One way to determine whether a child needs help with academic English is to talk to her about a story or about something that happened in another time and place. Invite the child to retell an episode from a book or from her experience, and listen well. If the child's language makes it hard to piece together what she is trying to say, she may need support with academic English. The term *academic English* does not refer only to the language that is used in discipline-based studies. It also refers to the language needed to communicate about times and places that are distant or unfamiliar. To meet this challenge, students need input from skilled teachers and people who can provide strong language models.

Scaffold students' work on talking and writing about reading with description and specificity.

At this stage, it is important for teachers to work on elaboration and specificity to help children use more descriptive and extended language. You might teach children adjectives or adverbs that can help make their language more specific (e.g., colors, textures, speeds, and so on). It is also important for these children to be partnered with others for whom English is their first language, who can function as strong language models. Often, when teachers have a handful of children who are in the earliest stages of language acquisition and a handful who are further along, teachers devote most of their special attention to the children who are the newest to English. However, if you set new arrivals up with the proper invitations to work, support structures from other children, and ways of being interactive, they can learn a huge amount from each other. Meanwhile, you can devote additional time to children who have a good command of social English but not of academic English and need help that is less readily available from the peer group.

Provide explicit instruction in tenses, pronoun references, and connectives.

Children who need help with academic English will profit from explicit instruction tailored to their needs. For example, when ELLs learn to read and write, connectives can become a source of confusion. Many readers assume that sentences are always arranged in chronological order, regardless of the connective used. That assumption may be incorrect, however, as in the sentence, "I went to the office because the principal called for me over the PA system." In small-group instruction, you can provide ELLs with explicit instruction to help them understand connectives, tenses, pronoun references, and so forth. This might be done with sentence strips and pocket charts, cards to be put in order, or transcripts of student conversations that include corrections.

Support students in building vocabulary using their own reading as the context.

ELLs also need support in developing a rich vocabulary. Explicit instruction benefits this aspect of language development as well. If a child overuses a word such as *nice* in describing a character, you might help him learn that there are a variety of more precise words to use. Is the character helpful? Kind? Friendly? Giving? You might help children develop word files, with the overused word at the center of a card and several variations around the edges. Remind children to keep these cards on hand throughout the day and look for opportunities to use specific words orally. You might even ask children to place a checkmark beside a word each time they use it orally. Illustrated charts, such as those showing feelings or traits, can also be supportive. Asking students to pose for the pictures can be extra engaging. You may find it useful to limit the number of new words introduced each week and to provide opportunities across the week for students to use those new words.

Similarly, if students are reading about a particular subject, you or an English-speaking buddy can help the ELL build domain-specific vocabulary to draw upon as she talks and writes about that text. If the child is reading about space, she would benefit from having lots of conversations about the topic, using terms such as *planet*, *star*, *solar system*, and *orbit*. Of course, this sort of vocabulary work is essential for any ELL but it can provide extra language support to the ELL who is ready to learn more precise vocabulary.

Provide small-group instruction for students to learn figurative language.

Children learning academic English will also need support as they come to understand and use figurative language. Literature is filled with metaphors, similes, and idioms, as are the minilessons in this series. Children who are just on the brink of learning academic English will profit from some small-group instruction that gives them access to literary devices. Again, shared reading can be a wonderful method to support students in studying, reading, and discussing figurative language. Word sorts where students read an idiom or phrase and determine whether it is positive or negative can give students exposure to new language in a fun way. You might even decide to introduce students to a new phrase each week, challenging them to use that phrase whenever they can across the week and then to add it to their bank of figurative language as the year continues.

Tailor your teaching to support reading goals and language goals.

When you approach a unit of study, think about the language needs of children acquiring English and ask yourself, "What are the language skills that students need to have to understand the work they are being asked to do?" You'll need to think not only about the reading skills and strategies that will be developed in a unit, but also about the language skills the unit will support.

Consider the vocabulary, idiomatic expressions, connectives, conjunctions, and grammar you want children to develop in a unit. You'll need a plan for content and a plan for language, side by side.

When approaching a unit on nonfiction reading, for example, you can anticipate that you'll be teaching children how to explain, describe, compare, categorize, and question. It's likely that they'll benefit from learning connectives such as *if*, *when*, *because*, and so forth. You can plan to provide scaffolds such as word charts, and you can plan to help children with academic terms such as *detail*, *example*, *reason*, *describe*, and *explain*. You may teach the language of comparison, including, for example, the use of the *-er* and *-est* word endings, as in *big*, *bigger*, *biggest*.

The power of written curriculum is that you and a group of colleagues can hold your hopes for teaching in your hands and talk and think together about how you can take your own good ideas and make them better. One of the most important ways to strengthen your teaching is to think, "How can we give all children access to this curriculum?" The reading workshop has built-in structures to support ELLs, and if you bring your best ideas to the table, you can make it even more supportive.

THE NEED FOR DIFFERENTIATION

We have come to realize one thing above all in our work—that assessments of our students' learning say as much about our teaching as they do about our students' skills—perhaps more. We cannot simply look at low scores, at students reading far below grade level, and say, "Well, these students don't have the background or the capacity or the ethic for success." What we must say is "What can we do to teach these students more effectively?" and we must ask, "Have we granted each student in our care with what they need to succeed in their reading lives, both inside and outside the classroom walls?" Nothing could matter more.

References

Ada, Alma Flor. 2004. *I Love Saturdays y domingos*. New York: Aladdin Paperbacks.

Allington, R. L. 2002a. "The Six Ts of Effective Elementary Literacy Instruction." *Reading Rockets*. Available at http://www.readingrockets.org/article/six-ts-effective-elementary-literacy-instruction.

———. 2002b. "What I've Learned about Effective Reading Instruction from a Decade of Studying Exemplary Elementary Classroom Teachers." *The Phi Delta Kappan* 83(10):740–47. JSTOR. Web.

———. 2008. "Response to Intervention: How to Make It Work." Speech, Teachers College Reading and Writing Project Principals as Curricular Leaders Conference, New York, October 8.

———. 2011. *What Really Matters for Struggling Readers: Designing Research-Based Programs*, 3d ed. Boston, MA: Pearson.

Allington, R. L., and P. Johnston. 2002. "What Do We Know about Exemplary Fourth-Grade Teachers and Their Classrooms?" In C. Roller (ed.), *Learning to Teach Reading: Setting the Research Agenda*, pp. 150–65. Newark, DE: International Reading Association.

Anderson, Carl. 2005. *Assessing Writers*. Portsmouth, NH: Heinemann.

Anderson, R. C. 1984. "Role of the Reader's Schema in Comprehension, Learning, and Memory." *Learning to Read in American Schools: Basal Readers and Content Texts* 29:243–57.

Anderson, R. C., P. T. Wilson, and L. G. Fielding. 1988. "Growth in Reading and How Children Spend Their Time outside of School." *Reading Research Quarterly* 23:285–303.

Anderson, R. C., and W. E. Nagy. 1992. "The Vocabulary Conundrum." *American Educator* 16(4):14–18, 44–47.

Barth, Roland. 2006. "Improving Relationships within the Schoolhouse." *Educational Leadership* 63(6):8–13.

Bear, Donald R., Marcia Invernizzi, Shane Templeton, and Francine R. Johnston. 2012. *Words Their Way: Word Study for Phonics, Vocabulary, and Spelling Instruction*. Boston: Pearson/Allyn and Bacon.

Beck, I. L., and M. G. McKeown. 2001. "Text Talk: Capturing the Benefits of Read-Aloud Experiences for Young Children." *Reading Teacher* 55(1):10–20.

———. 2007. "Increasing Young Low-Income Children's Oral Vocabulary Repertoires through Rich and Focused Instruction." *The Elementary School Journal* 107(3):251–71.

Bembry, K., H. Jordan, E. Gomez, M. Anderson, and R. Mendro. 1998. "Policy Implications of Long-Term Teacher Effects on Student Achievement." Paper presented at the Annual Meeting of the American Educational Research Association, San Diego, April 13–17.

Benjamin, R. G., and P. J. Schwanenflugel. 2010. "Text Complexity and Oral Reading Prosody in Young Readers." *Reading Research Quarterly* 45(4):388–404.

Betts, E. A. 1946. *Foundations of Reading Instruction*. New York: American Book Company.

Bomer, Randy. 1995. *Time for Meaning: Crafting Literate Lives in Middle and High School*. Portsmouth, NH: Heinemann.

Bruner, Jerome S. 1977. *The Process of Education*. Cambridge: Harvard University Press.

Calfee, R. C., P. Lindamood, and C. Lindamood. 1973. "Acoustic-Phonetic Skills and Reading: Kindergarten through Twelfth Grade." *Journal of Educational Psychology* 64(3):293–98.

Calkins, L. 1994. *The Art of Teaching Writing*. Portsmouth, NH: Heinemann.

———. 2001. *The Art of Teaching Reading*. Boston: Allyn & Bacon Educational Publishers.

Calkins, Lucy, et al. 2013. *Units of Study in Opinion, Information, and Narrative Writing*, Grades K–5. Portsmouth, NH: Heinemann.

Cisneros, Sandra. 1994. *Hairs/Pelitos*. New York: Knopf.

Clay, M. 1985. "Engaging with the School System: A Study of Interaction in New Entrant Classrooms." *New Zealand Journal of Educational Studies* 22(1):20–38.

———. 1987. "Learning to Be Learning Disabled." *New Zealand Journal of Educational Studies*. 22(2):155–73. Available at http://www.nzcer.org.nz/pdfs/9500.pdf.

———. 1991. *Becoming Literate: The Construction of Inner Control*. Portsmouth, NH: Heinemann.

———. 1993. *Literacy Lessons Designed for Individuals: Part Two. Teaching Procedure*. Portsmouth, NH: Heinemann.

———. 2001. *Change over Time in Children's Literacy Development*. Portsmouth, NH: Heinemann.

———. 2005. *Literacy Lessons Designed for Individuals*. Auckland, NZ: Heinemann.

Corcoran, T., F. A. Mosher, and A. Rogat. 2009. *Learning Progressions in Science: An Evidence-Based Approach to Reform* (CPRE Research Report #RR-63). Philadelphia, PA: Consortium for Policy Research in Education.

Cowley, Joy. 1999. *Mrs. Wishy-Washy*. New York: Philomel.

Cunningham, A. E., and K. E. Stanovich. 1991. "Tracking the Unique Effects of Print Exposure in Children: Associations with Vocabulary, General Knowledge, and Spelling." *Journal of Educational Psychology* 83(2):264–74.

Cunningham, Patricia M. 2013. *Phonics They Use: Words for Reading and Writing*. Boston: Pearson.

Cunningham, Patricia Marr, and Dorothy P. Hall. 2008. *Month-by-Month Phonics for First Grade*. Greensboro, NC: Carson-Dellosa.

Darling-Hammond, L., B. Barron, P. D. Pearson, and A. Schoenfeld. 2008. *Powerful Learning: What We Know about Teaching for Understanding*. San Francisco: Jossey-Bass.

Daro, P., F. A. Mosher, and T. Corcoran. 2011. *Learning Trajectories in Mathematics: A Foundation for Standards, Curriculum, Assessment, and Instruction* (CPRE Research Report #68). Philadelphia: Consortium for Policy Research in Education.

Dole, Janice A., Kathleen J. Brown, and Woodrow Trathen. 1996. "The Effects of Strategy Instruction on the Comprehension Performance of At-Risk Students." *Reading Research Quarterly* 31(1):62–88. Web.

Dooley, Norah. 1997. *Everybody Cooks Rice*. Minneapolis: First Avenue Editions.

Dorros, Arthur. 1997. *Abuela*. New York: Puffin.

Duffy, Thomas M., and Jamie R. Kirkley, eds. 2004. *Learner-Centered Theory and Practice in Distance Education: Cases from Higher Education*. Mahwah, NJ: Indiana University.

Dufresne, Michelle. *Bella Likes Purple*. Northampton, MA: Pioneer Valley Books.

———. *Food for Bella*. Northampton, MA: Pioneer Valley Books.

Duke, N. K., and D. Pearson. 2002. "Effective Practices for Developing Reading Comprehension." In A. E. Farstrup and S. J. Samuels (eds.), *What Research Has to Say about Reading Instruction*, 3d ed., pp. 205–242. Newark, DE: International Reading Association.

Duke, N. K., V. S. Bennett-Armistead, and E. M. Roberts. 2002. "Incorporating Informational Text in the Primary Grades." In C. Roller (ed.), *Comprehensive Reading Instruction across the Grade Levels*, pp. 40–54. Newark, DE: International Reading Association.

———. 2003. "Filling the Great Void: Why We Should Bring Nonfiction into Early Grade Classrooms." *American Educator* 27(1):30–35.

Dweck, C. S. 2000. *Self-Theories: Their Role in Motivation, Personality, and Development*. Philadelphia: Psychology Press, pp. 2–4.

Edmunds, K. M., and K. L. Bauserman. 2006. "What Teachers Can Learn about Reading Motivation through Conversations with Children." *The Reading Teacher* 59(5):414–24.

Ehri, L. C., S. R. Nunes, D. M. Willows, B. V. Schuster, et al. 2001. "Phonemic Awareness Instruction Helps Children Learn to Read: Evidence from the National Reading Panel's Meta-Analysis." *Reading Research Quarterly* 36(3):250–87.

Ehri, Linnea, Lois Dreyer, Bert Flugman, and Alan Gross. 2007. "Reading Rescue: An Effective Tutoring Intervention Model for Language-Minority Students Who Are Struggling Readers in First Grade." *American Educational Research Journal* 44(2):414–48.

Duke, Nell K., P. D. Pearson, S. L. Strachan, and A. K. Billman. 2011. "Essential Elements of Fostering and Teaching Reading Comprehension." In S. Jay Samuels and Alan E. Farstrup (eds.), *What Research Has to Say about Reading Instruction*, pp. 51–93. Newark, DE: International Reading Association.

Elley, W. B. 1989. "Vocabulary Acquisition from Listening to Stories." *Reading Research Quarterly* 24:174–87.

Elya, Susan Middleton. 2002. *Home at Last*. New York: Lee & Low.

Foorman, Barbara R., Christopher Schatschneider, Michelle N. Eakin, Jack M. Fletcher, Louisa C. Moats, and David J Francis. 2006. "The Impact of Instructional Practices in Grades 1 and 2 on Reading and Spelling Achievement in High Poverty Schools." *Contemporary Educational Psychology* 31:1–29.

Foorman, B. R., S. Herrera, Y. Petscher, A. Mitchell, and A. Truckenmiller. 2015. "The Structure of Oral Language and Reading and Their Relation to Comprehension in Kindergarten through Grade 2." *Reading and Writing* 28(5):655–81.

Fountas, I. C., and G. S. Pinnell. 2003. *Sing a Song of Poetry*. Portsmouth, NH: Heinemann.

———. 2012. *Genre Study: Teaching with Fiction and Nonfiction Books*. Portsmouth, NH: Heinemann.

———. 2013. "Guided Reading: The Romance and the Reality." *The Reading Teacher* 66(4):268.

Fox, Mem. 1989. *Koala Lou*. San Diego: Harcourt Brace Jovanovich.

Friedman, Ina R. 1984. *How My Parents Learned to Eat*. Boston: Houghton Mifflin.

Fullan, Michael, P. Hill, and C. Crévola. 2006. *Breakthrough*. Thousand Oaks, CA: Corwin.

Gardner, John. 1991. *The Art of Fiction: Notes on Craft for Young Writers*. New York: Vintage.

Gehsmann, K. M., and S. Templeton. 2013. "Reading Standards: Foundational Skills." In L. M. Morrow, T. Shanahan, and K. K. Wixson (eds.), *Teaching with the Common Core Standards for English Language Arts, prek–2*, pp. 67–84. New York: Guilford Press.

Gladwell, M. 2005. *Blink: The Power of Thinking without Thinking*. New York: Little, Brown and Company.

Goldschmidt, P., J. F. Martinez, D. Niemi, and E. L. Baker. 2007. "Relationships Among Measures as Empirical Evidence of Validity: Incorporating Multiple Indicators of Achievement and School Context." *Educational Assessment* 12(3 & 4):239–66

Goodlad, John I. 2004. *A Place Called School*. New York: McGraw-Hill.

Goodwin, Bryan. 2014. "Research Says / Get All Students to Speak Up." *Educational Leadership* 72(3):82–83.

Goodwin, Bryan, and K. Miller. 2012/2013. "Research Says / Nonfiction Reading Promotes Student Success." *Educational Leadership* 70(4):80–82.

Guthrie, John. 2004. "Teaching for Literacy Engagement." *Journal of Literacy Research* 36(1):1–29. Web.

Guthrie, J., and N. Humenick. 2004. "Motivating Students to Read: Evidence for Classroom Practices that Increase Reading Motivation and Achievement." In P. McCardle and V. Chhabra (eds.), *The Voice of Evidence in Reading Research*, pp. 329–54. Baltimore: Brookes Publishing.

Hall, Dorothy P., and Patricia Marr Cunningham. 2008. *Month-by-Month Reading, Writing, and Phonics for Kindergarten*. Greensboro, NC: Carson-Dellosa.

Hart, B., and T. Risley. 1995. *Meaningful Differences in the Everyday Experience of Young American Children*. Baltimore: P.H. Brookes.

Hattie, J. 2008. *Visible Learning: A Synthesis of Over 800 Meta-Analyses Relating to Achievement*. London: T & F Books.

Hayes, D., and N. Ward. 1992. "Learning from Texts: Effects of Similar and Dissimilar Features of Analogies in Study Guides." Paper presented at the 42nd Annual Meeting of the National Reading Conference. San Antonio: Education Trust.

Henkes, Kevin. 1991. *Chrysanthemum*. New York: Greenwillow.

Hoff, Syd. 1993. *Danny and the Dinosaur*. New York: HarperCollins.

Howe, James, and Melissa Sweet (illustrator). The Pinky and Rex series. New York: Simon & Schuster.

Isbell, R., J. Sobol, L. Lindauer, and A. Lowrance. 2004. "The Effects of Storytelling and Story Reading on the Oral Language Complexity and Story Comprehension of Young Children." *Early Childhood Education Journal* 32(3):157–63.

Johnston, Peter. 2004. *Choice Words: How Our Language Affects Children's Learning*. Portland, ME: Stenhouse.

Juel, C. 1988. "Learning to Read and Write: A Longitudinal Study of 54 Children from First through Fourth Grades." *Journal of Educational Psychology* 80(4):437.

Juel, C., and C. Minden-Cupp. 2000. "Learning to Read Words: Linguistic Units and Instructional Strategies." *Reading Research Quarterly* 35(4):458.

Jukes, I., and T. McCain. 2002. *Living on the Future Edge*. InfoSavvy Group and Cyster.

Kline, Suzy. 1989. *Horrible Harry and the Ant Invasion*. New York: Viking.

Kotaman, H. 2008. "Impacts of Dialogical Storybook Reading on Young Children's Reading Attitudes and Vocabulary Development." *Reading Improvement* 45(2):55–61.

Kraemer, L., P. McCabe, and R. Sinatra. 2012. "The Effects of Read-Alouds of Expository Text on First Graders' Listening Comprehension and Book Choice." *Literacy Research and Instruction* 51(2):165–78.

Krashen, S. D. 2004. *The Power of Reading: Insights from the Research*, 2d ed. Portsmouth, NH: Heinemann.

Krauss, Ruth. 2004. *The Carrot Seed*. New York: HarperCollins.

Kupperstein, Joel. 1997. *Mr. Noisy Paints His House*. Cypress, CA: Creative Teaching.

Lee, Hector Viveros. 1996. *I Had a Hippopotamus*. New York: Lee & Low.

Levine, Ellen. 1989. *I Hate English!* New York: Scholastic.

Lillegard, Dee. 1994. *Frog's Lunch*. New York: Scholastic.

Madden, N. A., R. E. Slavin, N. L. Karweit, L. Dolan, and B. A. Wasik. 1993. "Success for All: Longitudinal Effects of a Restructuring Program for Inner-City Elementary Schools." *American Educational Research Journal* 30(1):123–48.

Maine, F. 2013. "How Children Talk Together to Make Meaning from Texts: A Dialogic Perspective on Reading Comprehension Strategies." *Literacy* 47(3):150–56.

Michaels, Sarah, M. C. O'Connor, and M. Williams Hall. 2010. *Accountable Talk Sourcebook: For Classroom Conversation that Works*. Pittsburgh, PA: Institute for Learning.

Miller, Donalyn. 2013. *Reading in the Wild: The Book Whisperer's Keys to Cultivating Lifelong Reading Habits*. San Francisco: Jossey Bass.

Moats, L. C. 2000. *Speech to Print: Language Essentials for Teachers*. Baltimore: Paul H. Brookes Publishing.

Mosher, F. A. 2011. *The Role of Learning Progressions in Standards-Based Education Reform*. CPRE Policy Brief RB-52.

New Commission on the Skills of the American Workforce. 2007. *Tough Choices or Tough Times*. Washington, DC: National Center on Education and the Economy.

No Child Left Behind Act of 2001, Pub. L. No. 107-110, 115 Stat. 1425.

O'Connor, R. E., K. M. Bell, K. R. Harty, L. K. Larkin, S. M. Sackor, and N. Zigmond. 2002. "Teaching Reading to Poor Readers in the Intermediate Grades: A Comparison of Text Difficulty." *Journal of Educational Psychology* 94:474–85.

Pearson, P. D., and L. Fielding. 1991. "Comprehension Instruction." In R. Barr, M. Kamil, P. Mosenthal, and P. D. Pearson (eds.), *Handbook of Reading Research*. Vol. II. White Plains, NY: Longman.

Pearson, P. D., and M. Gallagher. 1983. "The Instruction of Reading Comprehension." *Contemporary Educational Psychology* 8:317–44.

Pellegrino, James W., Naomi Chudowsky, and Robert Glaser. 2001. *Knowing What Students Know: The Science and Design of Educational Assessment*. Washington, DC: National Academy.

Peterson, R. 1992. *Life in a Crowded Place: Making a Learning Community*. Portsmouth, NH: Heinemann.

Pinnel, G. S., C. A. Lyons, D. E. DeFord, A. Bryk, and N. Seltzer. 1994. *Reading Research Quarterly* 29:8–39.

Pressley, M. 1998. *Reading Instruction that Works: The Case for Balanced Teaching*. New York: Guilford.

———. 2001. "Effective Beginning Reading Instruction." Executive Summary and Paper Commissioned by the National Reading Conference. Chicago, IL: National Reading Conference.

Pressley, M., A. Roehrig, K. Bogner, L. M. Raphael, and S. Dolezal. 2002. "Balanced Literacy Instruction." *Focus on Exceptional Children* 34(5):1.

Pressley, M., A. Roehrig, L. Raphael, S. Dolezal, C. Bohn, L. Mohan, et al. 2003. "Teaching Processes in Elementary and Secondary Education." In W. M. Reynolds and G. E. Miller (eds.), *Handbook of Psychology*, Volume 7: *Educational Psychology*, pp. 153–75. New York: John Wiley.

Pressley, M., R. Wharton-McDonald, R. Allington, C. C. Block, L. Morrow, D. Tracey, K. Baker, G. Brooks, J. Cronin, E. Nelson, and D. Woo. 2001. "A Study of Effective Grade-1 Literacy Instruction." *Scientific Studies of Reading* 5:35–58.

Pressley, Michael, and Peter Afflerbach. 1995. *Verbal Protocols of Reading: The Nature of Constructively Responsive Reading*. Hillsdale, NJ: Lawrence Erlbaum Associates.

Randell, Beverley. 1996. *A Friend for Little White Rabbit*. Barrington, IL: Rigby Education.

Rasinski, T. 2005. "The Role of the Teacher in Effective Fluency Instruction." *New England Reading Association Journal* 41(1):9–12, 66.

———. 2010. *The Fluent Reader: Oral & Silent Reading Strategies for Building Fluency, Word Recognition & Comprehension*, 2d ed. New York: Scholastic.

———. 2011. "The Art and Science of Teaching Reading Fluency." In D. Lapp, N. Frey, and D. Fisher (eds.), *Handbook of Research on Teaching the English Language Arts*, 3d ed., pp. 23–246. New York: Routledge.

Ray, K. W. 2006. *Study Driven: A Framework for Planning Units of Study in the Writing Workshop*. Portsmouth, NH: Heinemann.

Rebell, M., and J. Wolff. 2008. *Moving Every Child Ahead: From NCLB Hype to Meaningful Educational Opportunity*. New York: Teachers College Press.

Rivkin, Steven G., Eric A. Hanushek, and John F. Kain. 2005. "Teachers, Schools, and Academic Achievement." *Econometrica* 73(2):417–58.

Rosenblatt, L. M. 1994. "The Transactional Theory of Reading and Writing." In R. B. Ruddell, M. R. Ruddell, and H. Singer, (eds.), *Theoretical Models and Processes of Reading*, 4th ed., pp. 1057–1092. Newark, DE: International Reading Association.

Rosenshine, Barak. 2012. "Principles of Instruction: Research-based Strategies That All Teachers Should Know." *American Educator* (Spring):12–39.

Rumelhart, D. E. 1994. "Toward an Interactive Model of Reading." In R. B. Ruddell, M. R. Ruddell, and H. Singer (eds.), *Theoretical Models and Processes of Reading*, 4th ed., pp. 864–94. Newark, DE: International Reading Association.

Sarason, Seymour. 1996. *Revisiting "The Culture of the School and the Problem of Change."* New York: Teachers College Press.

Simon, Charnan. 1996. *Sam the Garbage Hound*. New York: Scholastic.

Slobodkina, Esphyr. 1987. *Caps for Sale: A Tale of a Peddler, Some Monkeys and Their Monkey Business*. New York: Harper Collins.

Shanahan T., et al. 2010. *Improving Reading Comprehension in Kindergarten through 3rd Grade: A Practice Guide, NCEE 2010-4038*. U.S. Department of Education: National Center for Education Evaluation and Regional Assistance, p. 11.

Shanahan, Timothy, and Christopher J. Lonigan. 2013. *Early Childhood Literacy: The National Early Literacy Panel and Beyond*. Baltimore, MD: Paul H. Brookes.

Shanahan, Timothy, Douglas Fisher, and Nancy Frey. 2012. "The Challenge of Challenging Texts." *Educational Leadership* 69(6):58–62.

Sipe, L. R. 2002. "Talking Back and Taking Over: Young Children's Expressive Engagement During Storybook Read-Alouds." *The Reading Teacher* 55(5):476–83.

Smith, Doris Buchanan. 1973. *A Taste of Blackberries*. New York: HarperCollins.

Snow, Catherine E., M. Susan Burns, and Peg Griffin, eds. 1998. *Preventing Reading Difficulties in Young Children*. Washington, DC: National Academy.

Snowball, Diane, and Faye Bolton. 1999. *Spelling K–8: Planning and Teaching*. York, ME: Stenhouse.

Soto, Gary, and Ed Martinez. 1996. *Qué Montón De Tamales! (Too Many Tamales)*. New York: PaperStar.

Stadler, John. 1982. *Hooray for Snail!* New York: Crowell.

Swanson, H., M. Hoskyn, and C. Lee. 1999. *Interventions for Students with Learning Disabilities: A Meta-Analysis of Treatment Outcomes*. New York: Guilford Press.

Topping, K. J., J. Samuels, and T. Paul. 2007. "Does Practice Make Perfect? Independent Reading Quantity, Quality and Student Achievement." *Learning and Instruction* 17(3):253–64.

Teale, W. H., and M. G. Martinez. 1996. "Reading Aloud to Young Children: Teachers' Reading Styles and Kindergarteners' Text Comprehension." In C. Pontecorvo, M. Orsolini, B. Burge, and L. B. Resnick (eds.), *Children's Early Text Construction*, pp. 321–344. Mahwah, NJ: Erlbaum.

Torres, Leyla. 1997. *Subway Sparrow*. New York: Farrar, Straus, Giroux.

Trelease, J. 2006. *The Read-Aloud Handbook*. New York: Penguin Books.

U.S. Department of Education. 1999. *NAEP Reading Report Card for the Nation*.

Vygotsky, L. 1978. "Interaction between Learning and Development." In *Mind in Society* (trans. M. Cole.), pp. 79–91. Cambridge, MA: Harvard University Press.

Weinman Sharmat, Marjorie. 1977. *Nate the Great*. New York: Dell.

Wells, Rosemary. 1999. *Noisy Nora*. New York: Viking.

Wenger, E. 1998. *Communities of Practice: Learning, Meaning, and Identity*. Cambridge, U.K: Cambridge University Press.

White, E. B. 1952. *Charlotte's Web*. New York: HarperCollins.

Wiggins, Grant P., and Jay McTighe. 2005. *Understanding by Design*. Alexandria, VA: Association for Supervision and Curriculum Development.

Wood, George H., Linda Darling-Hammond, Monty Neill, and Pat Roschewski. 2007. "Refocusing Accountability: Using Local Performance Assessments to Enhance Teaching and Learning for Higher Order Skills." *FairTest* 16 May.

Wood, D., J. Bruner, and G. Ross. 1976. "The Role of Tutoring in Problem Solving." *Journal of Child Psychology and Psychiatry* 17:89–100.

Yopp, R. H., and Yopp, H. K. 2006. "Informational Texts as Read-Alouds at School and Home." *Journal of Literacy Research* 38(1):37–VIII.

Zion, Gene. 1984. *Harry, the Dirty Dog*. New York: HarperCollins.

Zipoli, R. P., M. D. Coyne, and B. D. McCoach. 2011. "Enhancing Vocabulary Intervention for Kindergarten Students: Strategic Integration of Semantically Related and Embedded Word Review." *Remedial and Special Education* 32(2):131–43.